Beginner
+
Intermediate Guide
to Serger

Table of Contents

Beginner's Guide to Serger Machine

A Comprehensive Guide On How To Set Up And Operate Your Serger Machine

Stotra

Introduction

Is it your first time to use a surge? This is an absolute beginner's guide that will teach you step-by-step basics on the use of a serger machine.

A serger machine is the most preferred sewing machine compared to a regular sewing machine due to its versatile uses. You can use this machine to create different types of stitches, seam fabrics while at the same time overcasting the raw edges, adding finishings, trimming edges, and sewing decorates stitches to your fabric.

A serger machine uses multiple threads to seam your fabric making the stitches more strong than those of a regular sewing machine. It gives your garment a neat and professional finishing.

In this tutorial, you will learn how to look for a good serger machine for your next sewing projects and some of the best serging machines in the market.

You will also learn how to set up your serger machines, the different parts of your machines, how each of the parts operates, and their functions.

Before you begin your first serging project, you need to learn how to thread your machine like a pro. In addition, you will be able to adjust your machine settings to ensure you have a perfect stitch for your projects. Depending on the type of fabric, you will know how to adjust the stitch length and needle tensions to create a balance.

Knowing all these essential techniques, then you're ready to begin your serging journey. You will be able to make a variety of custom made clothing and other accessories for you and your family!

With just the basics on how to operate the machine, you will be able to make your garment finishing like a pro. And with time, the serger will be the most useful tool in your sewing room.

Chapter One: Parts Of A Serger

Have you ever wondered how those perfectly stitch finishing on garments is done? Well, you can also add this professional finishing to your projects or garments. All you need is a Serger machine.

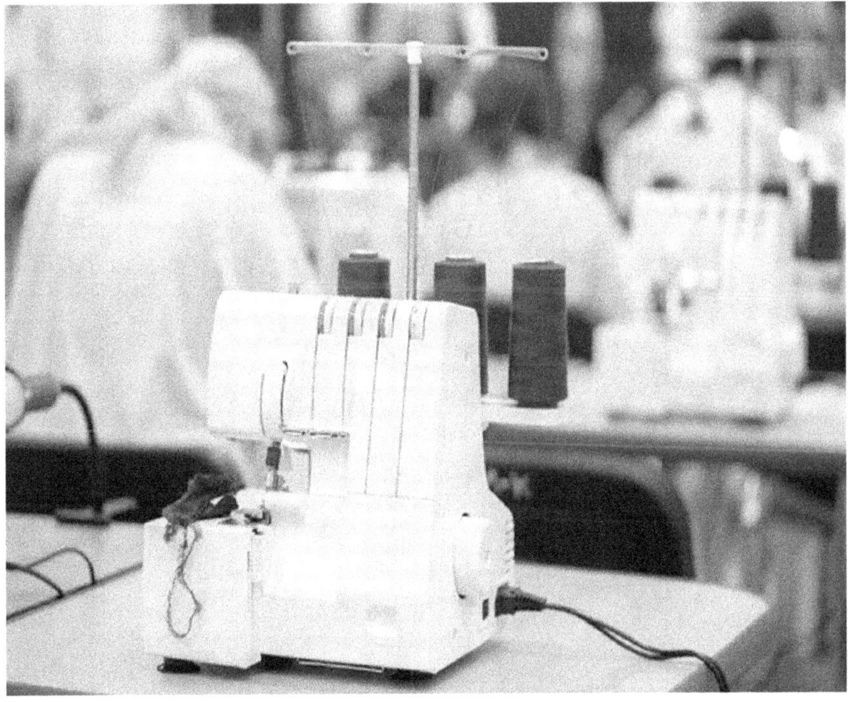

Image source: Andy Shell/Shutterstock

In this guide, I will walk you through all the essentials you need to know about the serger.

To start with, you need to know your serger, so in this chapter, you will learn about the serge, how to use it, and different parts of a serger. By the time we wrap up, you will be sewing with confidence!

What is a Serger?

A serger or overlock machine is a special sewing machine that trims the edges of the fabric, overcast it, and sews a seam around the fabric. It can also sew tightly rolled hems or bind fabrics together using an overlock stitch. You should not confuse it with a sewing machine. Both machines sew stitches but they do so differently.

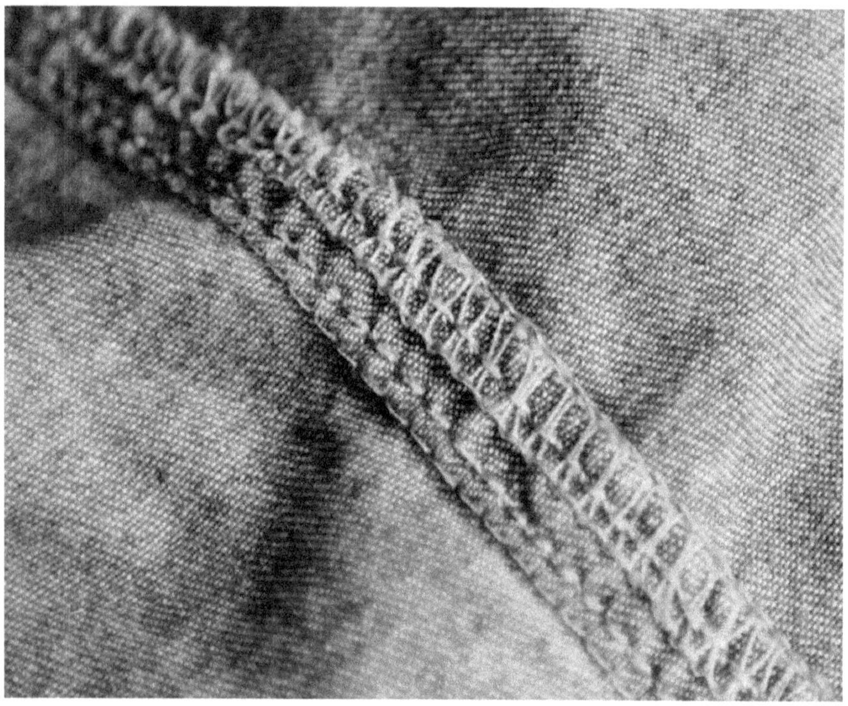

Image source: Keikona/Shutterstock

The serger not only binds fabric together but it also has a cutting blade that cuts the excess fabric at the same time. The cutting blade sits right before the needle unlike the normal sewing machine, you have to cut your project before sewing. As a result, it saves you time and at the same time sews clean and tidy seams.

A normal sewing machine uses only one thread to sew or two in case you have a double-needle machine. While a serger uses 3 to 4 threads to create interlocking stitches.

I personally prefer a serger machine to a sewing machine because it makes your sewing tasks much easier and faster. You don't have to spend more of your sewing time doing the unnecessary work associated with the sewing machine.

The stitches are better and strong especially if you're sewing children's clothes. In addition, you can use special stitches to make your garment look more attractive.

Why you need a serger

- A serger machine is a must-have if you love sewing stretchy fabrics, fleece, knits, and sweatshirt fabrics

- If you want to create a seam and an overlock stitch at once. When you want to cut the edges of the fabric as you sew, you can use the serger machine because it gives you clean raw edges.

- If you want to use thicker threads to create decorative edges.

- A serger is much faster and easier than a sewing machine.

- A serger gives you better, stronger, and durable stitches

- When you want to create rolled hems on your sheer fabric and other lightweight materials.

- When you want to use elastic threads, beading wires, cords, and pearls to serge the raw edges of your garment and have a beautiful finishing.

- If you want to add zippers to custom made pillows and simple bags.

- When you want to speed up your sewing and create gathering stitches much faster.

- If you want to prevent raveling of fabrics. The serger adds professional finishing to the raw edges of your fabric.

Parts of a Serger

Before you start using a serger, you need to know the different parts that make this machine. Look up at the handbook that comes with your new machine and make sure you can identify them.

Learning these parts of the serger will help you to achieve an excellent finish of your garments.

Although the sergers are different based on the model, most of them have similar parts.

Each serger has a vertical pole and a horizontal rod fixed at the top. There are several evenly distributed holes where threads are fed through. Below are spool pins that hold the thread. Each spool of thread has a tension control.

Some Sergers have a presser foot while others have a level to lift and lower the foot. On the right side of the needle, there is a blade that cuts excess clothing as you sew.

There are sergers with fabric catcher, a little box that is used to hold the pieces of the cut fabric.

Let's have a look at the main parts of the serger sewing machine. They include;

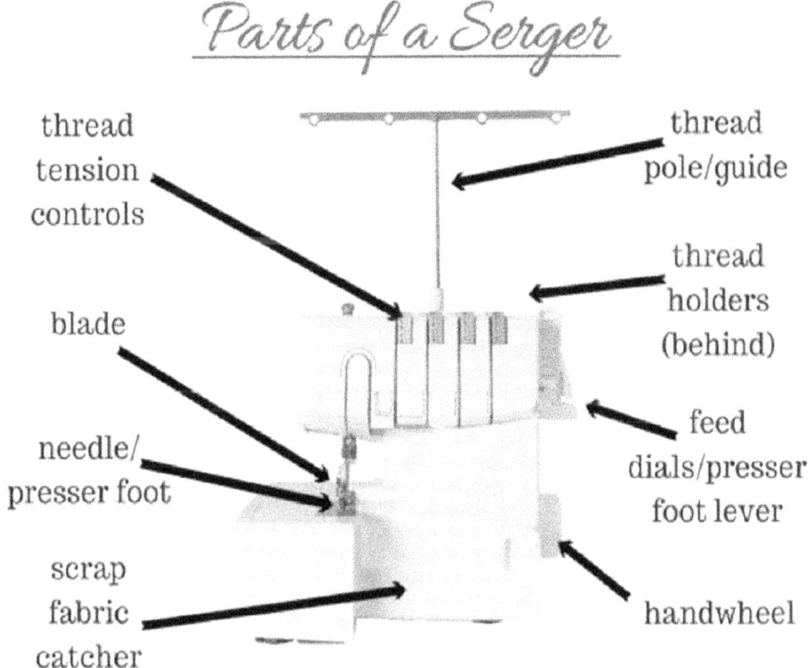

Image source: Serger manual

1. **Tension dials:** Tension dials help in balancing your stitch. It ensures you sew smooth stitches without any loops. Just like tension dials in a conventional sewing machine, you can adjust the tension dial on each of

the threads in a serger and have a perfect stitch. It works well in coordination with other parts of the machine to give you an appropriate stitch based on the type of fabric you're using.

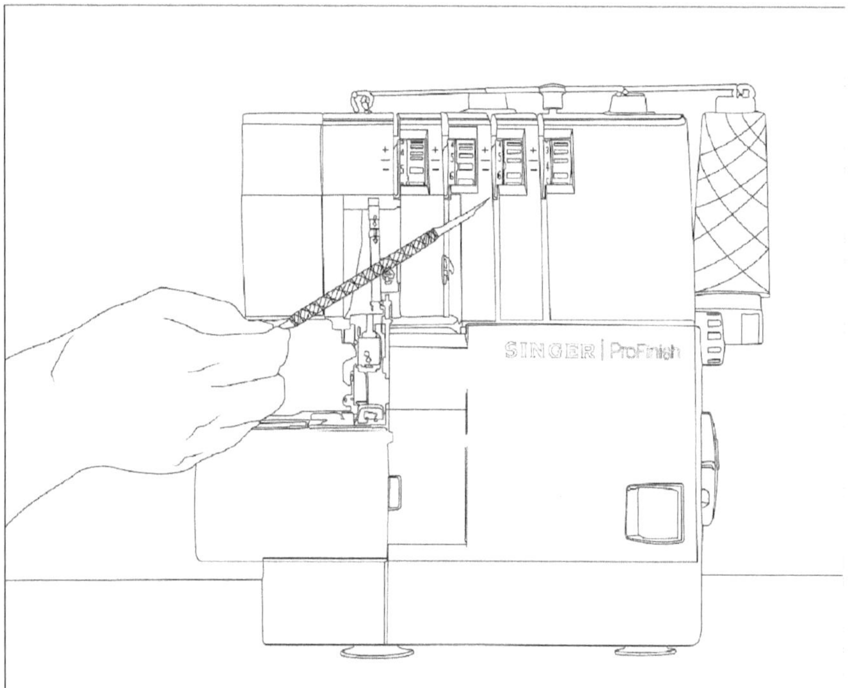

Therefore, you should set your tension dial based on the weight of the fabric or project.

A balanced stitch has the upper and lower looper meet at the edge of the fabric while at the same time there is no pucker or gape of the needle threads.

When tension is very high, there will be too much friction on thread leading to a tight sew and the machine will keep pulling the thread. So you need to adjust the tension to achieve a perfect balance in all the threads.

1. **Loopers:** Loopers are used to create stitches instead of using a bobbin. There are two types of loopers: the upper and lower looper. The stitches are created through the locking of the needle thread and the looper. It also uses the same mechanism to create finish seams.

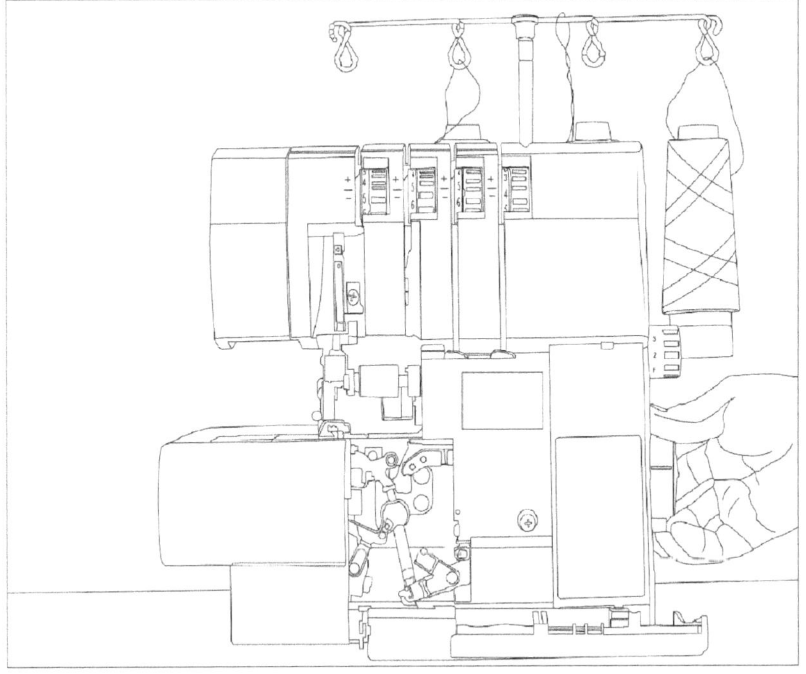

Looper threads do not penetrate the fabric but they do affect each other as you sew.

If your looper's threads do not meet at the fabric edges, this means one of the threads is pulled to the wrong side.

For example, if the upper looper tension is loose or the lower looper tension is very tight then you will have the upper looper pulled to the wrong side (bottom of the fabric). To correct this, you need to do proper adjustments based on the stitches affected.

This also applies to the lower looper thread. If the upper looper tension is tight while the lower looper tension is loose, then the lower looper thread is pulled to the right side or top of the fabric.

2. **Feed system:** This consists of the feed dog, a needle plate, and a presser foot. Feed dogs look like some jagged metal teeth and they're located on the stitch plate which is below the pressure foot.

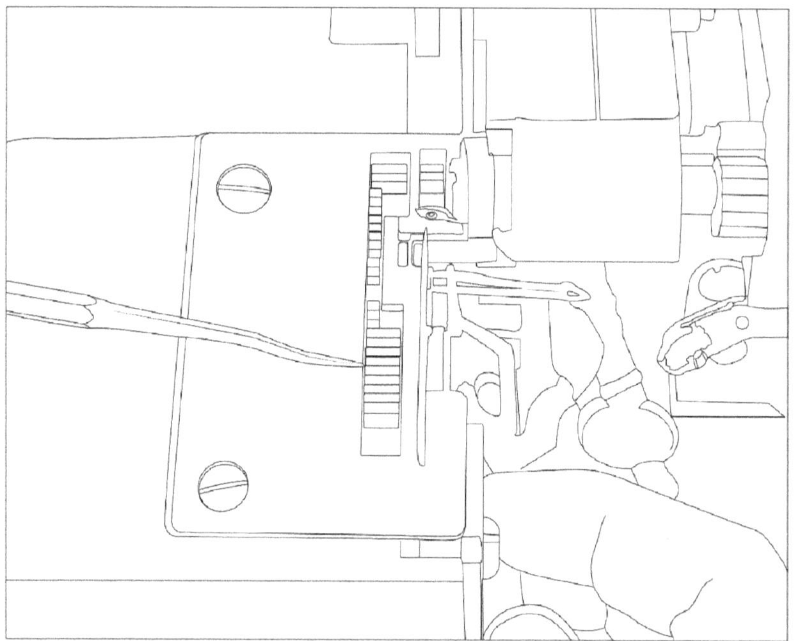

These feed systems work together to ensure the fabric is fed evenly through the serger. Some machines do have two different feed dogs which help prevent stretched seams.

3. **Stitch fingers:** It resembles a figure like shape and it is located close to the cutting blade and at the right side of the pressure foot. It acts as the center point for threads going through the serger and guides each thread to create a stitch on the fabric edges.

   Threads pass through the stitch finger when sewing and come off through the back of the pressure foot.

   In some brands, stitch finger is called stitch former and it works well in conjunction with pressure foot, needles, and threads.

4. **Cutting system:** It uses a movable upper knife to trim seam allowances while at the same time the lower knife remains stationary. The two knives work together in a coordinating manner and move at the same speed as that of the needles.

5. **3-4 thread spools:** Thread spools are designed to hold 2000 – 3000 yards of thread. In most cases, the threads are used in multiple of two or more spools. They are located at the back or at the top of the machine. Larger machines have more thread spools.

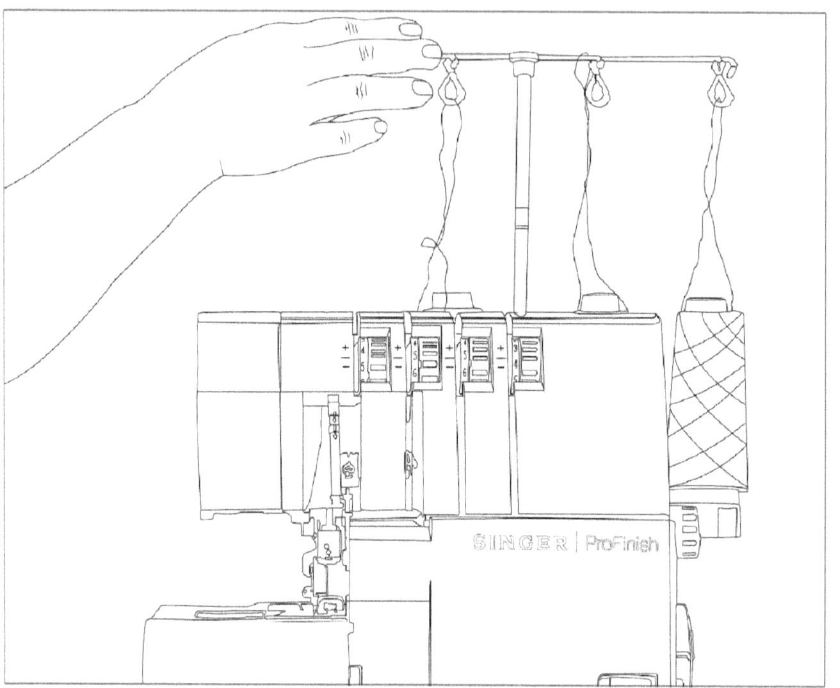

6. **2 needles:** A serger has two needles that have different heights when inserted into the sewing machine. The left needle is at a higher level than the right needle. Some old sergers only come with one needle while modern sergers have two needles.

   You can remove one of the needles and work with one but the serger will still function with three threads in both cases.

   If you're using 4 thread stitching, then you should adjust the thread tensions of the two needles. If you're using 3 thread stitching, you only adjust one needle thread tension.

   If you want to replace the needles, you need to unscrew the clamp screws that hold each needle and dispose of the old needle. Insert the new needle by pushing it deep into the slot. Make sure the shank flat side faces the front and then screw the clamp screw back into its position. Now test your serger machine.

7. **Stitch Length:** When starting up with your sewing, you don't think much about the stitch length. Most probably, you will use the default stitch length already set by the manufacturer.

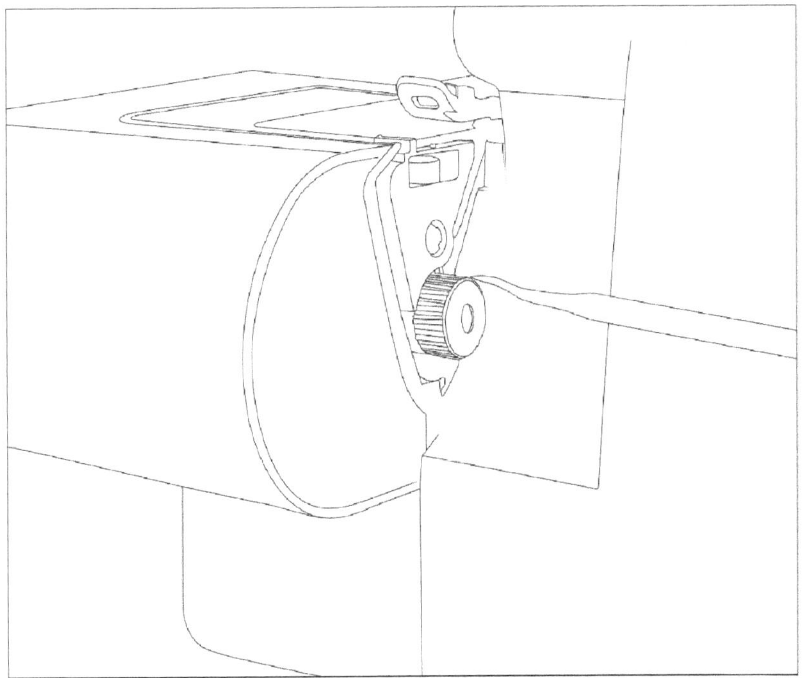

Default stitch length works for most beginner projects although this depends on what you're sewing.

But as you continue sewing more projects, you will need varying stitch length that suits the fabric and also the purpose of the stitch. To adjust how long each stitch is sewn, you need to adjust the feed dogs. Feed dogs control how

much fabric is to be pulled by each stitch. If you need a
longer stitch, then more fabric needs to be pulled through.

8. **A pressing feet:** Different presser feet helps you
   increase efficiency and better results in your project.
   These different serger feet makes it easy to achieve the
   specialty stitches and various sewing techniques.

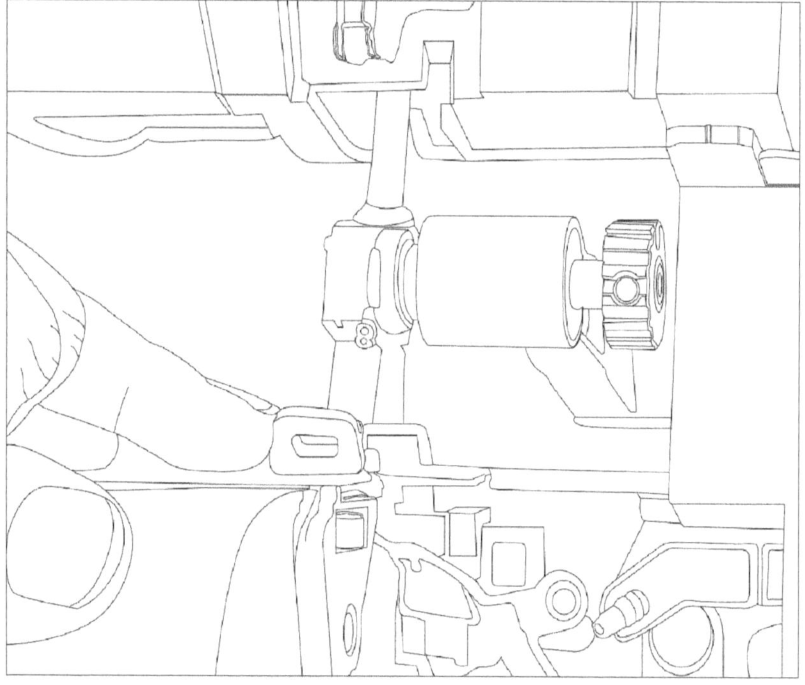

Although you're required to match the serger feet based
on your serger brand and model, you can also interchange
them.

The parts combine together to do multiple stitches
simultaneously. For example, when you want to sew a fabric
the feed dog ensures it is evenly fed through the serger, and
then moves the fabric until the knives trim all the edges. The

loopers and the needles sew the stitches on the fabric and then it is fed off the stitch fingers behind the needle.

In the end, you will have a professional finished edge of the fabric. The fabric can either be a garment or any home décor project.

Serger Feet

A serger foot can be part of your overlock machine or you can buy them as accessories. There are different types of serger feet.

The feet act as an attachment that enables the serger to create different forms of stitches when the fabric moves over the feed dogs. That is, it ensures thread is wrapped around the edges of the fabric to avoid unraveling.

The feet consist of:

- **Elastic/tape foot:** Used for adding an elastic or sewing tape to your garment.

- **Blind hem foot/ blind stitch foot:** Used for sewing seams on skirts and trousers so that they remain hidden. You can also sew cuffs on a knit fabric using this blind stitch foot.

- **Shirring foot:** It is used to create gathers in your fabric

- **Pearl/Sequin foot/beading foot:** This is ideal for sewing pearls, sequins, and beans on the garment.

- **Piping /Cording foot:** It is ideal for sewing piping on your garment. It also has a groove where the piping or the cording passes through and attaches to the garment.

- **Lace foot:** It enables you to add laces and ribbons at the edges of the fabric.

- **Gimp/ Yarn application tool:** This tool is suitable for attaching a thin thread or a wire at the cut edges of the fabric.

Functions of a serger

A serger or overlock machine can help you in;

- Sewing seams on knit fabrics

- Finish the seams on a fabric

- Sew rolled hems and edges

- Gathering

How a Serger Works

This special sewing machine performs multiple functions simultaneously to create a strong stitch.

When you want to sew a garment, the fabric is first fed to your machine through the feed dog. Then the fabric moves along as the knife trims the edges. After trimming, the loopers and needles sew stitches at the fabric edges, then the fabric is forwarded to the stitch finger behind the needle.

The machine repeats the same process for the next stitch until you're able to add a professional finish to your garment. However, for you to achieve this professional finishing, you need to know how to guide the fabric through the serger machine.

Once you're able to learn how the machine works, you will be ready to dive in and start sewing more projects.

Chapter Summary

- Before starting any sewing project, you need to first learn about your serger and how it sews. If you have been using a standard sewing machine, it will be much easier to learn how to use the serger.

- You need to identify the different parts of the serger machine. This is because the threading and thread tension in a serger machine is different from that of a standard sewing machine.

- A serger machine will cut some of the seam allowances in the fabric as you sew, thus saving you a lot of time.

In the next chapter, you will learn sewing tools and their uses.

Chapter Two:
Tools For Operating A Serger

There are a lot of sewing resources and supplies over the internet and probably wondering where do I begin?

If you're a beginner, it can be very overwhelming for you to choose the best sewing tools and equipment. While some of the sewing tools are a must-have, others are optional.

To help you solve your dilemma on sewing tools, I have put together some of the tools you need to start your sewing!

Also, you will be able to learn the work of each of the tools.

With this guide, you can determine what tools you need to buy before you go to your local supply store.

Have you ever walked to any sewing supplier store? Most stores have multiple sewing tools ranging from simple screwdrivers to other sophisticated equipment. That alone can leave you nervous if you're a beginner.

With this list, no more dilemma on what to buy. With the basic sewing tools, you're set to sew.

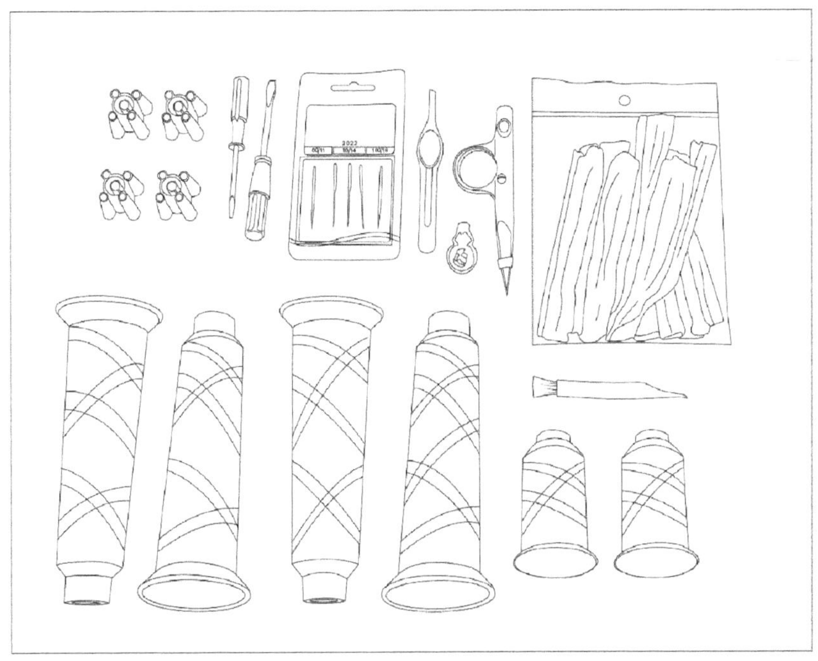

Basic Serger sewing tools

If you're on a budget, get these basic sewing tools and learn how to use each one of them correctly! They will get you started as well as help you complete a simple sewing project.

1. **Screwdriver:** This one of the most important tools for a tailor. It is used to change the needles or unscrew some hidden parts of your overlock machine that need to be cleaned or fixed.

2. **Serger needles:** There are types of needle brands that are compatible with certain brands of a serger. You can find some of these universal serger needles for your machine.

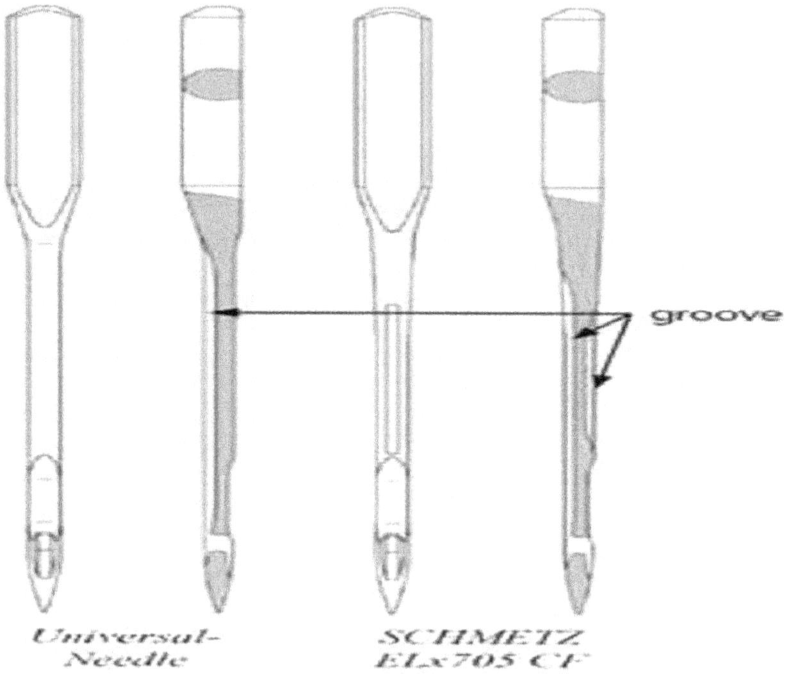

Other serger manufacturers recommend using certain types of needle brands. You may consider this option when shopping for needles for your machine. So choose your favorite brand of needles and go ahead to install it in your machine.

Different needles have different shank shapes. Some sergers use round-shaped shank needles while newer models have a flat shank. Needle shank thickness and size also vary. Therefore, using the recommended brand on a particular serger model will ensure it fits well.

Some types of sergers can still use the regular sewing needle although this depends on the model of the serger.

When inserting the new needle, always make sure it fits the same as if you're installing it in a regular sewing machine. If after fixing the needle doesn't fit well or not creating stitches as it is expected, then stick with the recommended brand on the user manual.

Always remember the right needle should extend down lower than the left needle.

3. **Needle inserter:** This is a must-have tool in your sewing list. Needle inserters easily hold needles when inserting in your sewing machine. It helps you to easily replace or remove serger needles. It has an ergonomic handle that makes it easy to use and comfortable on your hands.

   All you need to do is insert the needle into the needle inserter, fix it in your serger machine, and then tighten the clamp screws.

4. **Needle threader:** A needle threader helps you to easily insert the thread in the needle. You don't have all your projects delayed because you couldn't get the needle threaded. The threader works with all types of needles.

5. **Tweezers:** These are used to pick small objects that you can't pick with your fingers or reach to places with limited spaces. Keep one or two of these tweezers in your accessory box. With a tweezer, you can remove unwanted threads, reach the lower looper, insert needles in your machine, do beading, and do general crafts.

The curved shape of the tweezers makes threading very easy when using your overlock machine.

6. **Thread nippers:** Thread nipper is another must-have tool in your accessory kit. This tool is essential in craft projects that require more accuracy. In this case, the large scissors are inefficient.

   Therefore, thread nippers can be of great help in cutting unwanted threads in a garment while being keen on the clothes details. If your cloth or garment has some detailed craft, then thread nippers will help make it neat by removing or cutting unwanted pieces or small nips.

7. **Tiny lint brush:** After hours of sewing, removing lint, and cleaning your machine is very important. Therefore, the lint brush is great for the maintenance of your sewing machine.

   This tiny lint brush can clean those small spots or hard to reach parts of the serger machine.

8. **Spool net:** Spool nets are used to keep your threads neat, you don't have to waste your time sorting through a mess of entangled threads.

   If you're using a transparent nylon thread that winds off, you can put your thread inside the spool net. If the spool net is long, you can fold it to fit the size of the spool. This ensures your thread remains neat.

   A spool net tightens the upper thread tension therefore, you should adjust the upper thread tension to accommodate the spool net.

9. **4 spool holders:** A spool holder or spool cap is used
    to hold the spool on the pin. The spool cap ensures the
    thread is in place and your spool doesn't come off the
    pin as you sew. It also ensures the thread doesn't snag
    on the spool.

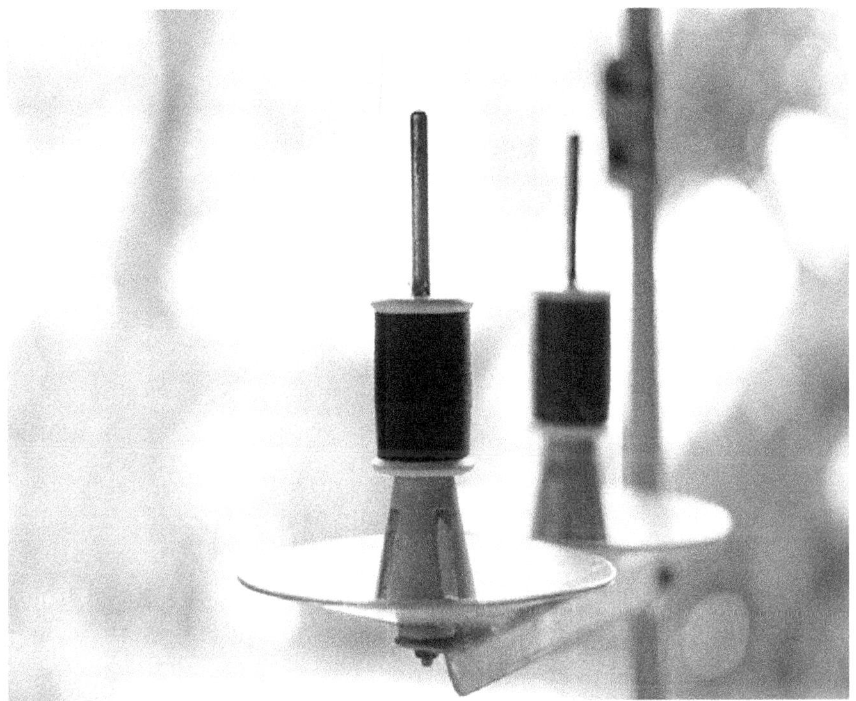

Image source: FaiPloypilin/Shutterstock

The spool cap shouldn't hold the thread tightly on the
spool pin. The spool needs enough space so that it
could rotate on the spool pin as the thread is pulled on
the spool.

10. **Thread spool holder:** This acts as a stand for the
    spools of your sewing thread. These spools are
    mounted on the pins such that they can rotate freely
    when the thread is unwound.

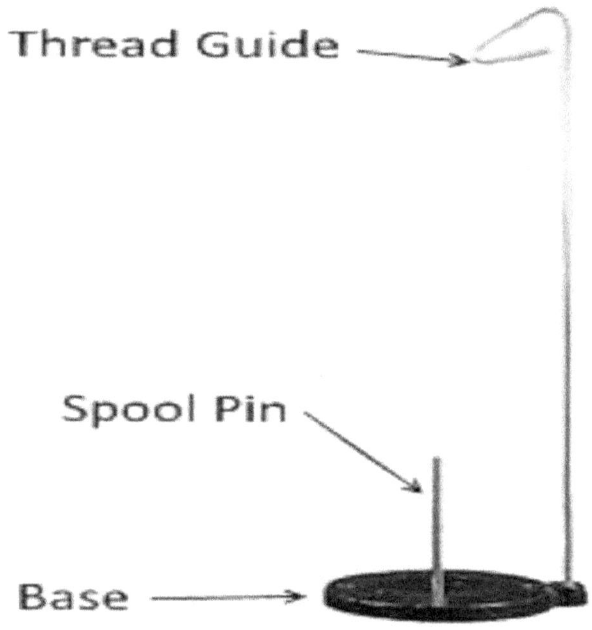

Image source: Serger manual

There is a wide variety of threads in the market and depending on how the threads are packaged, a spool pin cannot accommodate a larger thread. Therefore, in such cases, you need a stand for your thread cones and spools (thread spool holder).

11. **Rolled Hem presser foot:** It is also called the narrow hem foot and it is used when sewing a narrow hem. The foot helps in folding the edges of the fabric before it passes through the needle. This ensures you have a professional finish of your garment.

You can use a rolled hem foot when working with light and medium weight fabrics.

The rolled hem technique ensures all the finishes of the seam allowances are inside the hem.

12. **Upper knife & lower Knife:** Knives or cutting blades play a huge role in using a serger machine. The knives trim the edges of the fabric before sewing stitches. This results in a neat finished edge.

    The upper and lower knives work together to trim the fabric during stitching. The upper blade usually moves up and down while the lower blade remains stationary under the needle plate.

    You can disengage the upper blade if you want decorative sewing or when you don't want to cut the fabric when stitching. For example, disengaging the blades can help you use elastic, topstitch, or any other decorative stitch at the edges of the fabric.

    The blades ensure you have a neat and professional-looking garment. You don't have to spend more time going back to trim the seam.

    If you're planning to remove or replace the blades, make sure to disconnect the serger from the network. To remove the upper blade, unscrew it and pull it out.

    The lower knife is fixed with a screw that has a special washer and to remove it, you have to loosen the screws. Although this depends on the model of your serger machine.

13. **Awl or stiletto:** This is a pointed tool that allows you to feed your fabric next to the cutting blade and close to the presser foot. The awl will keep your fabric moving on areas you can't touch with your fingers.

14. **Wonder clips by clover:** If you have been sewing over the pins you're your sewing machine, it can be challenging when using a serger machine. If you serge over the pins, you can damage your knives. Instead of using pins that can cause an accident, you can hold your fabrics with wonder clip to avoid these problems.

How to use serger needles

Serge needles have sharp points that allow them to sew any type of fabric. Ballpoint needles are highly recommended by manufacturers when sewing performing knits. This is because the needles do not pierce the fabric instead, it goes in between the thread when sewing.

These needles have a groove both at the front and at the backside of the blade to reduce the number of skipped stitches. The long groove helps create chain stitches on a piece of fabric.

Older models of sergers have one needle while modern sergers come with two needles. You can also remove one, although this is optional.

Inserting new needles

When inserting the needles in your machine, they should not be parallel with each other. The left needle should sit higher than the right needle.

The serger has two needle clamps screws to hold each of the needles. Therefore, you have to unscrew the needle clamp and remove the old needle. Ensure the used needle is well disposed of.

Insert the new needle by pushing its shank deep into the needle slot. The flat side of the needle shank should face the front. Screw the clamp screws back in place and test.

Tips on working with needles

Before replacing the needles in your serger machine, ensure you have the right length. Different machines use different needle lengths so confirm with your serger manual the recommended needle length or number.

In addition, the size of the needle you choose should be suitable for the fabric you want to sew and the thread size you will use. Your sewing manual has an operator manual chart that highlights different needle sizes and recommended thread sizes for different types of fabrics. You can also get the manual from a reputable website.

Using a larger diameter needle for a thin fabric will result in an unattractive stitch with big needle holes left on the fabric. So always make sure you use the right needle size based on the fabric type.

Also, make sure the needle is inserted straight and doesn't have any burr or dull point.

When sewing special fabrics, choose the right needle for that. For example, use ballpoint needles when you want to sew knits and a wedge needle when you want to sew leather fabrics.

Parts of a needle

- **Needle plate/Throat plate:** Some manufacturers of certain models do recommend using a needle plate with an elongated hole to serge zig-zag stitches and a round hole when serging straight stitches.

Using the wrong needle plate may result in skipped stitches when serging straight stitches. This mostly happens when sewing synthetic fabrics.

- **Feed dog:** This a metal bar with diagonal teeth that emerges above the hole on the throat plate. It moves back and forth in between the needle plate and pulls (feed) the fabric in your sewing machine before the needle makes the next stitch.

  Adjust the setting such that the needle creates a seam with 10 to 12 stitches. If you're sewing a thin fabric, then a short stitch of 14 –16 per inch is more desirable. Leather and vinyl fabrics require a long stitch of about 6-10 stitches for each inch of the seam

- **Presser foot:** Your presser foot should have enough pressure for holding the fabric on the feed dog in order to make uniform stitches. If you're sewing a heavy fabric, then light pressure will be used to pull the fabric. Pulling the inner pin will increase the pressure while releasing the outer ring reduces the pressure.

  A roller-type presser foot can give you better feeding results than the standard pressure foot when sewing with vinyl fabric, velvet, loosely knit, or slippery fabric.

  Read your model instruction manual to know more about how to change the settings of the presser foot.

- **Thread tension:** To obtain a perfect stitch, you have to adjust the upper and lower tension dials. Different machines have the upper tension located in different areas. Some machines may have it located on the upper arm of the machine head, on the faceplate, or at the front of the needle bar.

  The lower tension dial is located on a bobbin case or on the shuttle. Just adjust the screw near the center of the spring holding the tension.

Lower tension adjustment

If you had removed the lower tension spring while cleaning, or changed the adjustment, then follow the normal adjustment procedure just like adjusting an ordinary sewing machine. In most cases, you have to assume the lower tension is correct unless proven wrong. You should make the adjustments on the upper tension.

If there were initial changes on the lower tension, then set the lower and upper tension such that there is a slight drag in each of the threads. Make sure the bobbin and spool have the same size of thread. After adjusting the tension, test the machine to see the stitch size formed. You can use different colors for the bobbin and spool for you to see the stitches clearly. Adjust the stitch length control to sew medium stitch length. Test the stitches again on a piece of cloth.

In a perfect stitch, threads should lock at the center or halfway between the layers of the cloth. There should be no loops formed at the top or bottom of the seam. If the top side of the seam forms a loop while the top thread remains straight, then you should loosen the upper tension thread because it is tighter than the lower tension thread. However, if the loop on the spool thread appears on the bottom of the seam and the lower thread remains straight, then you should tighten the upper thread.

How to choose the Best Serger

Looking for a new Serger can be a bit overwhelming with so many brands and models in the market. If you're new to the sewing world you may wonder what to look for and how to choose the best serger machine for your sewing projects.

Don't worry anymore. This guide will help in choosing the best serger machine.

Before you buy the serger you need to:

- Determine your sewing needs

- Features to look for (how often do you sew? Do you have eyesight issues? What kind of fabric do you sew?)

Sergers based on your sewing needs

Serger machines based on the needs of customers are classified into three:

1. Basic serger machines

2. Experimental serger machines

3. Automatic serger machines

Before you select the serger model to buy, ask yourself what kind of a tailor are you?

1. Do you need a basic serger to create professional finishing to the edges of a fabric? Do you use light or medium weight fabrics in your sewing projects?

2. Do you love experimenting with different types of fabrics? Do you like to practice sewing with woven fabrics, thick fabrics, and stretchy knits? Do you stitch athletic flatlock on sportswear? Or do you stitch rolled hems on a chiffon dress?

3. Looking for the easiest serger in the market? Do you struggle with threading and choosing the right settings to adjust the tension dial?

Whichever kind of tailor you are, there are different serger machines designed to handle different tasks. Let's have a look at these machines based on the above options

1. Basic serger machine

If you're able to answer yes to questions in number 1, then you need a simple budget-friendly serger machine.

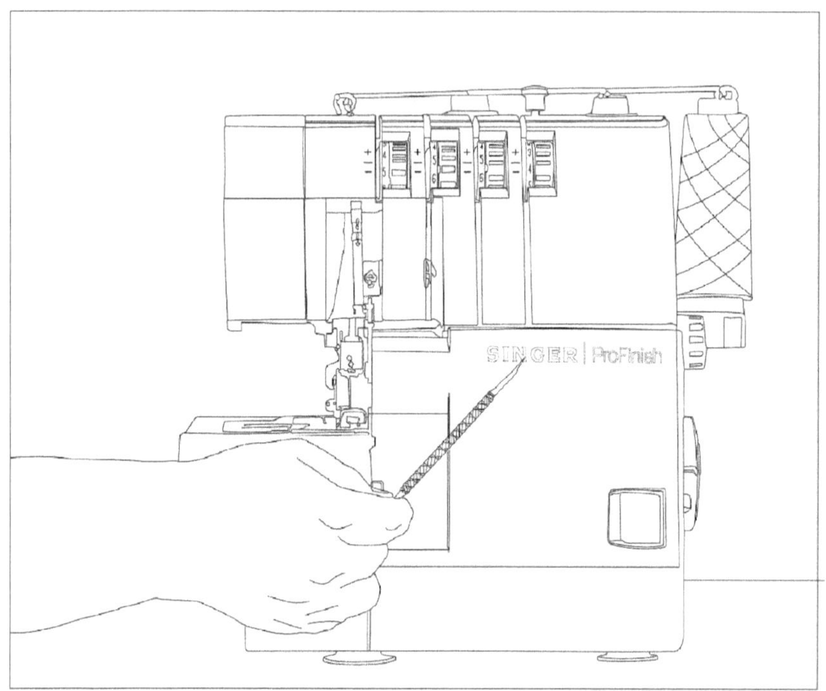

The basic serger machine is suitable for sewing simple fabrics of light to medium weight. You will not put your machine under pressure due to the use of heavy fabrics.

Features to look for:

3 and 4 thread stitches: It should have 3 to 4 threads ability to help you create desired stitches on the garment.

Easy to thread: You should choose a machine with an easy to thread lower looper. Look for a machine that has a printed color-coded threading diagram.

- Retractable knife: Whether the knife is retractable so that you can easily serge without cutting the edges of the fabric.

- Differential feed: A good serging machine should have a differential feed to prevent your fabric from puckering or stretching out. Differential feed ensures you create a flat and smooth seam.

You can adjust the differential feed settings to have the front and the back feed dogs serge at different speeds.

- Adjustable stitch length: Your basic serger machine should allow you to adjust stitch length and width.

- Waste bin: A waste bin is an added advantage to your sewing room. Serging can be messy sometimes therefore, you need a waste bin to clear all fabric fibers mess created by your serger machine.

- Free arm: I also recommend a serging machine with a free arm to sew tubes of fabric although you can still sew tubes without using the free arm. But if your machine has this feature, then it will save you a lot of time.

Most of the modern serger machines have features. However, some low-cost serger models do not have a waste bin or a free arm feature. So if you need to handle basic sewing projects, then this machine is suitable for you.

2. Experiment/Mid-range Serger machines

If you're the type of tailor who loves to experiment and create projects with different types of fabrics then you need to invest in a better-built serging machine.

Therefore, you need a serger that can sew 2, 3, and 4 thread stitches instead of just 3 and 4 stitching ability.

Features to look for:

- All the features mentioned in the basic serger machine

- 2, 3, and 4 thread stitches: This will allow you to create different forms of stitches. For example, 2 thread mock flatlock stitch, 2 thread overlock stitches, and 2 thread rolled hemstitches.

- Serger feet: Look for a serger that accommodates special presser feet and allows you to create more stitching effects. For example, a serger with gathering foot, buttonhole foot, ruffling foot, blind hem foot, etc.

- Built quality: To enjoy the quality performance you need to look for a more durable machine with excellent motor power.

- Rolled hem conversion: A good serger should make it easy to switch from normal overlocking stitches to rolled hemstitches.

- Adjustable pressure: The best serger machine should allow you to easily adjust tension dials with numbers or markings and not through the use of screws.

- High presser foot lift: Another factor you need to consider is the level of the presser foot lift. If you're serging thick fabrics, your serger should be able to support 5 to 6mm of the thickness or even allow 4mm fabric to fit underneath the foot.

3. Automatic/ Premium Serger machine

If you picked option 3, you're looking for a serger machine that is easy to use. This type of serger will automatically choose the tension dials for you. Just a push of a button and the serger will do the rest by itself.

These types of sergers are the most expensive in the market and worth the value for your money

Features to look for:

- Includes all the features in basic and experiment serger machines

- Looper air threading: The automatic serger should be able to thread fiddly looper by just pushing a button.

- Automatic tension: With automatic tension, you don't have to figure what is the right tension settings for the fabric. The Serger will automatically select the right tension setting for you.

- Built-in needle threader: If you have eyesight issues this feature will be of great help to you. It will thread the needles for you. No more wasting time trying to thread with your unsteady hands.

- Built-in spreader/ 2 thread converter: This makes it easy to switch to 2 thread stitches and serge more quickly.

Other features to consider

1. How often do you sew?

If you're always using your machine every day then you should go for a machine that is more durable. The build quality of your machine will determine the performance and lifetime of your machine.

Cheap sergers are made from weaker metals, and weaker motors so they will have less power. They also have more plastic inside and other poor quality materials. Buying these types of sergers will compromise the machine performance and it will not last long.

If you sew daily, then premium and mid-range sergers are more suitable for you. But if you only sew occasionally, then you can go for the budget serger machines.

2. **Do you use thick fabrics like canvas and denim to sew?**

If your answer is yes, then you should buy a serger with;

- Adjustable pressure: The serger should have user-friendly dials to allow you to easily adjust the tension dials. Modern serger machines have adjustable pressure that allows you to create more pressure when sewing thick fabric or reduce pressure when handling light fabrics.

  Older sergers come with unmarked screws for you to change the pressure. And this can be difficult for you since the screws are unmarked compared to when adjusting pressure by a simple numbered dial.

- Motor power: Buy a built-in machine with more motor power to give you better results. If you're serging thick fabrics they put more pressure on your machine. Therefore, you need a serger with more power and strong built-in quality to be able to handle the pressure.

- High presser foot lift: You can go for sergers with a presser foot lift of about 5mm or 6mm. A 4mm lift is also high enough and can support up to 8 layers of medium-weight denim fabric underneath.

3. Do you have eyesight problems?

Those who have issues with their eyesight find it difficult to thread the needles and the loopers. In such cases then you need to buy a serger that has:

- Built-in needle threader: This tool will automatically insert thread on the needles.

- Air-threaded looper: By just pushing a button, you can automatically thread the loopers. This feature is mostly found in premium serger machines. It uses a compressor air to insert the thread inside the looper hole.

4 Best serger machines for Beginners

The review on these four types of serger machines is based on the delivered quality, ease of threading, quality of construction and price.

1. Brother M343D Overlock Nachine

The brother range serger is a budget-friendly machine and one of the best in the market. It has a great threading system and comes with several free accessories such as a waste tray, free arm, and an extension table.

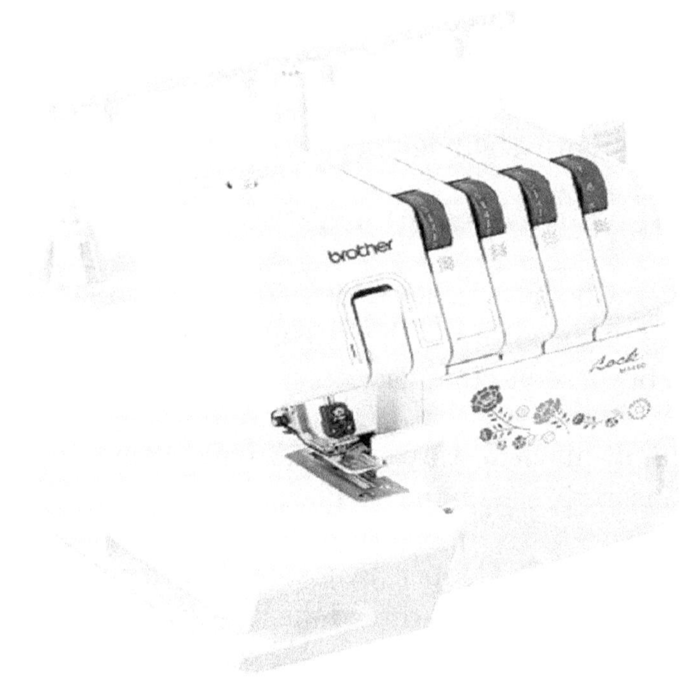

Image source: Amazon

This type of overlock is great for someone who sews occasionally.

With this budget overlock machine, you can only sew 3 or 4 thread stitches which is what most people use. If you're looking forward to doing 2 thread stitches, then you need to go for premium overlocks. It also uses the F.A.S.T lower looper threading system.

You can sew rolled hem, blind hem stitches, narrow hem, and mock flatlock with this type of overlock.

<u>2. Janome 6234XL Overlock</u>

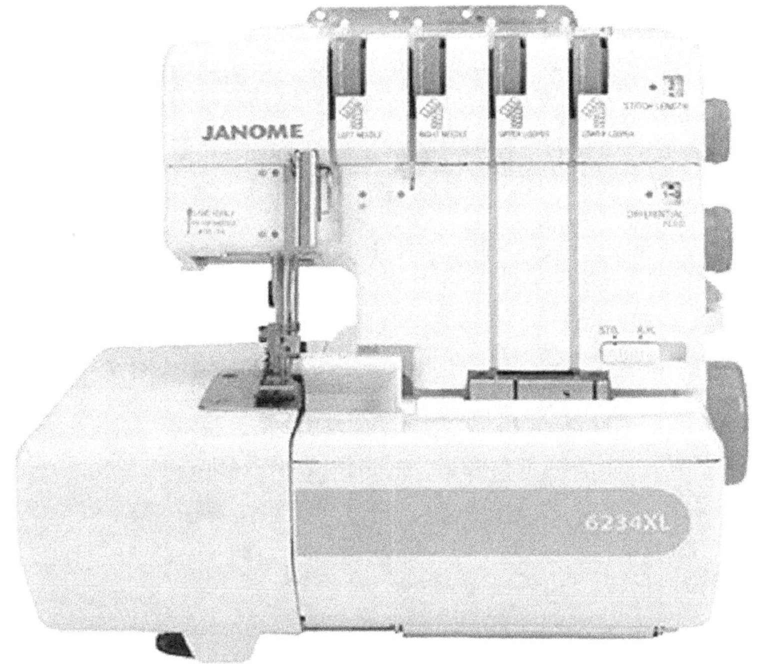

Image source: Amazon

This is great for creating professional looking stitches such as blind hem stitches, rolled hem, narrow, hem, and mock flatlock. You don't have to rely on 3 or 4 thread stitches, thanks to its 2 thread stitching ability.

This type of overlock has a better build quality that features a differential feed and a lower looper pre-tension setting slider. The color-coded thread guide makes your sewing much better.

Janome 6234XL is my overall best overlock machine for beginners.

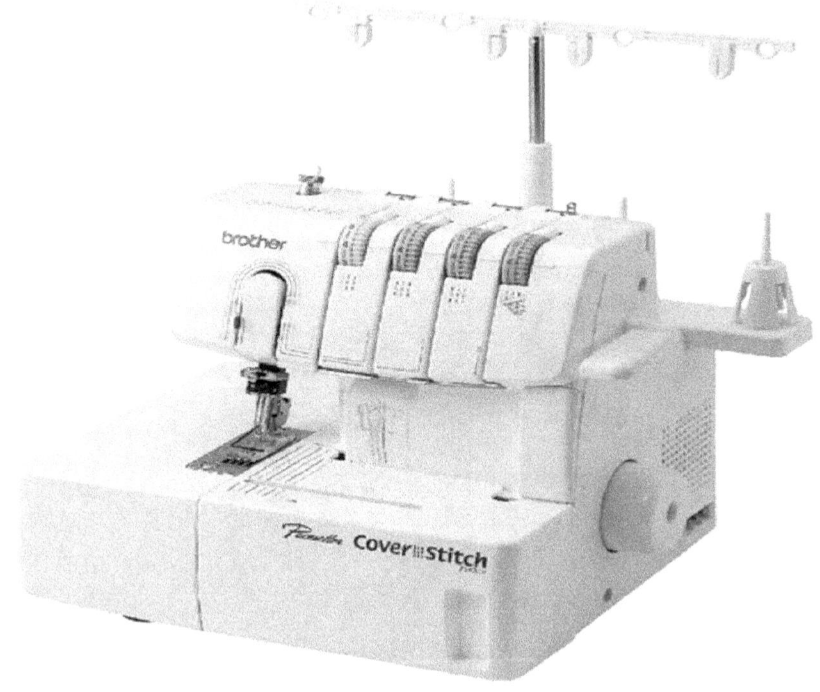

Image source: Amazon

Brother 2340CV is an easy to use overlock machine that supports 2, 3 and 4 stitch functions and adjustable stitch length. It features a tri-cover stitch with both wide and narrow cover stitches with easy to set color-coded threading.

You can easily adjust stitch length using a convenient dial. Test several stitch lengths to find the right stitch length for your project. A blind stitch foot is also included.

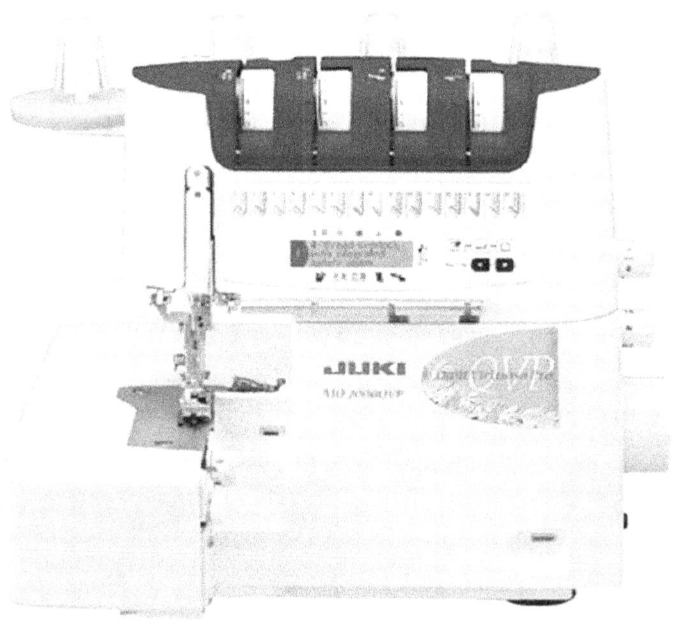

Image source: Amazon

This is great for those looking for an easy overlock machine that threads itself. It is among the best with an air threading technique and a needle threader. The machine will thread everything for you, you don't have to worry on how to thread your machine.

It has quality metal parts, high motor power, and other unique features. The lower looper converter can allow 2-3 thread conversion as well as do automatic rolled hemming. You can set up to 15 different stitches using this overlock.

Also, the overlock has an adjustable presser foot pressure and a wider throat area. An alternative to this is the Janome AT 2000D overlock or Juki MO-1000.

5. Baby Lock Enlighten

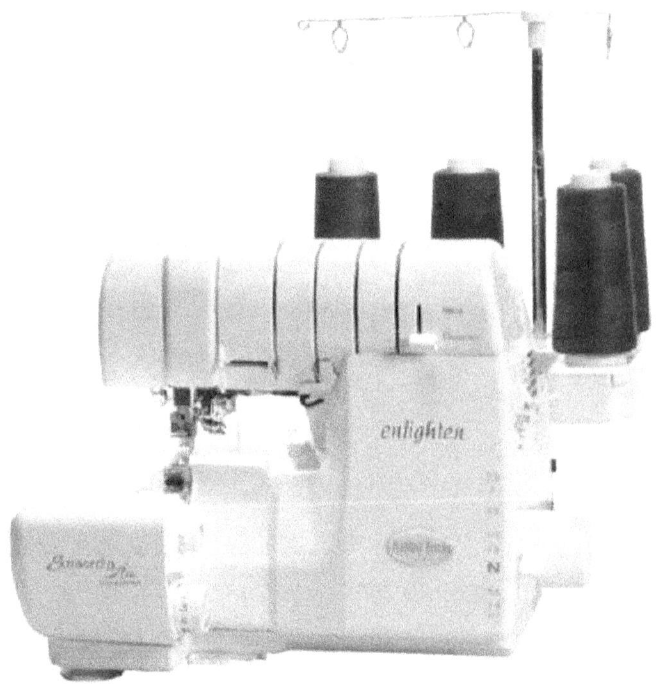

Image source: Amazon

This is an automatic air threading and automatic tension adjustment. It uses extraordinaire threading system to quickly thread your system and make life easy. It chooses your stitch settings automatically making it your dream machine.

Babylock has an excellent market reputation so you're assured of a quality product and it is worth the price.

If you're looking forward to the easiest overlock machine, then you will love this model.

Chapter Summary

- There are a lot of serging tools in the market but the above-mentioned tools should be part of your top list in your serger accessories toolbox. The tools help you get started sewing using your serger machine.

- Since you know the use of each of the tools, you can add them to your shopping list the next time you're walking to your local sewing accessory store.

- Make sure you buy the best tools for your serger brand.

In the next chapter, you will learn how to thread a serger

Chapter Three:
How To Thread A Serger Machine

Do you dread threading your serger machine? Well, you're not alone. Many people have frustrating moments when it comes to changing threads in the machine.

You always have to open the overlock lid then ensure the thread passes through the right place and threaded correctly. Otherwise, your machine will not stitch.

In this chapter, you will learn step by step procedure on how to thread your serging machine and how to adjust your tension and stitches.

Tip: You must follow the threading order. In most machines, the order is the same but sometimes it can vary from one machine to the next. You should confirm the threading order from your serger manual before proceeding. Most machines follow Upper looper, lower looper, and needles order.

Let's get started!

Before you get started, make sure you have these basic tools for your 4-thread overlock machine.

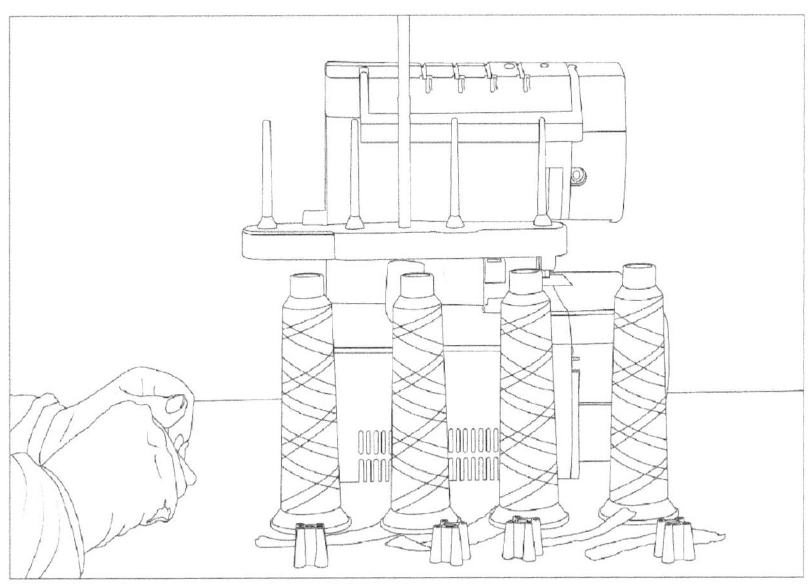

They include:

- Overlock/Serger machine (In this case we will use Brother 1034D)

- 4 spools of thread (Preferably a cone thread because it's not easy to get snagged in the small thread clip as the regular thread spools do)

- Tweezers

- Small thread scissors or thread snips

- Scrap fabric

- Overlock manual

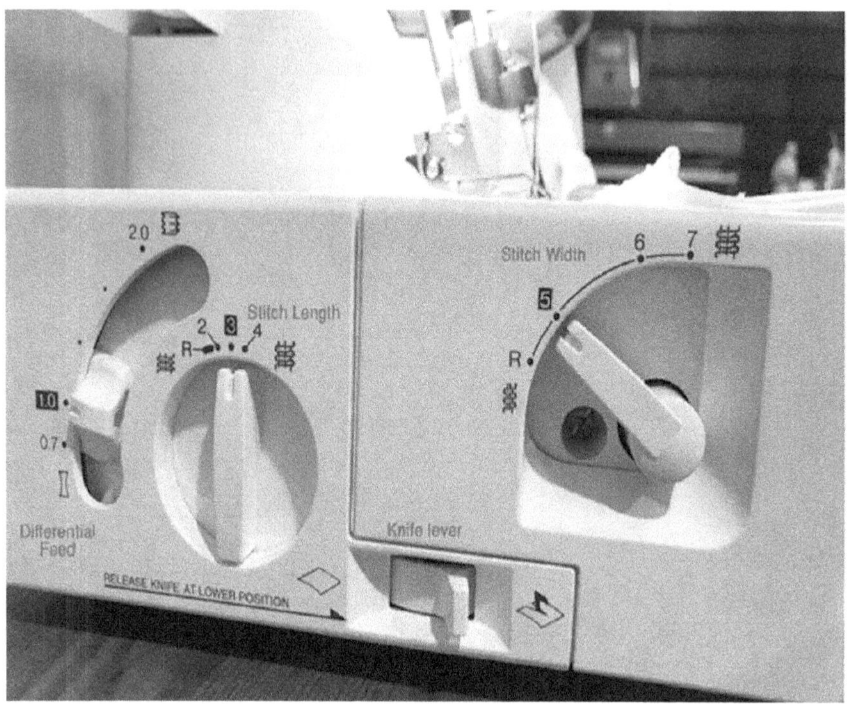

Before you start threading, always have a look at the settings of your overlock machine.

- Stitch length: This determines how long your stitches should be. Based on your machine, you can choose your preferable stitch length. In this case, the numbers are in millimeters so I will choose 3mm.

- Stitch width: This determines how thick or deep your stitches should be. They range from 5-7mm. You can choose a standard 5mm width since we are not doing any special hem.

- Differential feed: It is used to control front and rear feed dogs' movements. That is, how will the feed pull the fabrics through? Set this to 1 so that the fabric is pulled evenly by both the front and rear feed dogs.

- Knife/Blade lever: You can keep the blade down if you want to cut excess fabric while sewing.

- Tension dials Setting: You can start by adjusting the tension to 4. This will make it easier when you want to adjust the stitch tension.

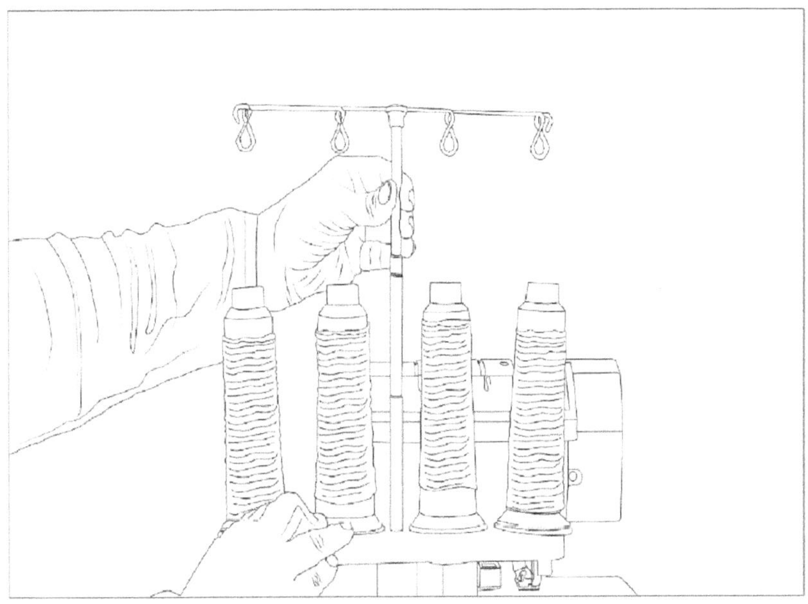

Threading a 4-thread Serger Machine

To practice with, you can use 4 different thread colors. You can choose colors similar to the tension dial colors. This will help you to know which dial you need to adjust later.

Place the 4 cone thread spools on each of the spool pins and extend the thread tree.

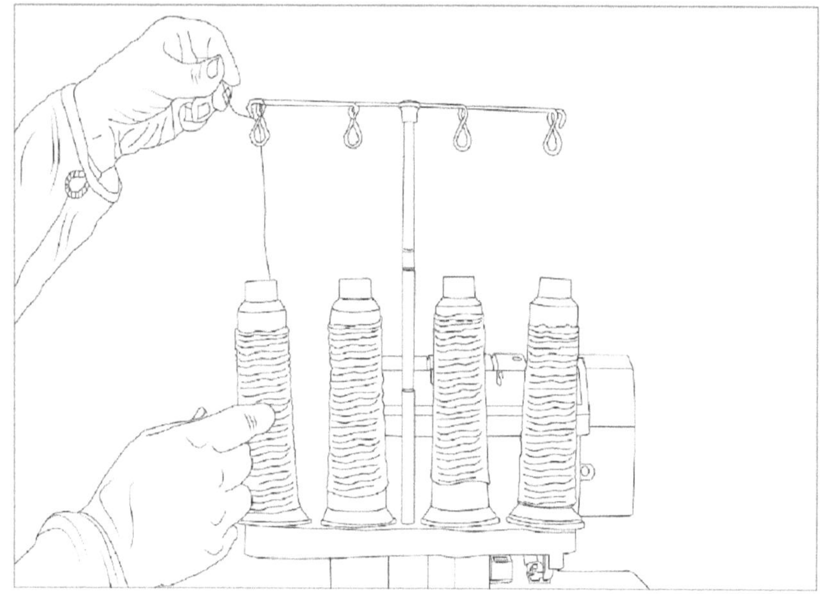

Each individual machine comes with an instruction manual on how to thread it. Your machine may have a slight difference from this one. Always consult your instruction manual for accurate threading.

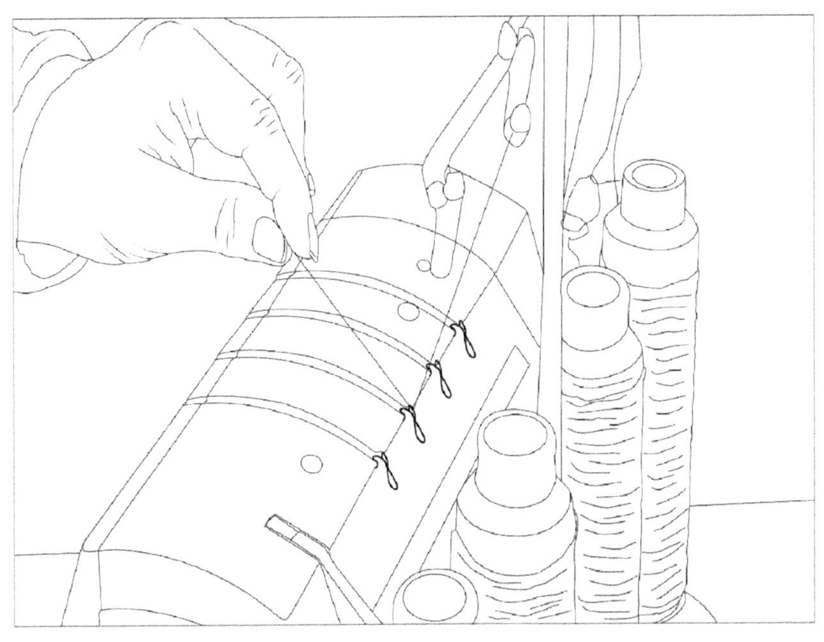

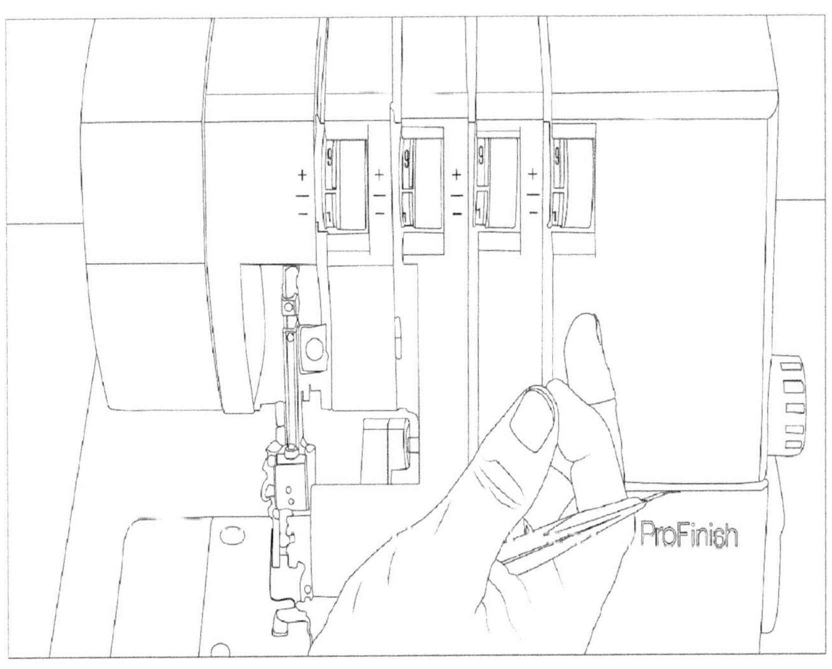

ProFinish

Steps to follow;

Threading the left needle

Step 1:

To thread the left needle, we will use the yellow thread color.

Pull the thread from the thread tree and pass it through the first guide hole on top of the machine as shown below.

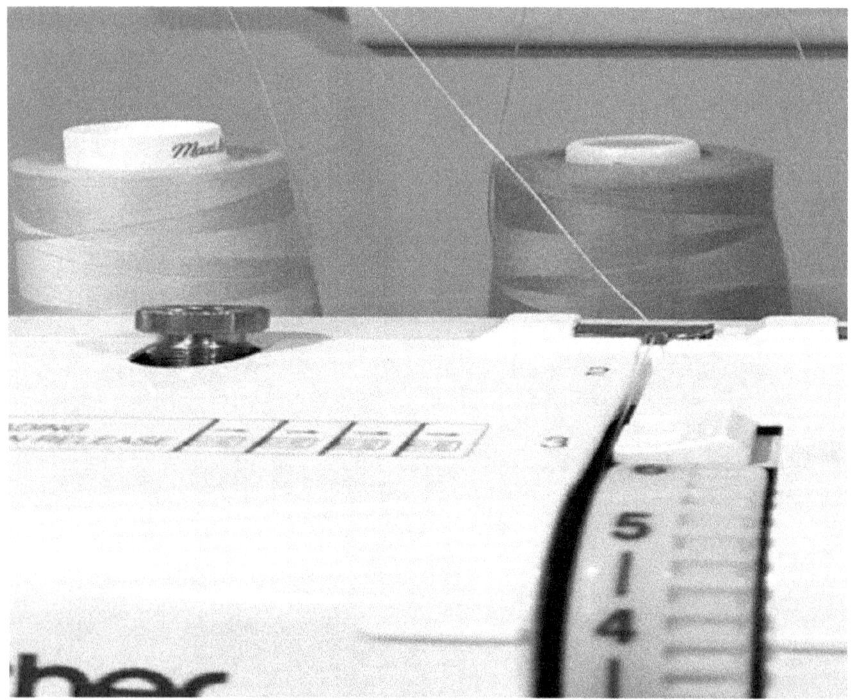

If your machine has some markings, you can follow them.

Step 2:

Pull the thread to pass through the tension disc (next to the first tension dial). Follow the instructions on your machine and get ready to thread the needle.

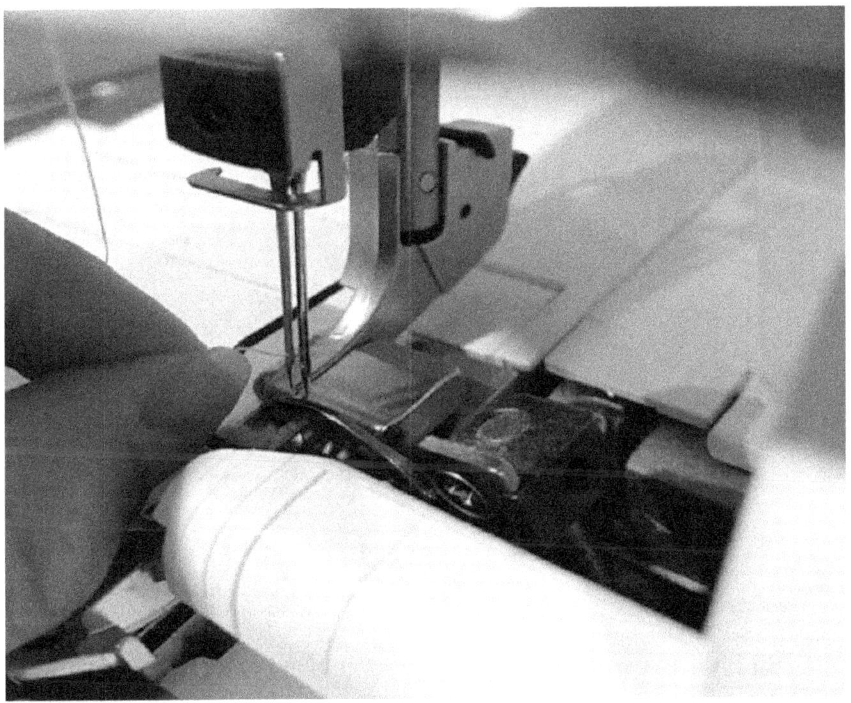

Step 3:

Thread your needle by passing the thread from front to back. You can use tweezers or use a needle threader to quickly thread your needles.

Step 4:

After inserting the thread, you can use tweezers to pull the thread to the back of the machine.

Threading the right needle

Step 1:

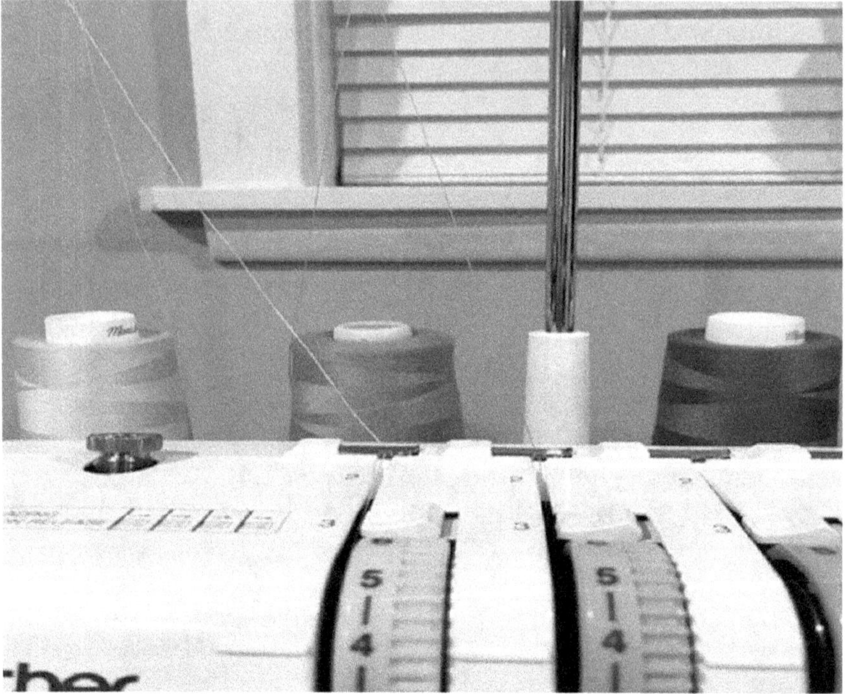

Pick your pink thread and pass it through the 2nd guide hole in the thread tree. Pass the thread through 2nd guide on the top of the machine as shown above. If your machine has markings always follow them.

Step 2:

Pull the thread to pass through the 2nd tension disc next to the tension dial. Pull the thread up and around the channel just like you threaded the left needle.

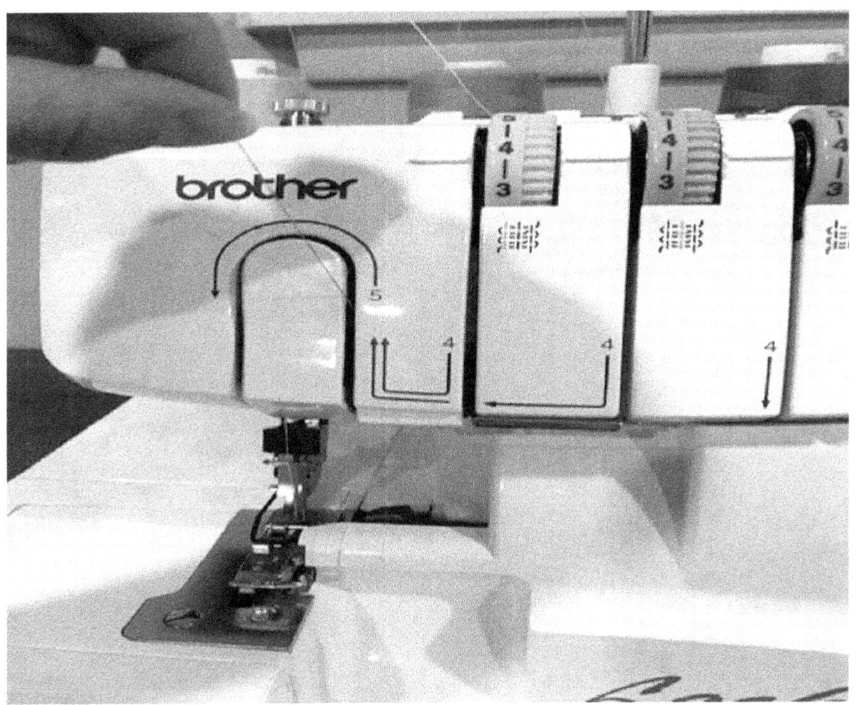

Step 3:

Insert the thread in the right needle from front to the back direction and push the thread to the back. You can also use tweezers to pull the thread.

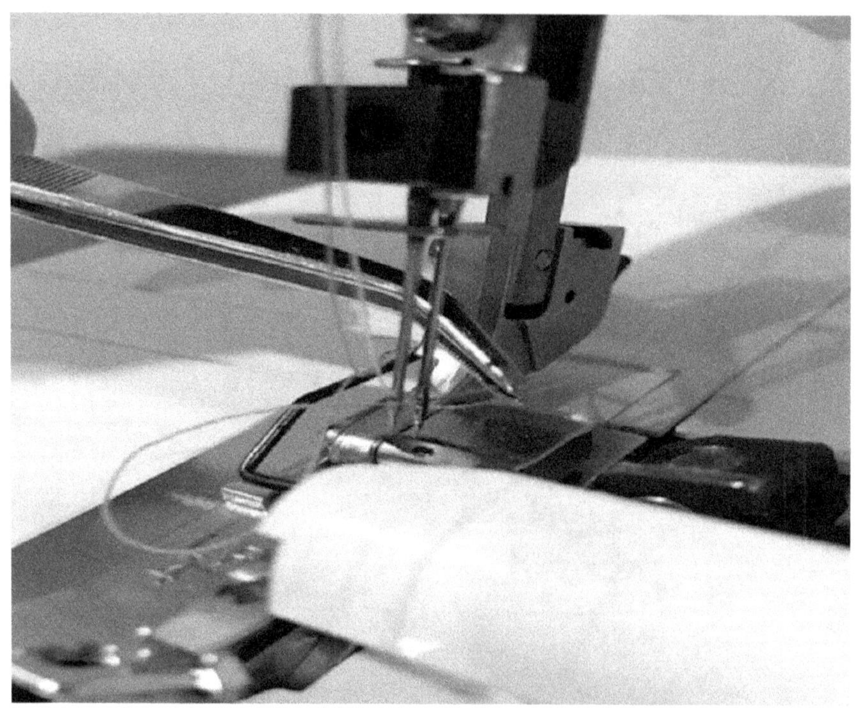

Now both threads (yellow and pink) should be lined up at the back of the machine.

Threading the upper looper

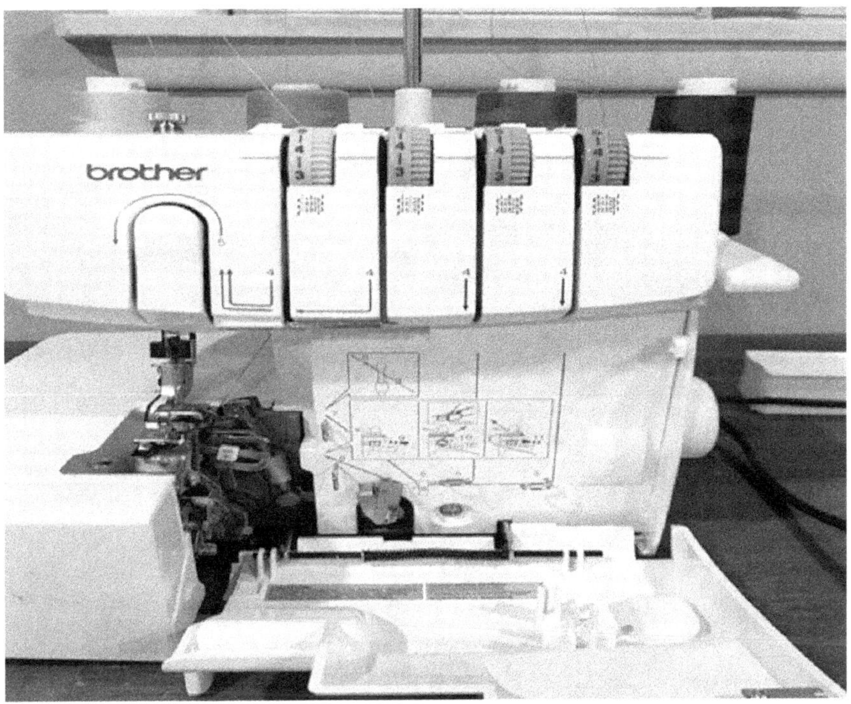

Start by pulling out the trim trap, you can slightly lift up the machine to make it easy to pull the trim trap and pull the front cover. This will enable you to access both lower and upper looper.

After pulling the front cover, there is a diagram that guides you on how to thread the upper and the lower loopers. Some machines might have a slightly different diagram so make sure to follow your machines diagram for you to thread correctly.

Step 1:

Using our third thread (green color), we can now thread the upper looper or the third needle.

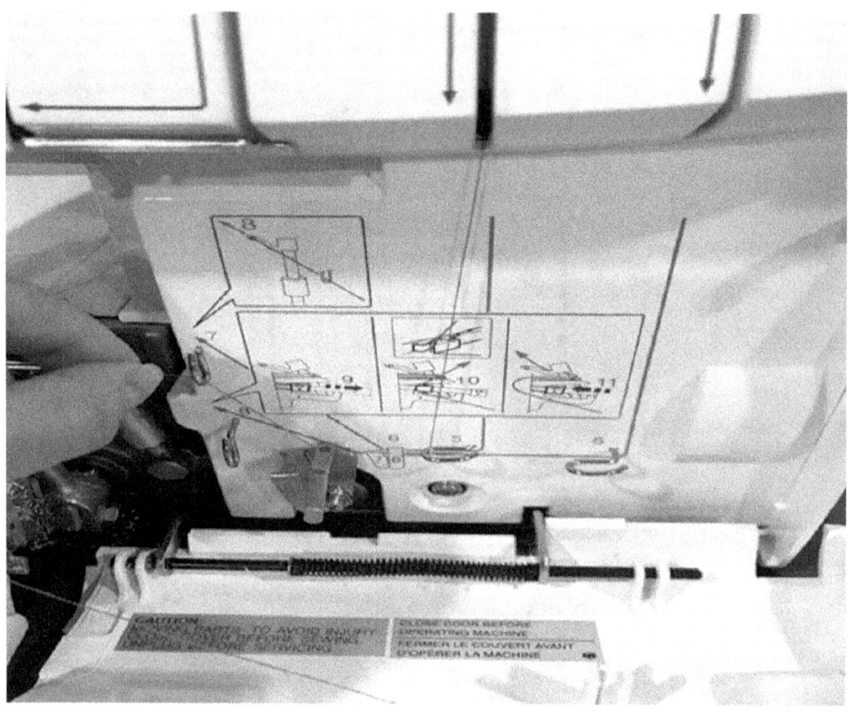

Just like threading the left and right needles, the third thread passes through the 3rd guide hole on the thread tree. Then pass the thread through the 3rd guide on top of the machine.

Pull the thread to pass through the tension disc (next to 3rd tension dial). Pull the thread through guides indicated by the diagram on the front cover.

Step 2:

Once you pass the thread through the indicated guide, you can now thread the upper looper needle. You can use tweezers to pull the thread front to the back.

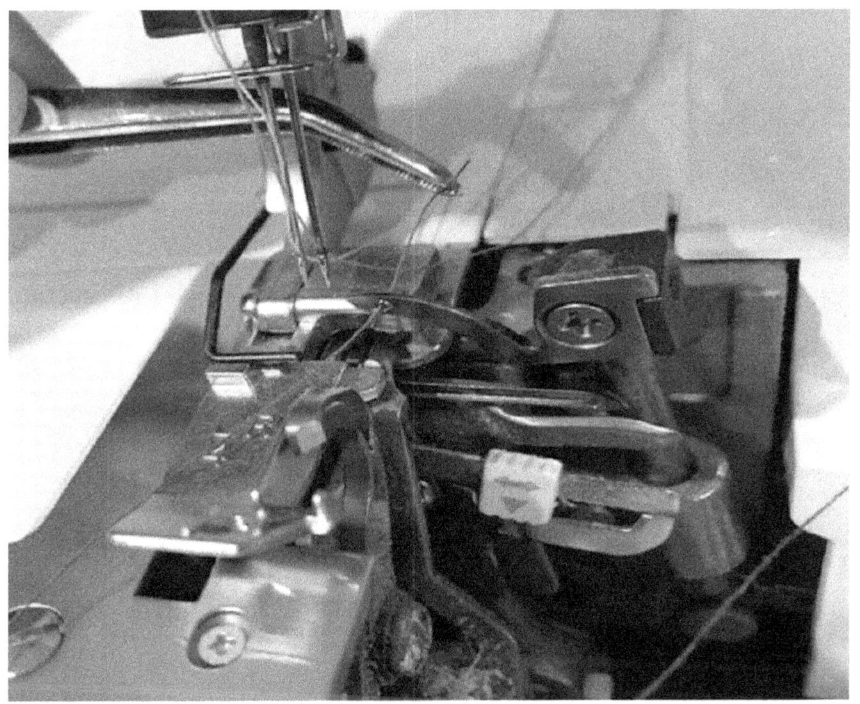

Pull the threat to the back of the machine as you have done with other threads.

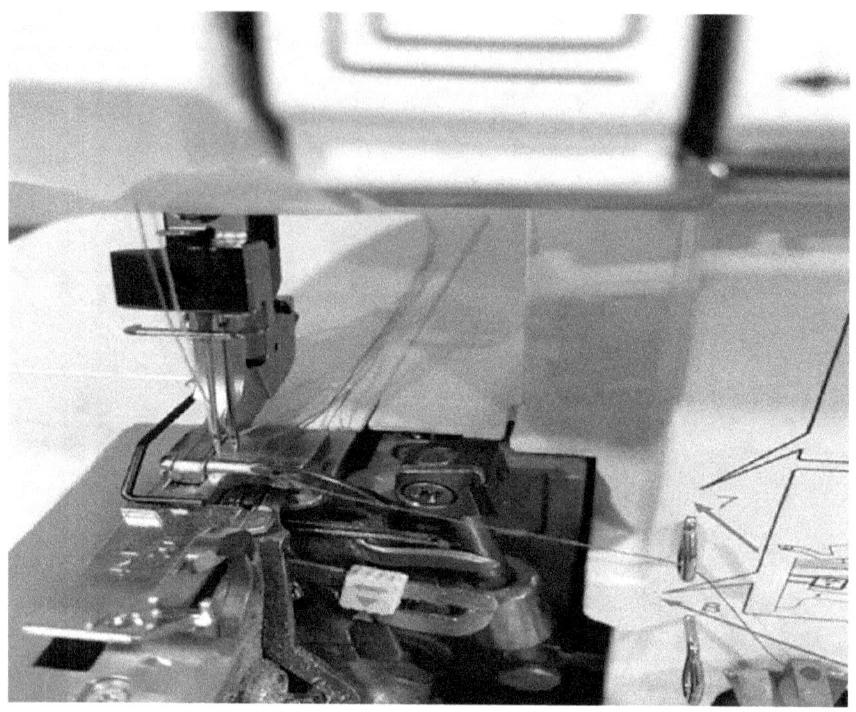

Threading the lower looper

We are going to use our 4th thread (blue color) to thread the lower looper.

Step 1:

Pass the blue thread via the hole in the thread tree and then pull it through the 4th guide at the top of the machine. Pass the thread through the 4th tension disc next to the last tension dial.

Step 2:

Follow the marked instructions on your machine and pull your thread through a series of steps on the front cover.

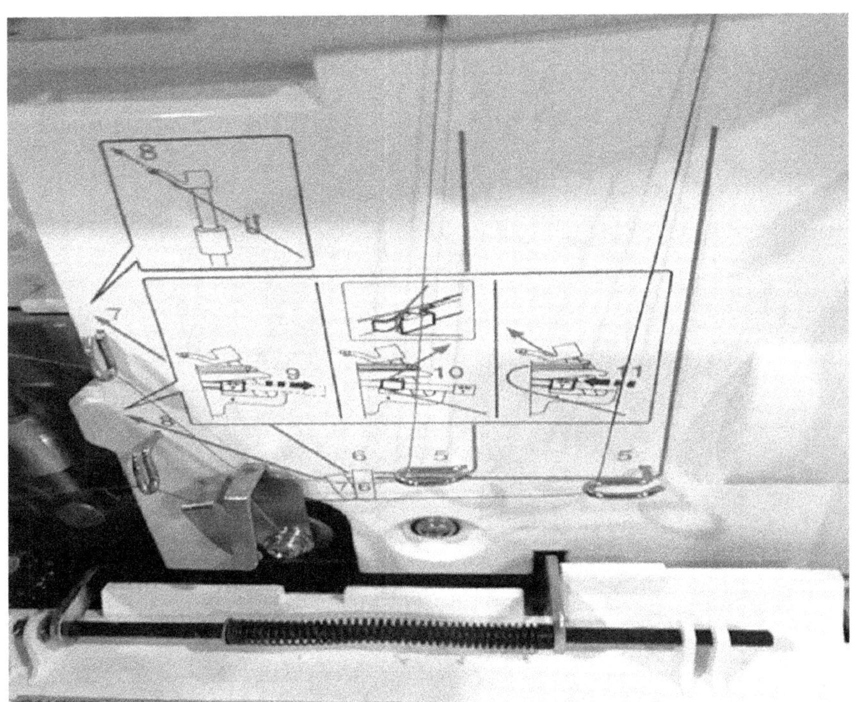

Now thread the lower looper with your thread. Thread on the two holes on your lower looper needle. Some machines do have an auto thread guide that automatically threads the first needle hole. Follow your machine instruction manual to know how the lower looper needle needs to be threaded.

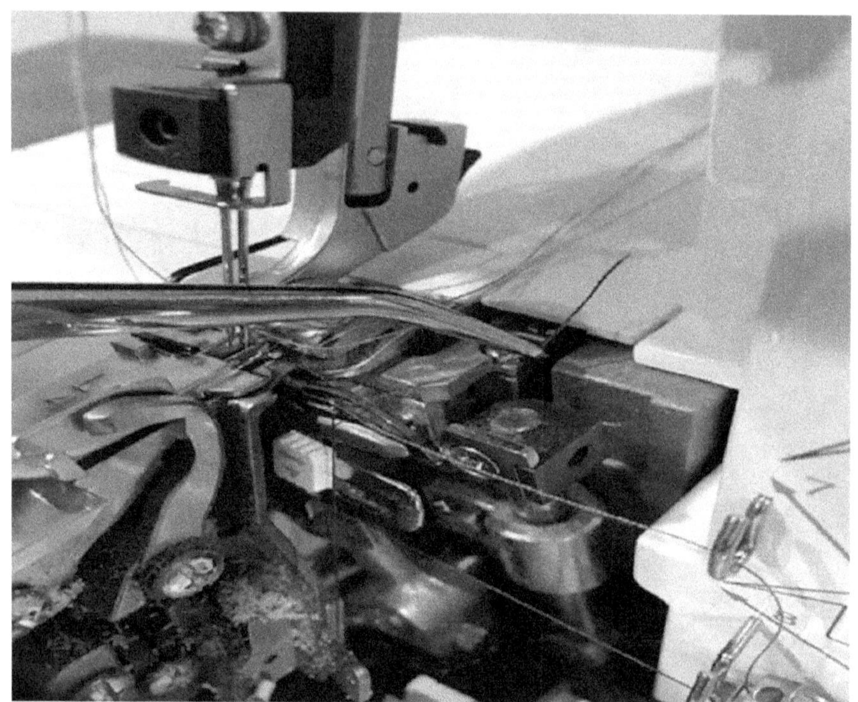

Step 3:

After threading, use tweezers to pull the thread to the back. The lower looper thread should always be placed at the top of the upper looper thread.

Step 4:

You can now close the front cover and return the trim tray back to its position. Line all 4 threads at the back of the machine before you start stitching.

Step 5:

Use the lever to lift up the presser foot of your serger machine and pass the 4 threads under the presser foot. Make sure the threads are pulled to the back. Now you're good to go!

Step 6:

Turn on your machine and step on the pedal. This will enable you to create a chain of threads. This also acts as a way of testing that the threads run through.

Since there is no breakage of any thread, you can now test the accuracy of your thread using the scrap fabric.

Place your fabric on the feed dogs to feed through. Align it with the edges of your machine and push the blade down. When the blade is pushed down, it will trim the excess fabric as you sew. The trimmed pieces will be collected in the trim trap.

When sewing, do not pull or push the fabric, let it feed through.

After stitching the scrap fabric, you can remove it from the machine and compare the tension.

Reviewing your overlock stitch and fixing issues

Once you make your first stitch on the scrap fabric, view the stitches formed at the front, back, and sides. Inspecting the stitches will confirm whether you have set the right tension dials based on the fabric type or whether there are issues that need to be fixed.

From our scrap fabric sample, if the blue thread (lower looper) at the front appears to be loose, this means you have to tighten the lower looper. This is done by adjusting the tension dial with the blue color thread.

Since the other colors look okay from the front view.

Proceeds to view the back of the fabric. If the yellow and pink color appear ok, then no adjustment needed on the tension dial. However, if the green and blue color thread appear loose, you need to tighten the tension dial with green and blue color (upper and lower looper tension) so that they can lay flat on the fabric edges.

Do the same for the side view of the fabric. Look at the overlock stitches on the sides where the two fabrics meet each other. If the settings are correct, you should see the loops perfectly lined down at the center. If any of the colors appear loose, you need to tighten it.

Having proper settings for the tension dials will leave your stitches looking professional.

How to change threads

Once you have already threaded your serger machines, it becomes easy to change the threads.

You don't have to open the lid in order to change the threads. You don't have to go through the threading process again. You can do that in just a few steps.

"How to change your serger thread and never re-thread again" is one of the best sewing hacks for every sewer. If you have been sewing for some time and you don't know this trick, it's time to learn it! And you will never be frustrated again while threading your machine. It will also save you time!

Step 1:

Turn off the machine and lift up the presser foot and ensure the needles are set at the highest point

Step 2:

Cut the thread close to the thread cone. Leave the piece of thread hanging and remove the thread.

Step 3: Your secret trick

Now put the cones of the new thread where you removed the old thread. Make sure the thread is placed in the right place.

Take the ends of the cut old thread and the new thread and tie a knot to them. Make sure the knot is strong and small. A simple knot is enough.

Step 4:

Pull the corresponding old thread color at the foot. Start by separating the 3 or 4 threads.

Step 5:

Pull the threads one by one until the new thread you have replaced is pulled to the back of the machine.

If the thread gets stuck along the way like in the tension disc, you can use your free hand to pull the thread. Continue pulling until the new thread comes up to the needle hole.

Due to the knot you made, the thread may not pass through the needle hole so you need to cut the knot then thread your needle again with the new color thread.

As simple as that, you're able to re-thread your machine. Repeat the same for all other threads you need to change and start sewing

Chapter Summary

- Before you start your sewing projects you need to know how to thread your overlock machine. With the above steps, you will be able to correctly thread your needles and both upper and lower loopers. Incorrect threading may result in the breakage of thread.

- After threading the needles, you can test them on your scrap fabric and adjust the tensions accordingly.

- After the initial threading of your machine, changing the thread colors becomes easy and can be done in seconds. All you need is to cut the old thread around the thread tree and replace it with the new thread color. Take the edges of the cut old thread and the new thread edges and tie them together to create a knot. Then pull the replaced thread at the back of your machine until the new thread color reaches the needle hole, cut the knot, and thread the needle with the new color thread.

You can re-thread the other colors based on your preferences and you're good to start stitching.

In the next chapter, you will learn how to stitch overlock stitches.

Chapter Four:
Introduction to Stitching Overlock Stitches

In our last chapter, we discussed how to set up your overlock machine and thread it. After threading your machine, now you're ready to start stitching. An overlock machine allows you to create a variety of stitches. A standard overlock machine should allow you to create at least 16 different forms of stitches.

Simple settings to your machine including adjusting the tension will help you create these different stitches. Your ability to customize the control settings is what makes the overlock machine great.

The most essential stitch to create is the overlock stitch. So whenever we talk of serging, most people only think of the overlock stitch but there are other diffcrent forms of stitches you can create with your overlock machine.

An overlock stitch is a special stitch that sews the edges of a piece of cloth by either adding hems, seams or edges.

You can sew an overlock stitch in different ways but the most used method is to sew a seam while at the same time finishing the raw edges of the fabric.

Overlock stitches are versatile since you can use them for decoration, construction, or for rcinforcement of the fabric.

These stitches are created when one of the needles (or two needles) penetrates through the fabric to sew a seam and the knife blade trims the edges of the fabric while the looper thread wraps the clean raw edge of the fabric.

A stitch can be formed using different ways based on the number of threads used. The key factor is the durability of your stitches.

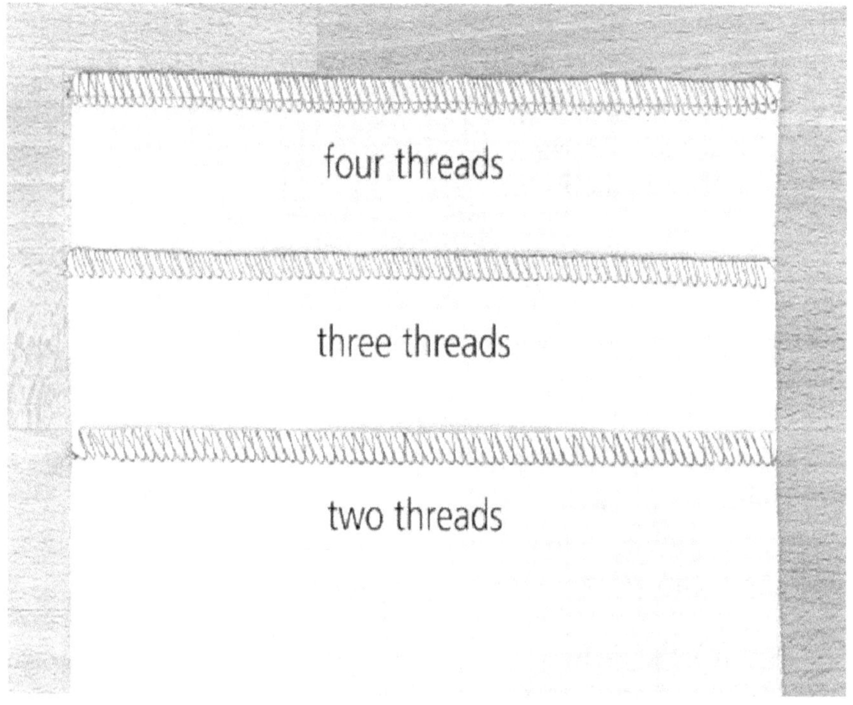

Types of overlock stitches

There are different types of overlock stitches that are classified based on the number of threads used in making the stitch. Most overlock machines use 1, 2, 3, 4, and 5 thread formations.

Each of these threads serves a unique purpose and benefits. For example;

1. Thread: It is great for doing end-to-end seams or butt-seaming on a piece of garment finishing.

2. Thread: Great for edging and seaming on knits and woven. You can use this type of stitch to finish seam edges, stitch an elastic lace to lingerie, stitch flatlock seams, and hem.

    In 2-thread stitch, the needle thread appears at the bottom of the fabric while the looper threads are on top of the fabric. Both needle and looper threads intersect at the edges of the fabric.

    This thread is suitable for sewing lightweight and stretchy fabrics.

    2-thread stitches are are not strong enough to create a seam, they're only suitable for finishing the raw edges of your fabric.

3. Thread: It is used to sew pintucks, blind hems, create finishing on fabric edges, create narrow rolled hems, create decorative edging, create seam knits, and woven fabrics.

    The stitch only uses one needle, you can choose either the left or right needle to create simple edge finishing on lightweight fabrics. It is the most used stitch due to its wide application. If you want to sew a loose t-shirt, you can use this type of stitch.

4. Thread: Used to create decorative edges and finishing, seam high-stress areas, and to create mock safety stitches that add extra strength on the stitches while at the same time retaining flexibility.

The 4-thread overlock stitch uses two needle threads to sew two rows of stitches in fabric while the looper thread wraps the edges of the fabric. The stitch is suitable for sewing medium to heavyweight fabrics, or sewing seams in fitted garments.

A 4-thread overlock allows you to sew more flexible seams and the stitches are more durable. Since more threads are used, you may end up with a bulky seam especially if you use thicker threads.

5. Thread: Mostly used in apparel manufacturing. They utilize the use of two needles to create a very strong seam.

Stitch formation

- As the needle goes through the fabric, a loop of thread is formed at the back of the needle.

- As the needle moves downward into the fabric, the lower looper moves from left to right. The tip of the lower looper needle passes behind the needle via the loop of thread that has already been formed behind the needle.

- The lower looper continues to move towards the right side. As it moves forward, the lower thread is carried along via the needle thread.

- When the lower looper moves from left to right, the upper looper moves from right to the left. The upper looper tip goes behind the lower looper needle and picks the lower looper thread and thread the needle.

- After needle threading, the lower looper moves back to the far end of the left position. While the upper looper continues moving to the left it firmly holds both the lower looper thread and the needle thread in place.

- The needle will again begin its downward move and pass behind the upper looper to promptly secure the upper looper thread. The needle will pass between metal and thread. This will result in a complete overlock stitch formation. This process continues until you finish sewing the fabric.

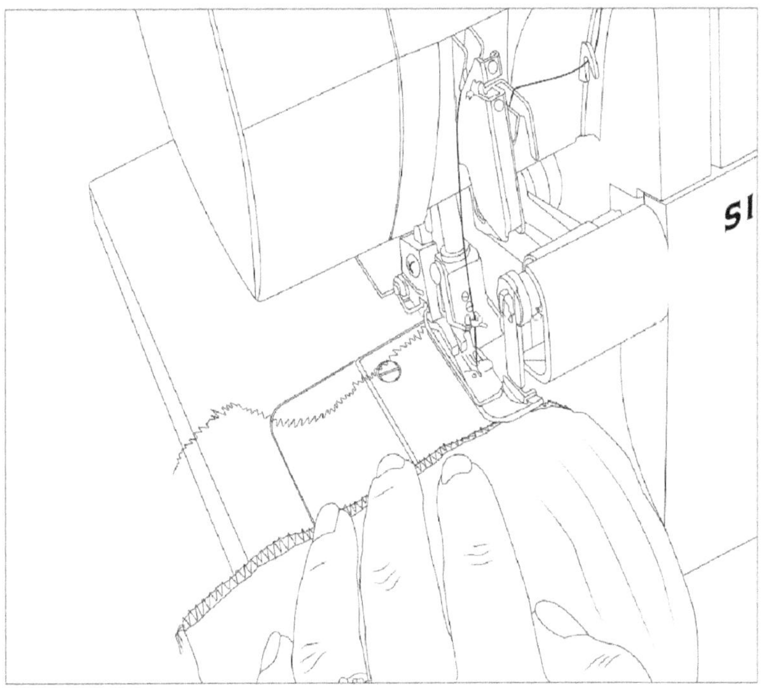

When to use an overlock stitch

Overlock stitch is ideal for sewing garments and creating general edge finishing regardless of the number of threads you use. You can use the stitch to construct a complete garment and finish the edges at the same time.

Overlock stitches help you join two pieces of fabric together. Some fabrics require you to create overlock raw edges before you can sew them. For example, the fabrics that need to be pressed open after you have sewn on them in order to reduce the fabric bulkiness. In such cases, you have to overlock the raw edges, then you can later construct your garment.

If your garment needs to be fitted with patterns that require extra attention, then you have to construct the patterns to the garment and then later you can add finishing edges with your overlock machine.

Therefore, based on what you want to sew, there are cases where you sew the garment and at the same time create finishing edges. While there are cases where you have to start sewing the fabric and later add the finishing edges. Alternatively, start with finishing edges then sew your garment.

Creating a Perfect overlock stitch

Since overlock stitch is the default stitch in all serger machines regardless of the number of threads used, the default stitch settings are always indicated on the machine using a small dot. These dots are on the tension dials next to number 4.

#	Stitch Type	Needle Positions	Tension Dial: Numbers shown are average settings on medium weight fabric with standard #80 polyester spun thread					Page
			Blue	Green	Orange	Yellow	Upper Looper or Spreader	
1	Two-Threaded Wrapped Edge Overlock (502)	3.5mm		3.0		1.5	Spreader	30
		5.7mm	3.0			1.0	Spreader	
2	Two-Threaded Standard Rolled Hem Stitching (503)	3.5mm		0.5		6.0	Spreader	31
		5.7mm	0.5			6.0	Spreader	
3	Three-Threaded OverLock (504)	3.5mm		3.0	2.5	2.0	Upper Looper	32
		5.7mm	2.5		2.5	2.0	Upper Looper	
4	Three-Threaded FlatLock (505)	3.5mm		0.5	5.5	5.5	Upper Looper	33
		5.7mm	0.5		5.0	6.0	Upper Looper	
5	Three-Threaded Wrapped Edge Overlock	3.5mm		3.0	0.5	7.0	Upper Looper	34
		5.7mm	3.0		0.5	7.0	Upper Looper	
6	Four-Threaded Ultra Stretch Mock Safety Stitch (514)		2.5	2.0	2.5	2.0	Upper Looper	35

The same is applicable to the differential feed, stitch length, and also the cutting width, If you have all the settings adjusted to the recommended numbers, then you have a solid overlock stitch.

But depending on the fabric you want to be sewn and the type of thread, the default settings may not work for you.

Probably if you're a beginner, you may not know whether you have the perfect stitch for your fabric. But as you continue to learn to use the machine, you can fine-tune the stitches. I suggest you follow the above steps mentioned in our previous chapter to fine-tune the stitches. That is, thread the machine with colored threads that match the marked or labeled path of your machine.

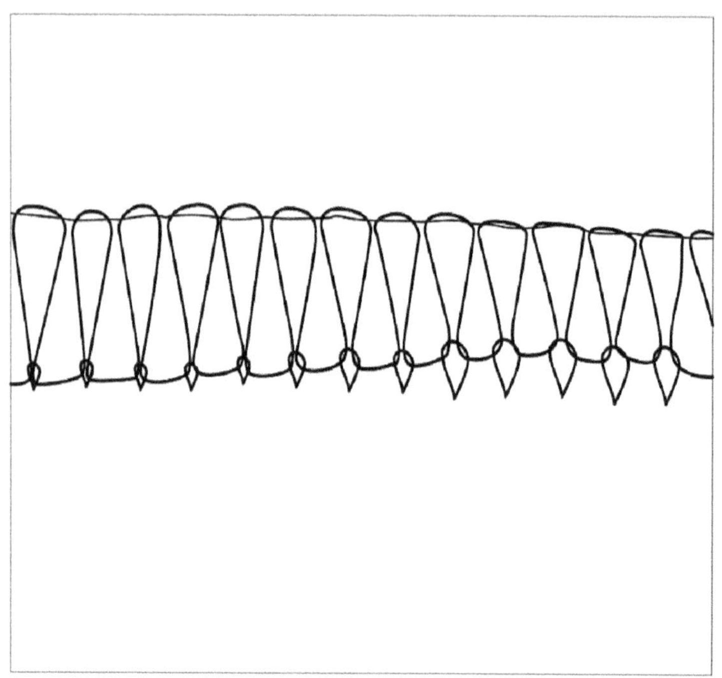

With different colors, you can identify the loose color thread or a tight color thread and adjust the corresponding thread color tension dial accordingly.

The looper threads should always meet at the edge of the fabric so if there is an issue with the tension, you will notice that based on how they appear on the sewn fabric. If the upper looper thread is pulled to the back of the lower looper thread is pulled to the front, you need to adjust the tension and strike the balance on the two looper threads.

If you can see the looper threads on the front side where the needle penetrates the fabric, then you have a tight needle thread and you need to loosen the needle tension.

However, if the needle tension is too loose, you will not have clean and straight line stitches. This is because the looper thread will keep pulling the needle thread to the front and back of the seam allowance on the fabric.

Lastly, if the seam allowances are pulled too tight and the looper threads hang loosely on the edges of the fabric then you need to adjust your micro thread control (MTC). Micro thread control is a lever that is used to control the stitch finger.

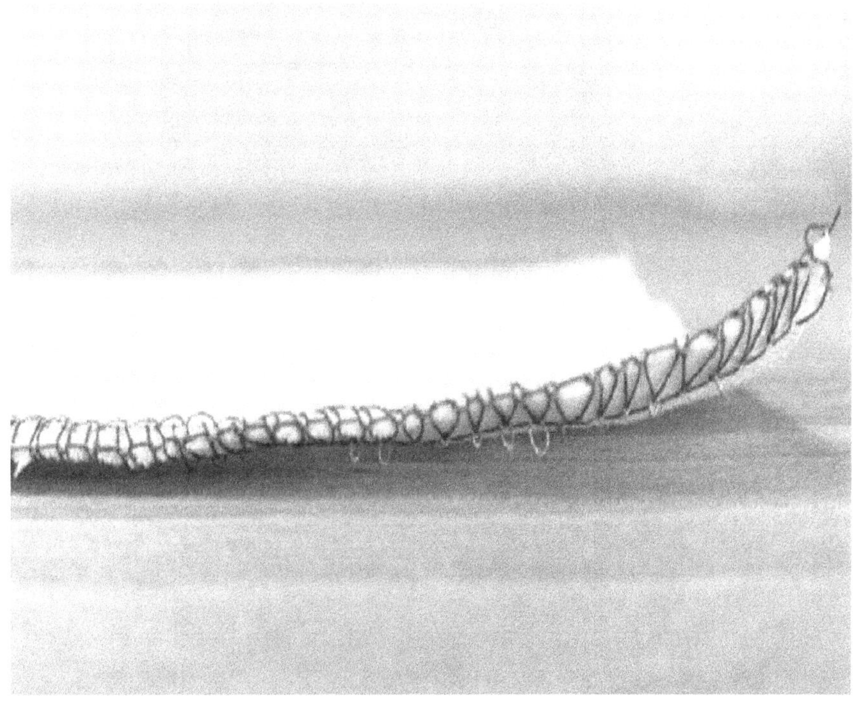

A stitch figure is a small metal around the needle area that supports the fabric as the loopers wrap the raw edges. If you increase the MTC (micro thread control) tension, the stitch finger will move out creating more space between the threads and the fabric. Reducing the tension will force the stitch finger to move in and bring the threads closer to the raw edges. This eliminates looping and results in tunneling of stitches.

If MTC is too tight, the looper thread digs into the raw edges of the fabric. This prevents the tunneling effect and the seam will not lie flat. If MTC is too loose, there will be slacks created between the looper threads and the edges of the fabric.

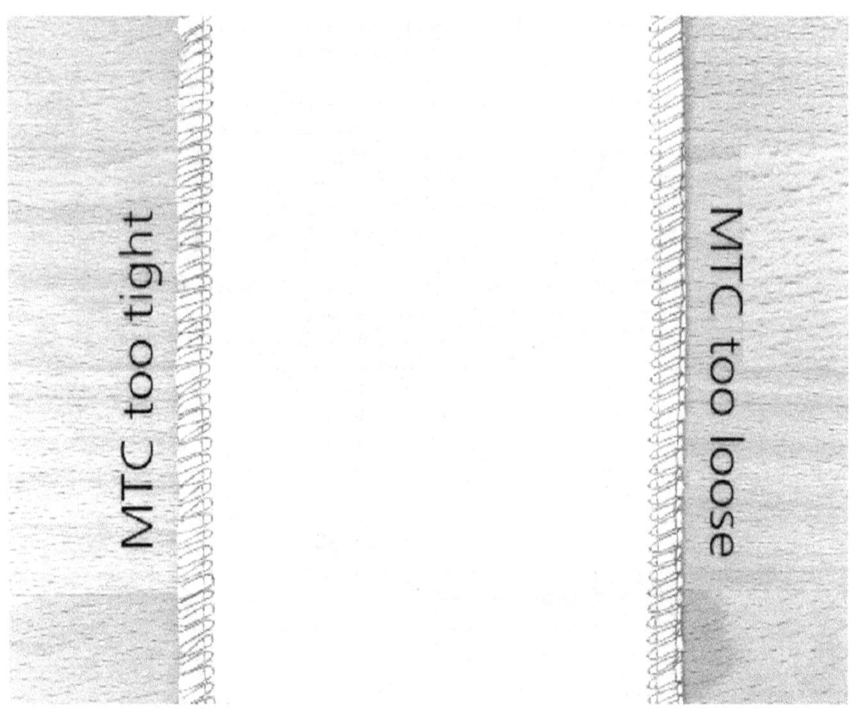

Therefore, to create a perfect stitch, you need to create a balance between the thread loopers and the needle threads.

Choosing the right serging stitches for your project

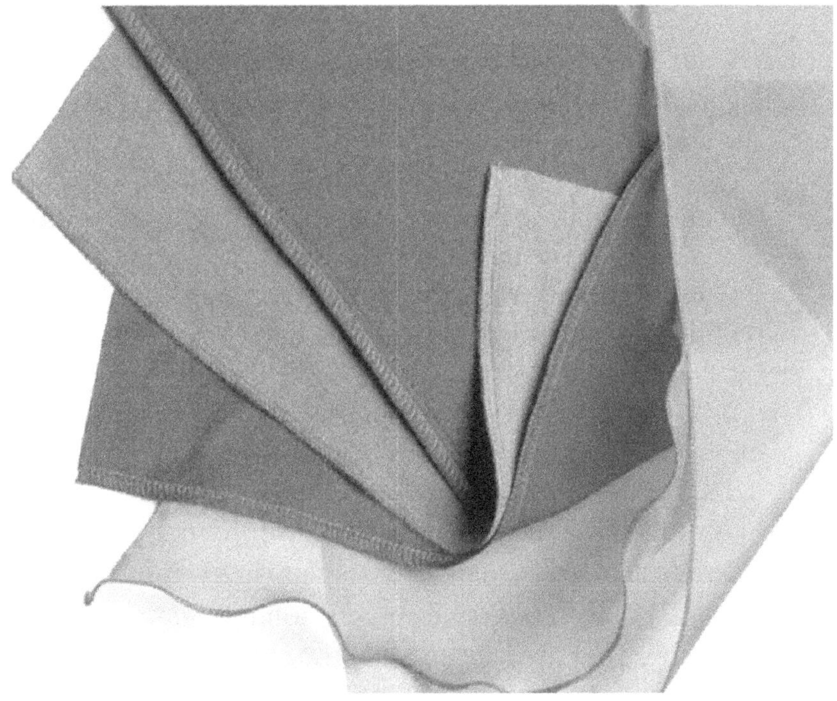

When serging, probably you have come across different stitches and you have been wondering what different stitches mean and how you can do them. Don't worry, you in the right place.

Overlock stitch, rolled hem and narrow hem are the most known stitches, but there are a variety of stitches you can form with your serger machine.

A serger stitch strengthens seams, add stretch to fabric, simplify edge finishing, and embellish your garment.

With the different types of stitches, sometimes you may be confused on which stitch to use and when. For you to choose the best stitch for your fabric, you need to first know the standard serger stitches.

Again, keep in mind that not all sergers that do all these stitches, so be sure to check with your brand on what type of stitches it can do. When buying a new serger, go for the one with the stitches you need.

The main stitches done by an overlock machine include:

- 3 and 4 thread overlock: It helps create seams and eliminate fraying of the fabrics raw edges.

- 2 thread overlock: It helps create lightweight stitches and also create finish stitches on lightweight fabrics.

- Wrapped stitches: In this, the lower looper thread wraps around the edges of the fabric from front to the back. You can use a 2-thread seam to create wrapped stitches that are strong and stretchy. You can use a decorative thread on the loopers to make the finish look good.

Rolled hem and narrow hem: These types of stitches helps add finishing to a single layer of fabric. If your serging a sheer fabric, a rolled hem will add a beautiful finish to your garment. ·   In a rolled hem, the edges of the fabric are folded and then wrapped with threads. The hems are great for finishing edges on a silk scarf, chiffon dress, and edges of a ruffle.

You can use this stitch with lightweight fabrics to stop them from frying but it cannot be used for creating seams.

A narrow hem works the same as rolled hems but have a line that runs along the edges of the fabric. Narrow hems don't have full stitch look so you may have some gaps between the stitches. Therefore, if you're using a fabric that frays, then rolled hem will the most suitable stitch for your fabric.

Flatlock: A flatlock helps you join two pieces of fabric side-by-side and create a flat seam. This type of seam is mostly found in sportswear garments because they need to be more comfy on the inside. When you sew wrong sides together, the lower looper thread remain outside the stitch but when you sew right side, the needle thread is placed outside.

This stitch is good for stretchy fabrics or when you want to sew a reversible stitch that look neat on both sides.

The flatlock only joins two pieces together without forming a seam allowance that rubs against your skin when exercising. If you want to join thick layers of fleece fabric, use this stitch to join them.

Blind hem stitches: They are used to create invisible finish of the hems. You can use blind hems on your dresses and trousers made of woven fabric. You can also use bling hem in a stretchy t-shirt. Loosen the needle thread if you want the created hem to stretch with the fabric.

Picot edge: This type of stitch is used to create decorative finish on the edges of a single layer of fabric. The serger folds the edges and wraps them with a thread

Therefore, when you want to create edge finishing or seams, choose the best stitch that will match your fabric needs.

One of the best stitch rules is to choose overlock stitches when handling standard seams on knits and wovens, a wider overlock stitch when dealing with bulky fabric, a narrow stitch with few threads when serging lightweight fabrics, and a wrapped stitch when knitting seams for maximum stretch.

If your machine can stitch 2-thread or 3-thread stitches, you can decide to use the left needle to sew wider stitches, or use the right needle for narrow stitches. Alternatively, you can decide to use rolled-hem stitches to create decorative narrow stitches. Since both loopers do not pierce through the fabric, you can decide to use a heavy or decorative thread in one or both of the loopers to make your edge finishing more attractive.

Chapter Summary

- An overlock stitch is the most used stitch to join pieces of fabric together or add finishing to your garments. Creating this type of stitch is very easy, all you need is to learn how to customize your thread tension and you're good to go.

- There are different types of stitches you can create like French seams, zigzag stitches, blind hems, and much more. For you to be able to create the different types of stitches using different thread types, you need to know how to create a perfect stitch for your projects.

- Balancing the looper threads and needle threads can make it easy to sew a clean garment. The stitch ensures the edges of the fabric have a great finishing.

- Also, if the stitches are far apart, then you will not have a strong seam especially if your serging on a loosely woven fabric. Therefore, you should adjust the thread tensions depending on the fabric you're using.

In the next chapter, you will learn how to stabilize your Serging stitches

Chapter Five:
Stabilizing Serging Stitches

In our previous chapter, we have talked about how to balance your threads to have a perfect stitch. Based on the fabric you're using, you will find you have to adjust the tension dials for you to have a clean stitch.

Your fabric type affects how your stitches will turn out. If you're using a medium weight fabric, you may find adjusting the tension to a certain number will give you a good stitch. However, this stitch setting may not look good when used on thin or heavy fabric. The looper threads may appear either too loose or have a tight thread if used on heavyweight fabric.

So there are instances where adjusting the tension alone or even the presser foot may not balance your stitches. Therefore, implementing the stabilization of seams can help improve the quality and look of your stitches. Especially if you have a very thin fabric.

You may also want to reinforce the stitches in some of the high-stress areas or probably want to ensure your seams are sewn in a straight line and do not warp out of shape. Since overlock stitches do stretch as the fabric stretches, stabilizing the stitches will a great way to improve the stitches' look.

There are some great ways to stabilize your stitch such as using stay tape, using a ribbon, binding, or using a clear elastic.

These methods are great for stabilizing high-stress areas such as the shoulder seams.

In this chapter, you will learn how to stabilize your seams and reasons why you need to stabilize.

Stabilization of seams

Stabilizing helps prevent the fabric from stretching out. They act as a reinforcement to the seams especially if you're using knit fabric.

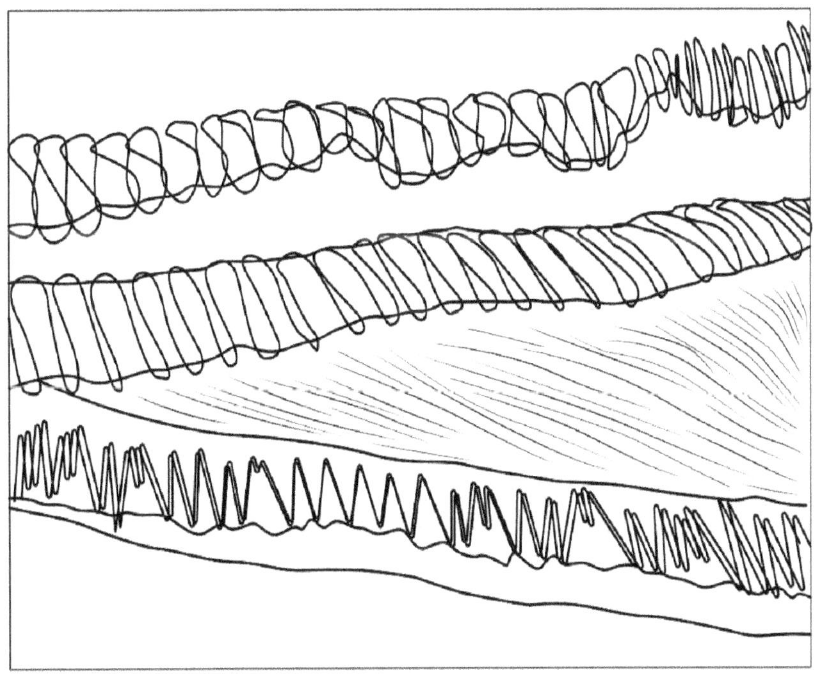

Most people always stabilize the shoulder seams because they are at high risk of stretching out when sewn and when you wear the garment.

The front piece of shoulder seam is sewn slanted thus, increasing the stretch of the garment. This makes you end up with a wider shoulder seam than your original pattern.

For this reason, you have to reinforce shoulder seams on t-shirts and on knit-tops.

There are various ways you can do this, but what is the best method for you to use? keep reading to learn how you can reinforce seams and when to use each of the methods mentioned.

Stabilizing methods

- Clear elastic

- Power fusible

- Fabric strip

- Fusible bias tape

1. Clear elastic

This is the most common stabilizing method because it has the ability to stretch and recover just like the 4-way stretch of spandex knits. Therefore, clear elastic has a perfect stretch for almost all the fabrics and makes your fabric stay in shape.

Clear elastic is suitable for sewing any close-fitting stretchy tops. It ensures you don't end up with an uneven shoulder seam.

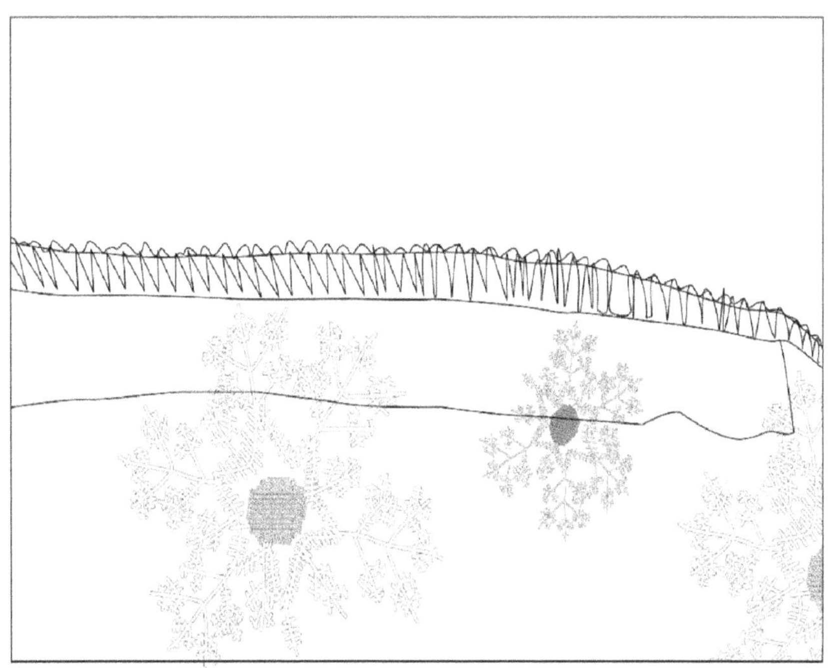

The width of this clear elastic is equivalent to your seam overlock stitch, so you can use the clear elastic to cover your shoulder seam.

No need to fuse the clear elastic thus making it suitable for use with synthetic knits. It is also easy to serge clear elastic especially if your presser foot has a built-in narrow elastic slot.

However, the clear elastic doesn't work well if you're sewing a neckline using an attachment binder because you have to open the shoulder seam making it difficult to add the clear elastic later. Again, not all people who like to have the silicon feel of the clear elastic on their clothing. Also, the clear elastic learning curve can frustrate you.

You should always sew the clear elastic together with shoulder seams at the same time and only cut the elastic after you have sewn both seams.

You can also use clear elastic when gathering the fabric in order to add some shirring to your garment.

2. Power Net/Power Fusible

Power net is a piece of a heavy stretch mesh that is used to reinforce stability on lingerie and shapewear products. Just like clear elastic, the power net has a good balance for stretch and recovery properties making it great for sewing stretchy knit fabrics.

You don't need to fuse it and due to his versatile nature, you can use this stretchy mesh on any type of fabric.

3. Fabric strip/Ribbon

This one of the greatest methods that relies on the use of fabric scraps and it the most commonly used method in the garment industry. Scraps made from 100% cotton jersey or a blend of cotton and jersey are the best in stabilizing shoulder seams.

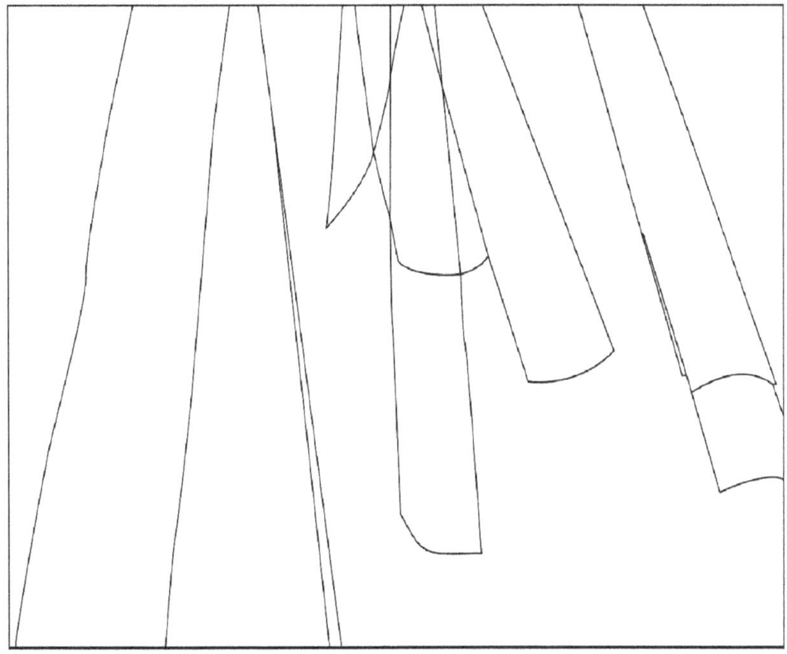

Make sure to use a thin knit with a smidgen stretch length to reinforce seams. Cut the strips vertically and use them to sew the seams. The fabric strip adds stability to your garment and also gives your knits the right amount of stretch.

A fabric strip is versatile and can be used in reinforcing almost any type of fabric. Although, when used on shoulder seams, it can add some bulkiness to them.

When stabilizing shoulder seams and knits, place the reinforcement strip on the back shoulder piece and sew the seam.

You can also attach the fabric strip to your garments by using either glue or zigzag stitch and then go ahead and sew the shoulder seam. This ensures the strip doesn't slip while sewing the seam.

4. Fusible bias tape

A fusible tape is great for adding a balance between the stability of the garment and its stretch. Make sure to use the bias tape to get better results. It is easy to sew since you only stuck the tape on the fabric and sew the shoulder seam.

The tape doesn't fuse well when sewing synthetic fibers.

Alternatively, you can use stay tape or cotton twill tape which is soft and made of natural fiber. These tapes prevent stretching of seams since the tapes themselves do not stretch

How to stabilize the shoulder seam

- Prepare a piece of your stabilizer. You can cut it to about 1 to 2 inches longer than the seam.

- Place the two pieces of the bodice together with the wrong sides facing together.

- Place the aligned pieces of fabric under the presser foot.

- Place the stabilizer fabric on top of the bodice pieces at an exact place intended for the seam line and the excess length remains under the presser foot.

- Serge at the middle of the stabilizer up to the end of the seam

- Trim the excess stabilizer on both ends of the seam.

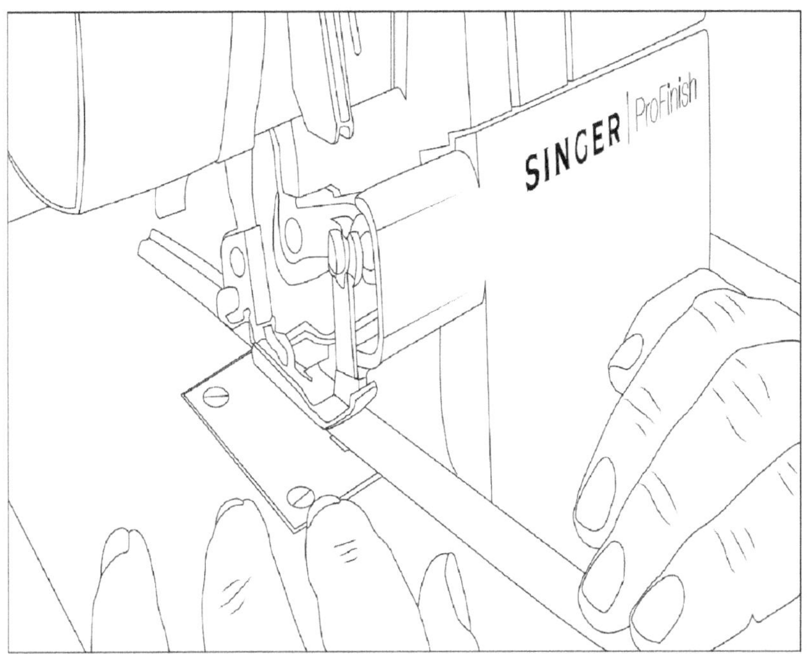

Chapter Summary

- Stabilization of seams is one of the greatest methods you can use to strengthen your seams, especially when dealing with stretchy fabrics or lightweight fabrics. They make it to reinforce stitches when dealing with a very thin or light fabric.

- It also helps prevent fabrics from stretching out. Some stabilizing methods enhance the design of the garment by hiding the seam allowance.

- You can use binding strips, clear elastic, twill/stay tape to stabilize your seams. Depending on the material you're using, you can use any of the stabilizing methods to strengthen your seams.

In the next chapter, you will learn how to add corner curves both inside and outside and circle curves.

Chapter Six:
Working With Corner and Curves

A serger machine makes the finishing of your fabric look clean and more professional. However, serging finishing edges around the corners and curves can be difficult not only to beginners but also to those who have been sewing for some time.

Sewing corners can be great if you want to add pockets, collars, bows, straps, and other decorations to your garment.

This curve and corner serging guide will help on how to easily make a clean and even finish for your curves and corners. At the end of the chapter, you will be able to add professional finishing to the garment no matter the shape.

How to serge corners in a fabric

Step 1:

To make it easy for you to sew corners in your garment, you can draw a seam line at the corner using chalk or a removable pen to help you know when to pivot.

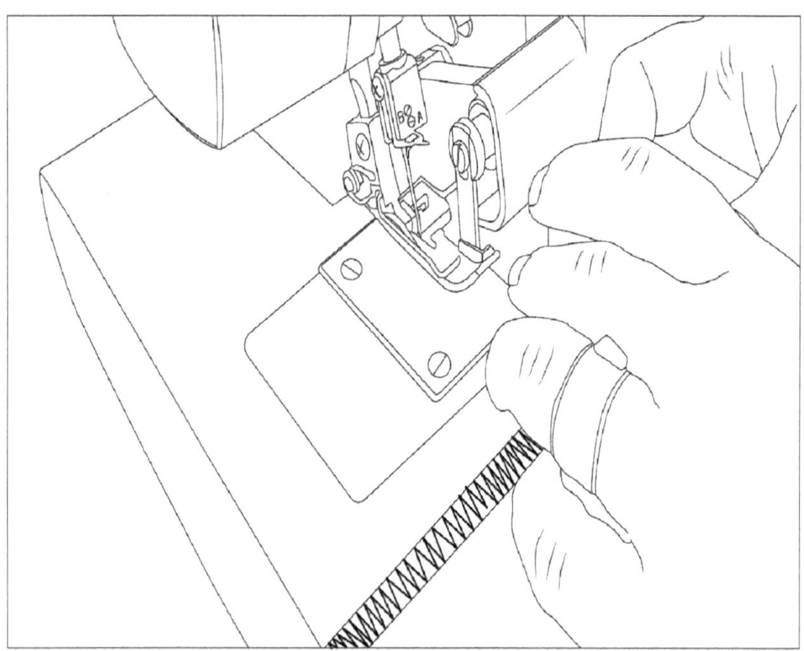

Step 2:

Start sewing along the seam line and slow down your serging speed when you're almost to the corner of the fabric.

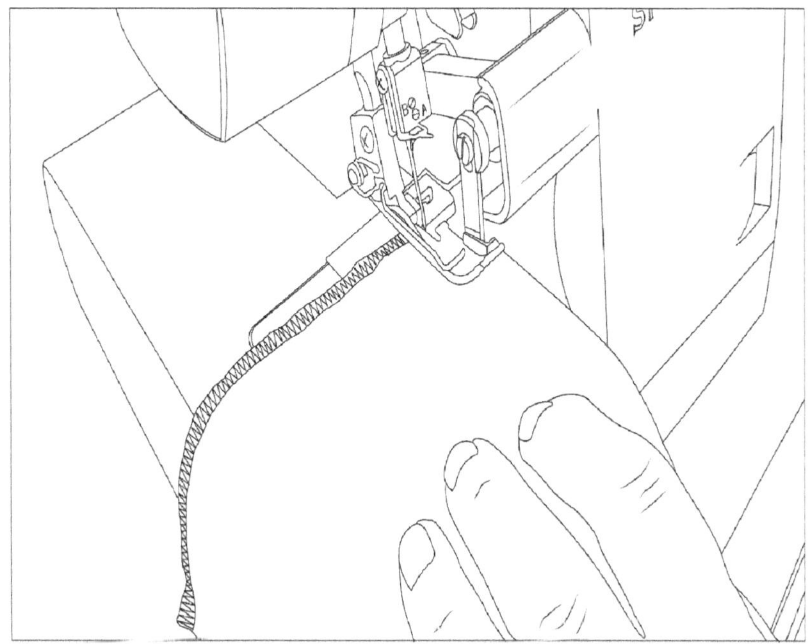

Step 3:

Add one or two stitches past the end of the corner. Let the needle remain down the fabric, and lift up the presser foot and turn the corner of the fabric to face the new direction. Lower the presser foot down and continue serging in that direction.

Step 4:

After sewing the corners, you need to trim and clip your fabric. If there is excess fabric you need to trim it away before you turn the garment on the right side out.

When serging corners of garments, we mostly use the 90 degrees corners. For example, for the corners of pillows, bags, etc. you only need to snip the corners off at 90°.

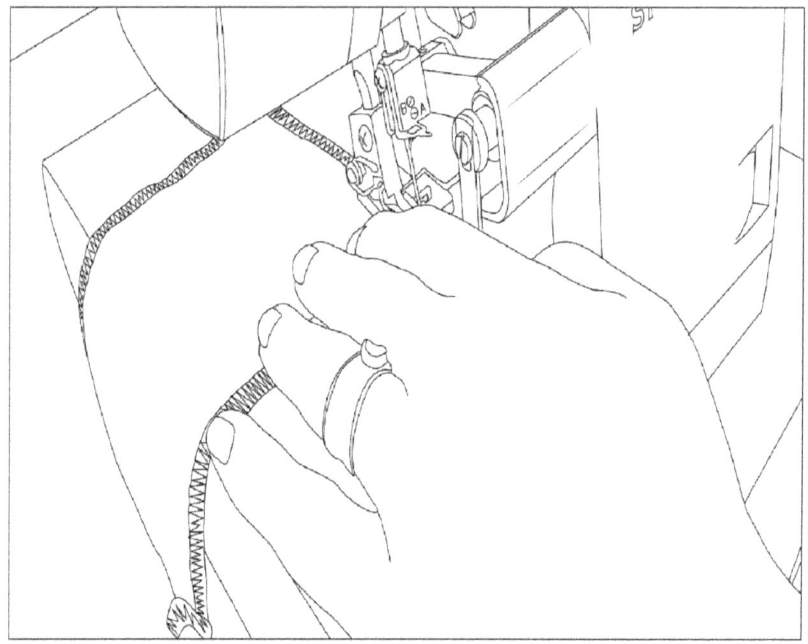

If you have a seam allowance with a width of more than 6 mm (1/4 inch) then you can trim off the sides.

If you're serging on sharp corners like the ones you add on collars, then you need extra trimming of the excess fabric. If the fabric is thick or it has various layers, you may consider grading the seams for better results.

Extra narrow corners

If you want to serge narrow corners, you should consider stitching across the corners several stitches in order to lessen the point. This will result in enough room for seam allowance once you turn the fabric in the right way.

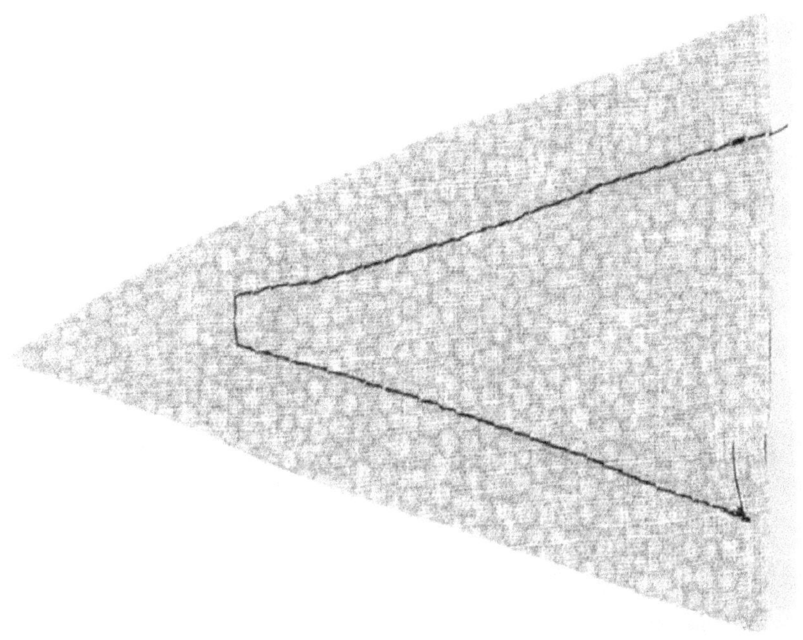

Then trim the excess fabric on both ends to leave a narrow corner.

Inside corners

If you want to add inside corners to the fabric, then you have to snip into the corners up to the stitching line as shown below.

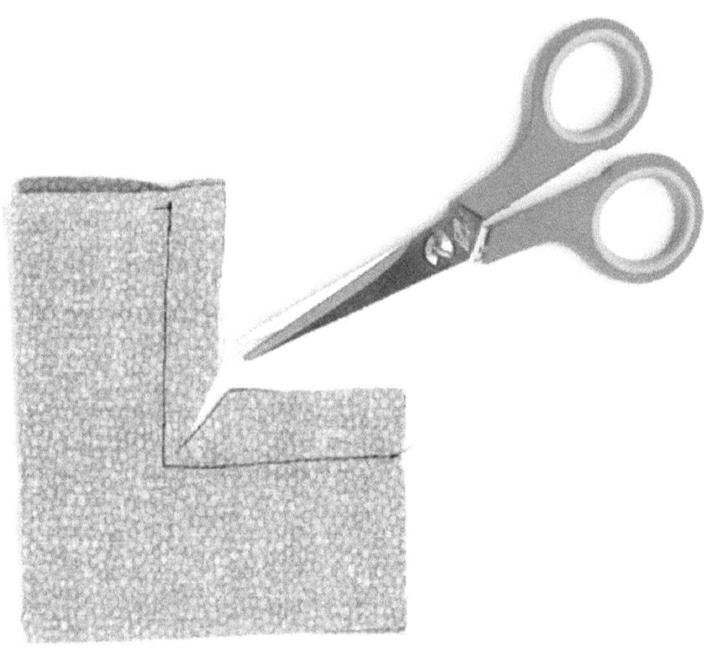

After sewing the corners, you need to turn the corners the right way out. You can use a pointy tool to poke the corners out. Do not use any sharp object because you can accidentally poke a hole or cut the fabric.

Serging mitered corners

You can also serge a 90 degree mitered corner with hems at the edges or a binding. After serging the mitered corner hem, you will not turn the fabric the right way out. Mitered corners are used on items such as napkins, curtains, tablecloths, and quilts.

The corners help reduce bulkiness in the fabric and help and leaves you with flat attractive hems on fabrics.

There are two techniques you can use to serge this type of corner. These techniques depend on whether you will have a narrow hem or wide hem. In a narrow hem method, you will create an opening at the diagonal of the corner. If a wide hem technique is used, then you will shut down the diagonal opening.

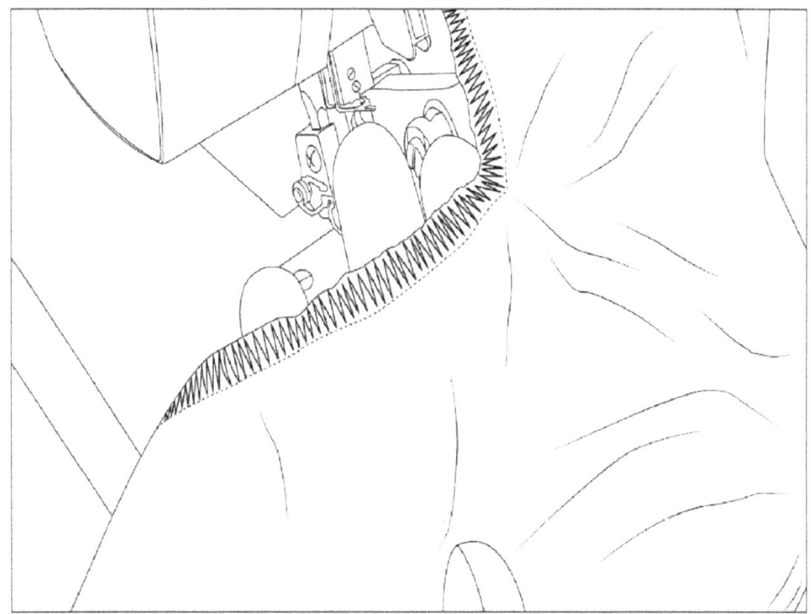

Serging Circle Curves/ Convex Curve

A convex curve is a form of the curve that faces outward just like a circle. This curve is mostly used to sew pockets edges, bag flap, or clutches.

Step 1:

Use the tailor's chalk to mark the seam allowance line that you will follow when sewing. It gives you the accuracy of the curve. Without the drawn line, it makes it difficult to visualize the curved seam and know when to turn so as to sew a perfect curve.

You can use a seam gauge or even a ruler to help you create a few dashes or marks on the fabric then join the dashes together.

Step 2:

Place pins vertically on the fabric to make it easy for you to follow the drawn curve without any interference. The heads of the pins should be left hanging outside of the curve to make it easy to remove them.

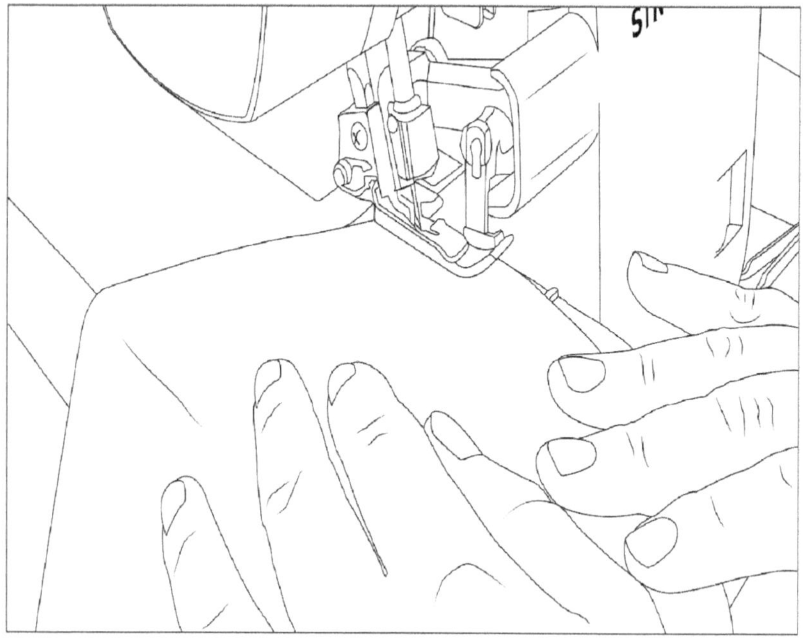

Step 3:

It is now time to sew the curves. First, set your overlock machine to use a small stitch length. You can set a stitch length between 2.0 to 2.5.

Then start stitch slowly. Gently guide the fabric with your fingers and continue serging following the marked seam line.

Step 4:

After sewing all the corners, then you need to trim the excess fabric in order to maintain a smooth curve when you turn the right way out. You can do this by cutting triangle notches from the seam allowance of your convex curve.

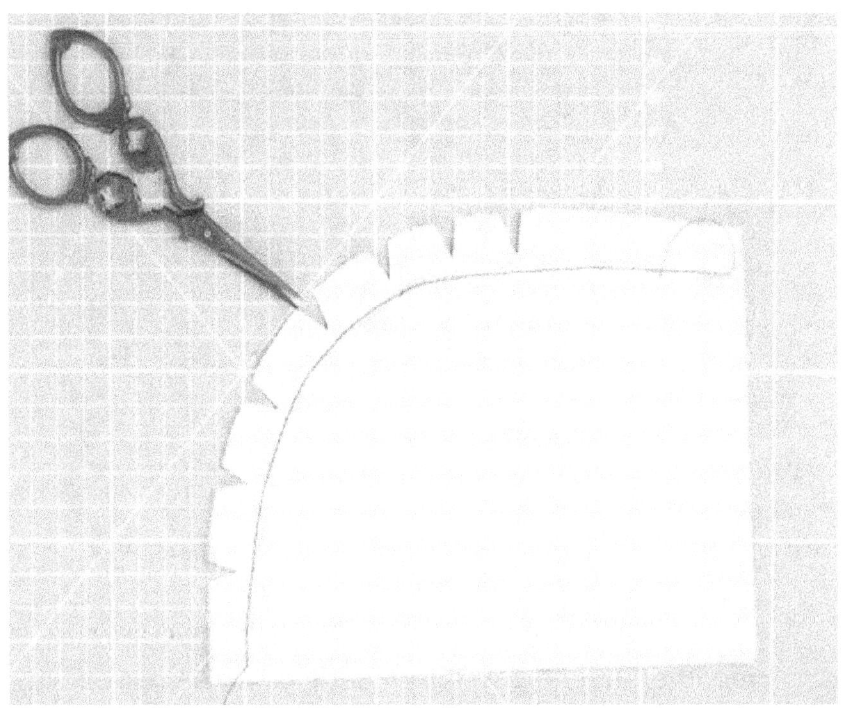

Step 5:

Turn the fabric to have the right side out and then press the curves.

Serging Concave Curves

Concave curves are mostly used in creating necklines and armholes in a garment. You can use the same steps as the sewing convex curve but clipping of the seam allowance is different from that of the convex curve.

Instead of clipping notches in concave, you place snips before the stitch line

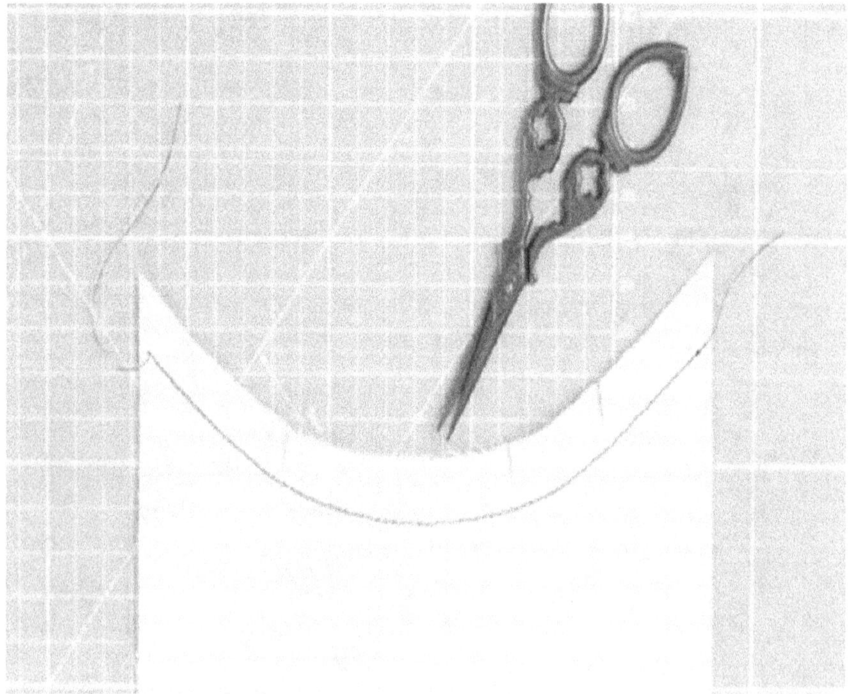

Press the curve to give it a smooth look. The reason why you have to clip the curves is that once you turn them right side out, the seam will appear flat and smooth. If the seam is

left without clipping, your curves and corners will look wrinkled and pull out. Am sure you don't want to see this on your garment.

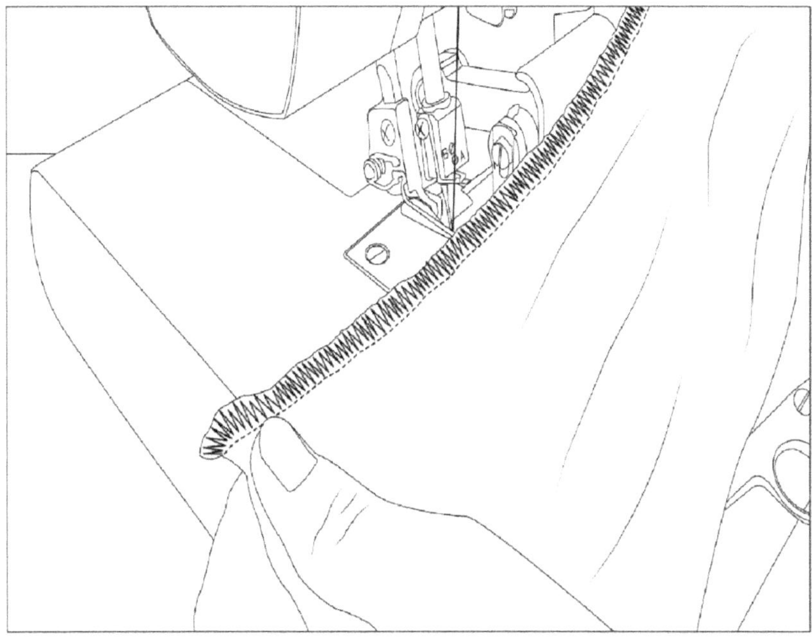

Clipping Curves and Corners

After sewing the curves and corners, clipping them will leave your garment with a professional look.

Clipping is applied to finished projects to prevent them from pulling out strangely or bunching after sewing them. Clipping of corners and curves depends on the fabric shape.

Clipping corners

There are two types of corners: the outward corner and the inward corners.

Clipping outward corners

The edges of your blanket have clipped outward corners. These corners are created by clipping a point diagonally on the seam allowance in order to prevent bulkiness. Then turn your garment on the right side out then use a pointed tool to push the corners out.

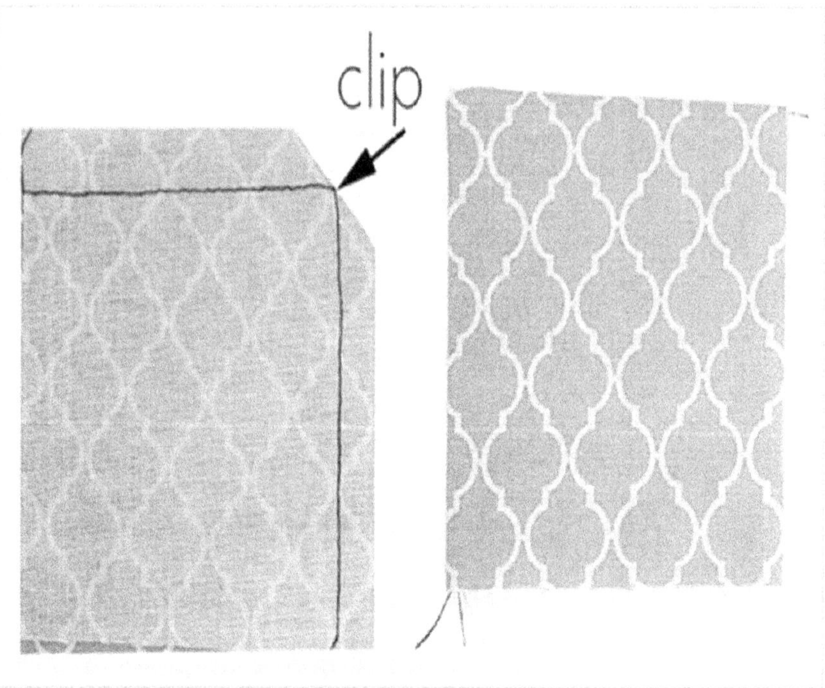

Of the corner of the garment is sharply pointed, you have to trim the excess fabric from the seam allowance for you to have a flat look.

Clipping inward corners

Inside corners are used to make neckline seams. To do this, you need to make a small cut at the corner of the seam allowance. This will make it easy to open up the seam and have a great shape when you turn the fabric the right way out.

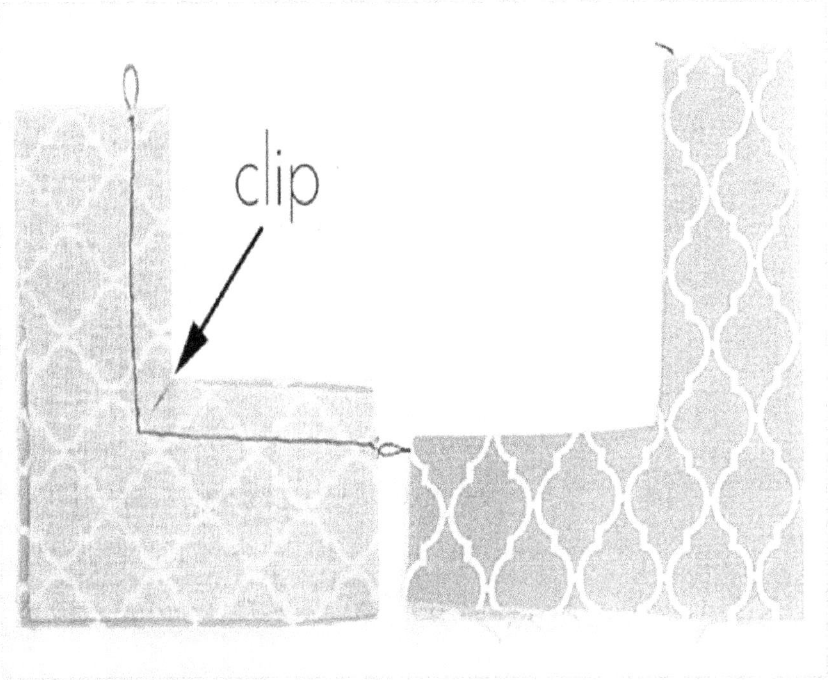

Clipping Curves

Just like corners, you have curves that curve outward and those curve inwards

Clipping convex curves

These mountains like curved shapes can be used to serge necklines, scalloped hems, and other round-shaped projects.

To clip your curved fabric, you need to cut v-shaped notches around the curves. Clipping these curves will eliminate some bulkiness on the fabric when you turn the right way out.

This is because the notch edges will curl up and pack close together to make your garment look flat when turning the right way out.

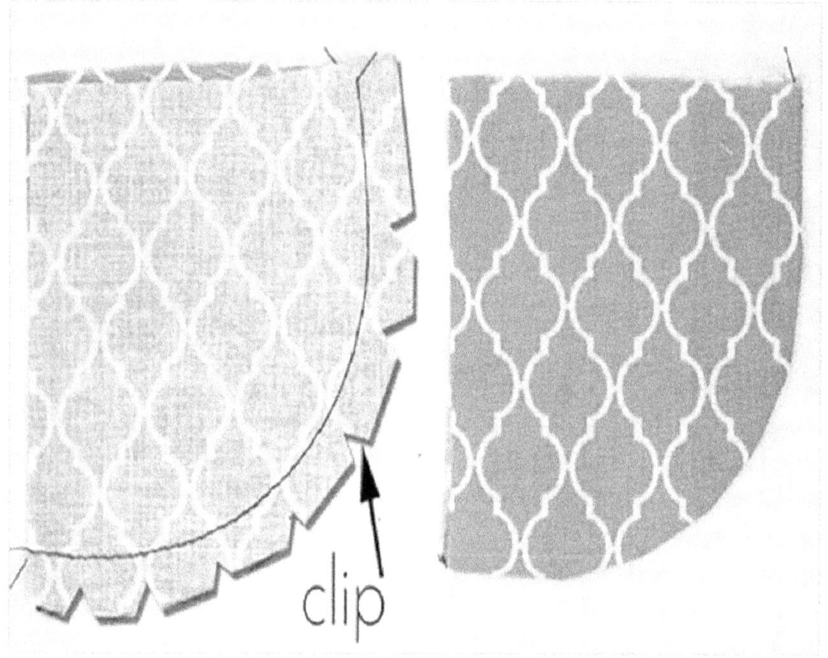

You can use pinking shears to cut the notches faster. These shears cut zigzag edges near the seam line.

Clipping concave curves

When clipping concave curves, you use snips close to the seam line. Be careful not to cut the stitch line. Embroidery scissors can do a faster job of snipping. If you have created a gentle curve then you need less clipping compared to when you have created a steep curve.

After clipping, turn the right way out and press the fabric to have a flat and smooth curve.

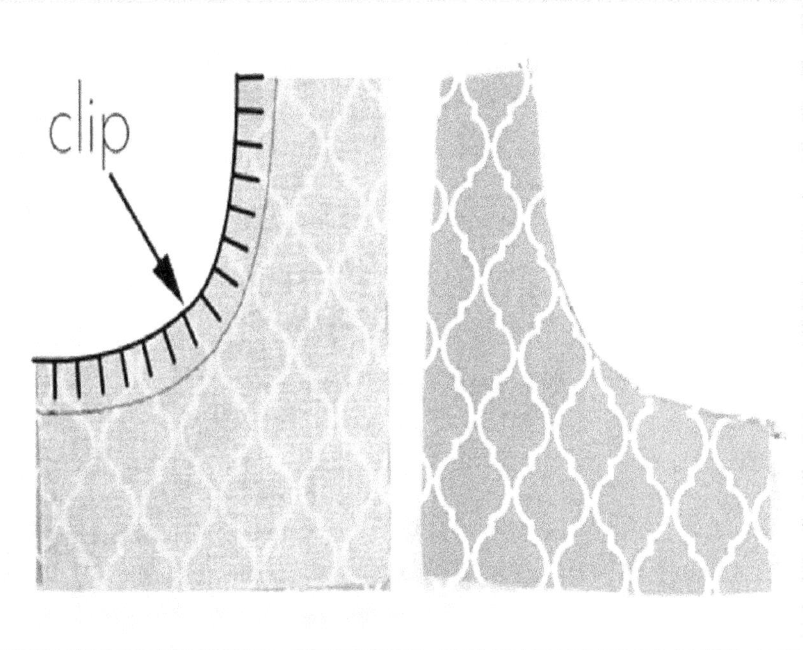

Serging with rolled edges

To create a rolled edge, you only need to have one needle. To use either the right or the left needle depends on whether you want to sew narrow or wide hems. If you use the left needle, you will create a wide edge while the right needle will create a narrow edge.

You should also have your cutting blades engaged to trim the excess fabric and give you a cleaner finish.

Step 1

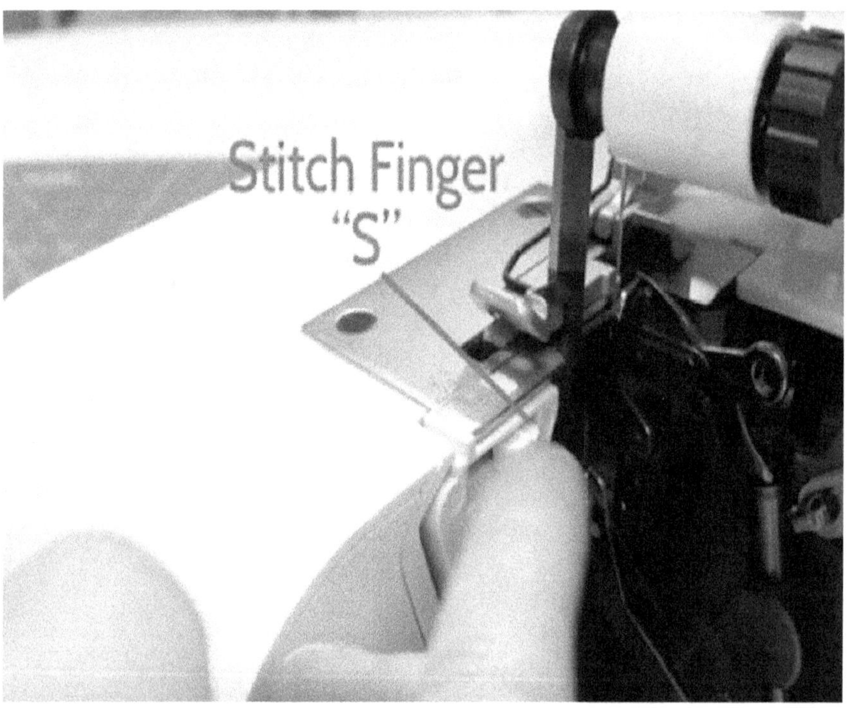

Switch the stitch finger from the standard "S" setting to the "P" setting which is the rolled hem setting.

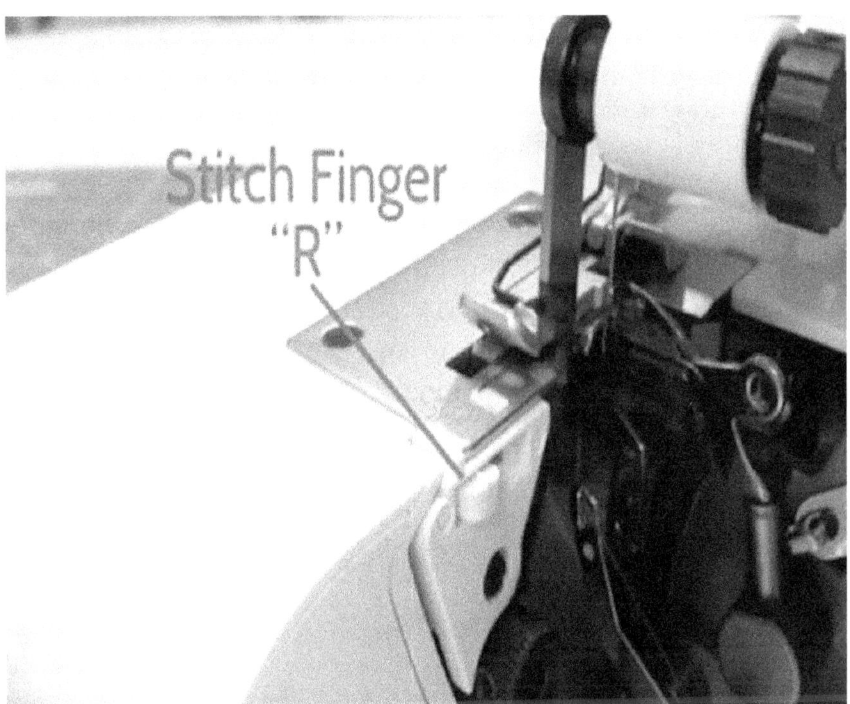

Step 2

Depending on the type of overlock machine you have, you can use a retractable stitch finger to make rolled hems. If your machine doesn't have this feature, you can buy a special rolled hem plate and install it on your machine.

If you're creating rolled edges with 3 threads, you need the upper looper, lower looper, and the right needle.

Adjust the thread tension in order to create the rolling effecting at the edges of the fabric.

Loosen the lower looper so that more thread is allowed into the stitch and also ensure the thread appears on the top and bottom side of the fabric. Increase the lower looper tension to the highest level. Some machines have lower looper tension up to 9 so you can set your machine to use the maximum number in the lower looper tension control and start sewing. Tighten your upper looper thread.

Step 3

Set the stitch length to 3" and stitch width to 4" to create a wider edge using the left needle. As you stitch the rolled hem, the fabric rolls over as you continue stitching. The stitches not only appear on the top side but also they're visible on the hem's bottom side.

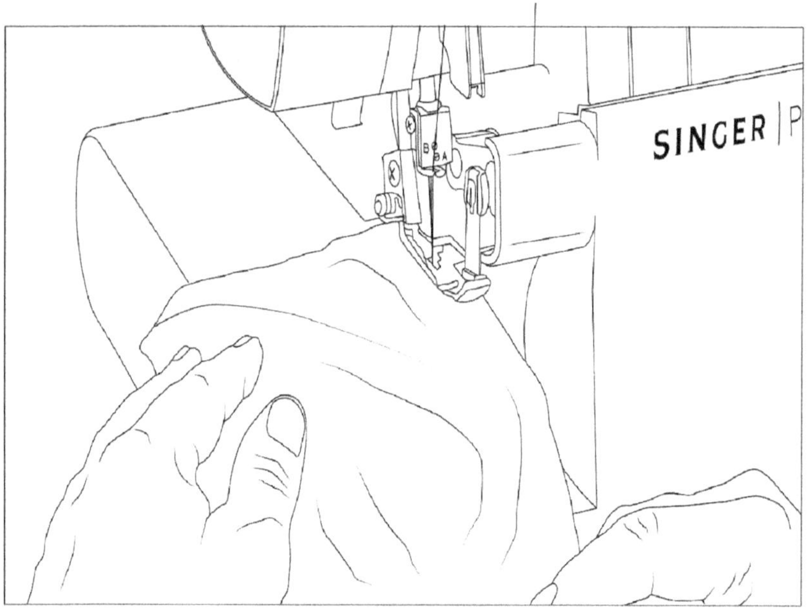

Step 4

Adjust the stitch settings to sew shorter stitch length. A rolled edge stands out when you use a shorter stitch length because a shorter stitch length helps you create a narrow edge with more decorative stitches.

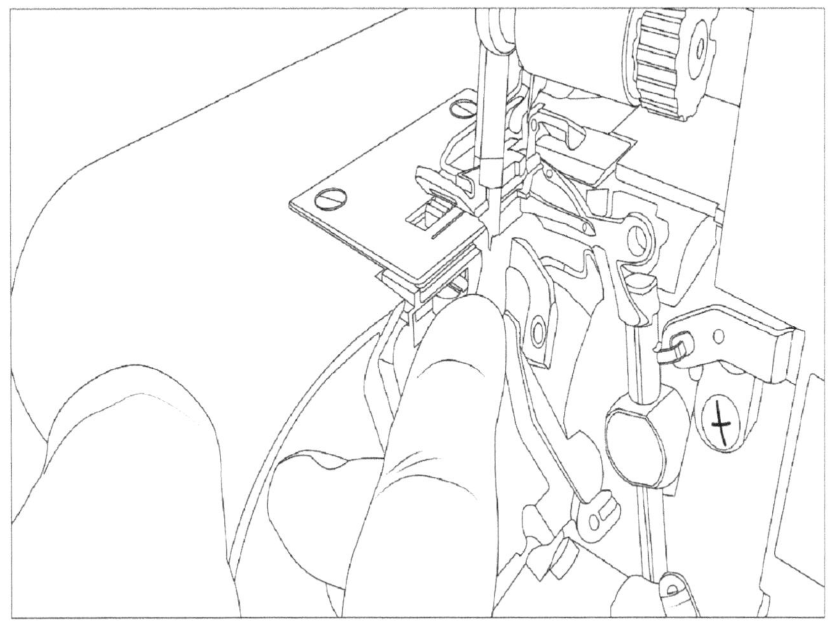

Step 5

Setting a shorter stitch length in your machine will create fuller rolled edges with little space left between the individual stitches. A shorter stitch length uses more thread and looks very cool.

If you use a longer stitch length, then there will be more space between the stitches. Always make sure to have a balance between the stitch length and the tension in order to get better results.

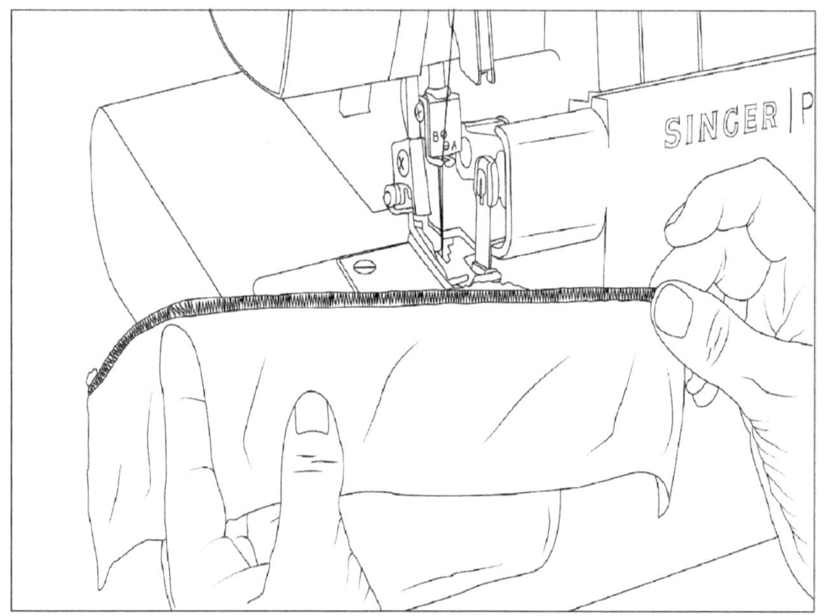

Step 6

If you need to have a narrow hem that is completely covered with no spaces and using the right stitch for your project then you should consider using nylon thread. When you use textured nylon thread for both the upper and lower looper there is no fabric shown between the stitches. This is because nylon thread is thicker and fills in the gaps between threads. When using this thread, you can have a longer stitch length and still get fuller stitches on the fabric.

Step 7

If you need a saddled rolled edge, switch to use the right needle that helps you create a super-thin rolled edge. It also allows you to switch to a narrow 2 thread rolled edge that saves you a lot of thread and reduces the bulkiness of the seam.

Not every machine is 2-thread compatible but if yours is compatible, it should have a 2 thread spreader/ converter which is inserted into the upper looper. Use your serger manual to know how to insert the spreader/converter correctly.

Step 8

With a 2-thread rolled edge, you only use the lower looper and the right needle. While the upper looper is disengaged by inserting the spreader. This will also give you better results just like you're using a 3 thread stitch.

With these two methods, you can easily create rolled edges on your garment and make it look more attractive. It also gives you a clear finishing to the garment. If you don't want your garment to have bulky finishing, you can use your 2 thread converter/ spreader.

Chapter Summary

- You can easily add corners and curves to your garments to make them look more attractive. There are different methods of adding the corners depending on whether you need sharp corners or narrow corners. You can also create convex and concave curves that look great and attractive.

- After sewing the corners and curves, you have to clip them to give your garment a flat and smooth look. Slipping will ensure you don't have any bulkiness in your garment when you turn the right way out.

- With these simple steps, you can make your projects look professional.

In the next chapter, you will learn about Flatlock

Chapter Seven: Flatlock

So far, we have learned the basics of using an overlock machine. Lets' now dive into more advanced topics.

An overlock machine is used to make a variety of stitches and one of the stitches you can create with your overlock machine is the flatlock stitch.

A flatlock stitch is a type of stitch you can create using either a 3-thread or 2- thread form just like the rolled edges. This type of stitch can be used in a wide range of applications due to its unbulky nature on the finished project. The raw edges of the fabric are encased within the looper threads making the stitches less bulky.

Flatlock stitch is mostly used for hemming activewear garments like stretchy sports clothing, hiking garments, and innerwear. Having a seam allowance inside the garment may chafe athletes' skin.

What are flatlock seams?

In a normal seam, you usually put two pieces of fabric together with the right sides facing each other and then sew along the fabric edges. This creates a flap inside the garment due to the seam allowance used. To avoid this, you can use flatlock seams on your fabric.

In flatlock seams, you put two pieces side-by-side and sew the raw edges of the fabric together. This ensures there is no bulkiness in the fabric.

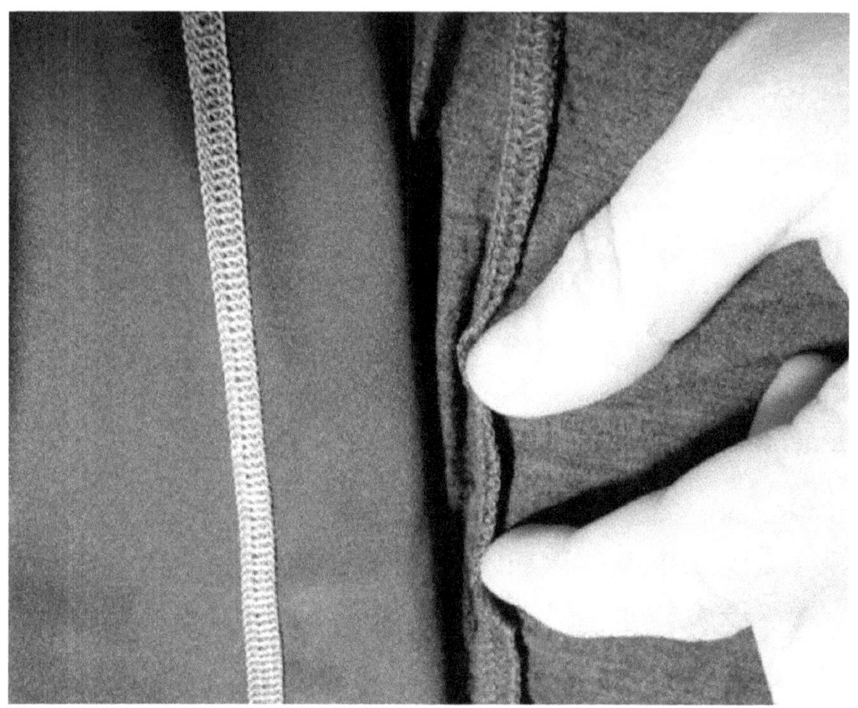

In the above example, the left fabric uses flatlock seams while the second fabric is using normal seams. The flatlock seams don't have any layers left hanging around because the seam allowance is wrapped inside the seam. While the normal seams have seam allowance left hanging around on the wrong side of the garment.

Flatlock seam is suitable for garments worn next to your skin. For example, long-sleeve shirts, t-shirts, pants, gloves, hats, etc. When wearing these garments, they should make you feel more comfortable. You don't need a piece of clothing that causes any discomfort or chafe your skin.

When to use flatlock seams?

Flatlock seams are great for sewing pants and thick garments like fleece jackets. If you use normal seams on these garments, they will be very bulky. The hanging fabric on the inside will also make you uncomfortable and limit your motion.

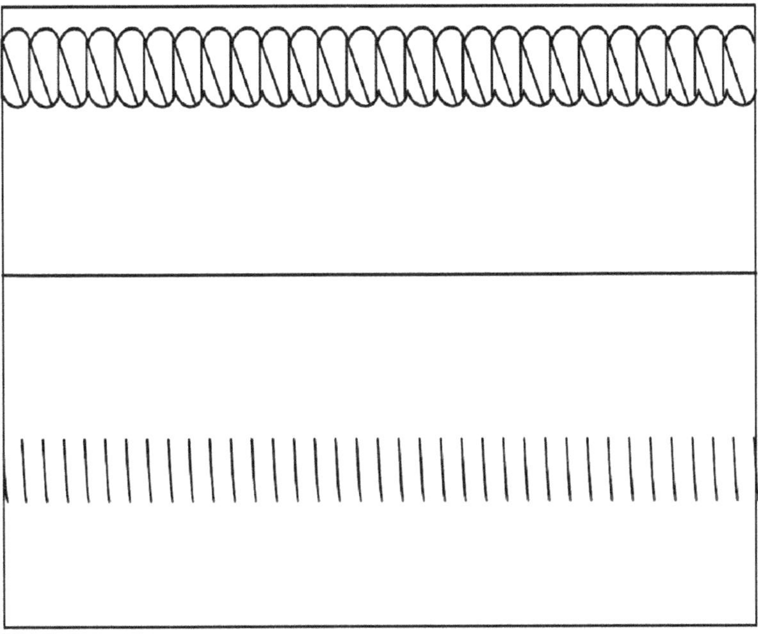

You can also use flatlock seams on base layers made of polyester or nylon fabric. Polyester is very rough and using a normal seam on the material, it will chafe your skin. Further, polyester fabrics have a compression fit and tight fit that presses seams tight against your skin

Two faces of flatlock seams

A flatlock has two sides where the right side of the fabric show stitches that look like a ladder or small bars of threads from the needle thread.

While the wrong side of the stitch displays looper threads as they sew back and forth and create loops across the raw edges on the two sides of the fabric.

If you want the loops to show on the right side of your fabric, then you should sew on the wrong sides together.

Creating these types of stitches looks more decorative. Flatlock stitches on the right side of the fabric can be used to create a blind hem look. However, the wrong side will have stitches that are more decorative. If decorative threads are used then you will have good looking seams.

With these types of stitches, there is no wrong and right side, and the stitches are mostly referred to as ladder or loops (front and back stitches).

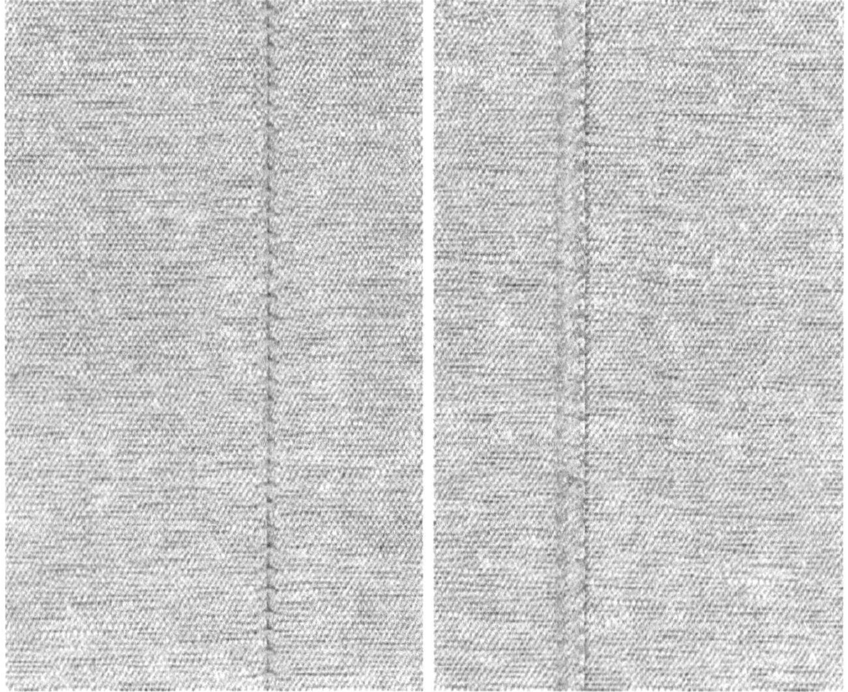

Strength in numbers

The number of threads used to make an overlock stitch correlates to how strong the seam will be. Using a three-thread stitch you will have a strong flatlock seam than when using a two-thread stitch.

When stitching flatlock on high-stretch fabric for sportswear, you should use three-thread stitching. Activewear garment experience a lot of stress and pulling every time, so you need a stronger thread version to support the stretching.

However, if you want to create a hem or a decorative stitch on a loose-fitting garment, then you can use a two-thread version.

Wide vs. Narrow stitches

From our previous topic, we learned that the type of needle you use determines whether you will have a narrow or a wide stitch. Therefore, your needle placement determines the length of your stitches. If you're using the left needle for your stitching, you will create wider stitches while the right needle helps you create narrow stitches.

However, choosing whether to use a narrow or a wide stitch is determined by the thickness or weight of the fabric. Although, sometimes you can choose the stitch width of your preference because the seam is visible and can act as a decorative stitch.

Machine setup

To use flatlock stitches, you need to set up your machine.

Although you can still use a standard serger foot (on the right), it is easy to sew a flatlock seam using an adjustable blind hem foot shown on the left. Ensure you buy a replacement foot that is compatible with the model of your serger machine.

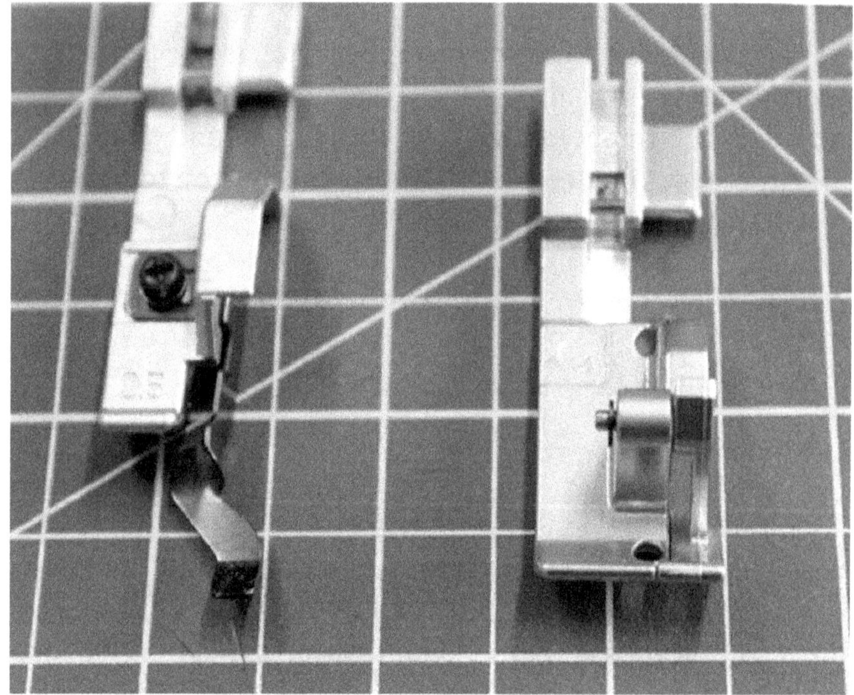

If you're using a standard foot, align the trimmed raw edges of the fabric between the needles.

If you have installed an adjustable blind hem foot in your serger machine, use a piece of scrap fabric to help adjust the slider. Based on the stitches formed, you can decide either to move the adjustable slider to the right or not and tighten the tiny screw on the slider.

When using flatlock stitches disengage the blades because you don't need them. If you leave the blades engaged and you're sewing flatlock stitches on a fold, the blades may cut parts of your fabric. So it is better you be safe than sorry!

When using a flatlock stitch to attach the edges of two pieces of fabric together, you should start by straightening the raw edges of the fabric first to make them even.

Setting up three-thread stitch

You can start by setting up your three-thread flatlock. In this case, you will be using one thread. Use the chart below to adjust your settings.

THREADING/THREAD TENSION SETTING				MACHINE SETUP				
Left needle	Right needle	Upper looper	Lower looper	Rolled hem lever	Upper looper converter	Cutting width	Stitch length	Differential feed
1.5	-	3.5	7	▲	-	6.5	2.5	1

After stitching, you may not notice anything unusual but when you pull the two-layer of fabric, the ladders of the stitch are well exposed while the loops lie flat on the other side.

Three-thread flatlock uses more thread and usually sew strong seams

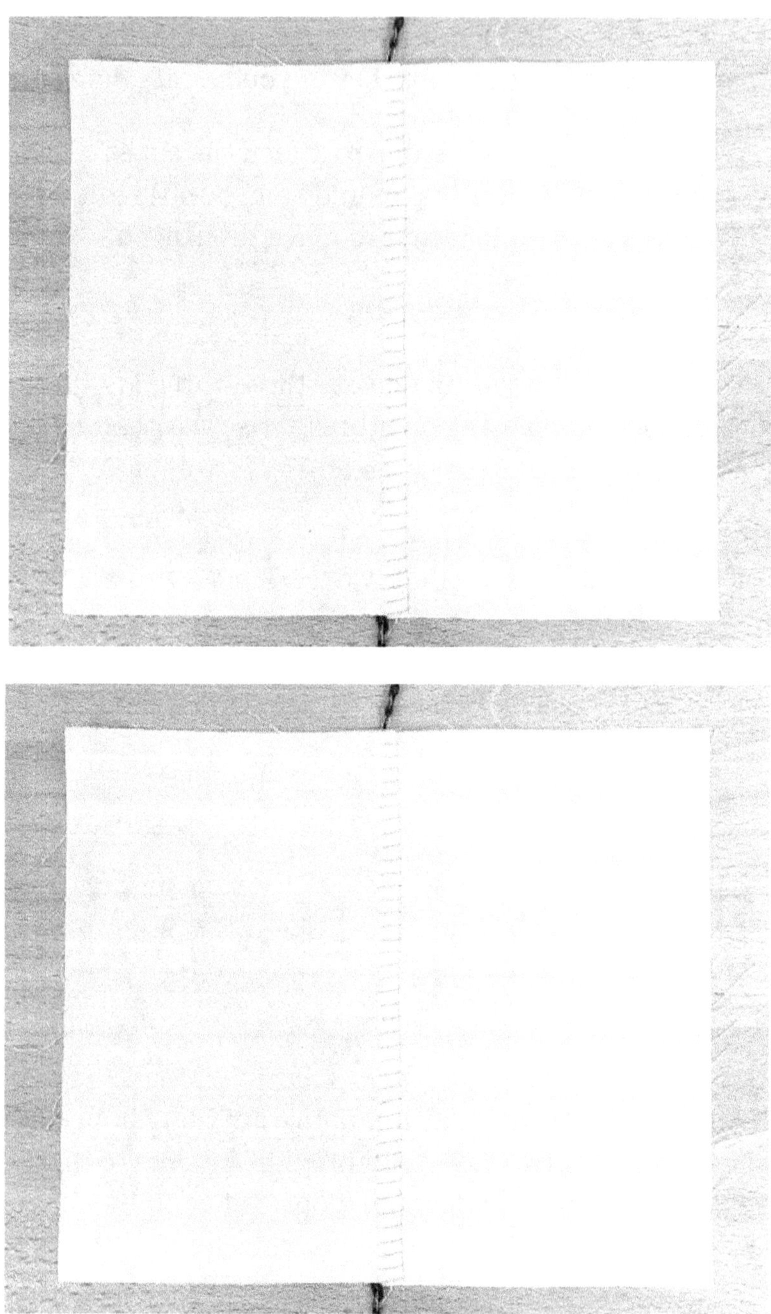

Setting up two-thread stitch

If you want to use a two-thread flatlock, adjust your machine to have the following settings.

2-thread flatlock sews weaker seams compared to the 3-thread flatlock. It also uses less thread.

THREADING/THREAD TENSION SETTING				MACHINE SETUP				
Left needle	Right needle	Upper looper	Lower looper	Rolled hem lever	Upper looper converter	Cutting width	Stitch length	Differential feed
2	.	.	4	▲		6.5	2.5	1

With a two-thread flatlock, you need to install a snap-on upper looper converter (ULC). Different models of overlock have a different snap-on converter so check your manual.

The converter tool stores the looper door when you open the machine. You only slide the blunt end of the upper looper converter into the groove at the top.

Ensure the pointed end is carefully pulled at the back of the looper and hooks through the looper eye.

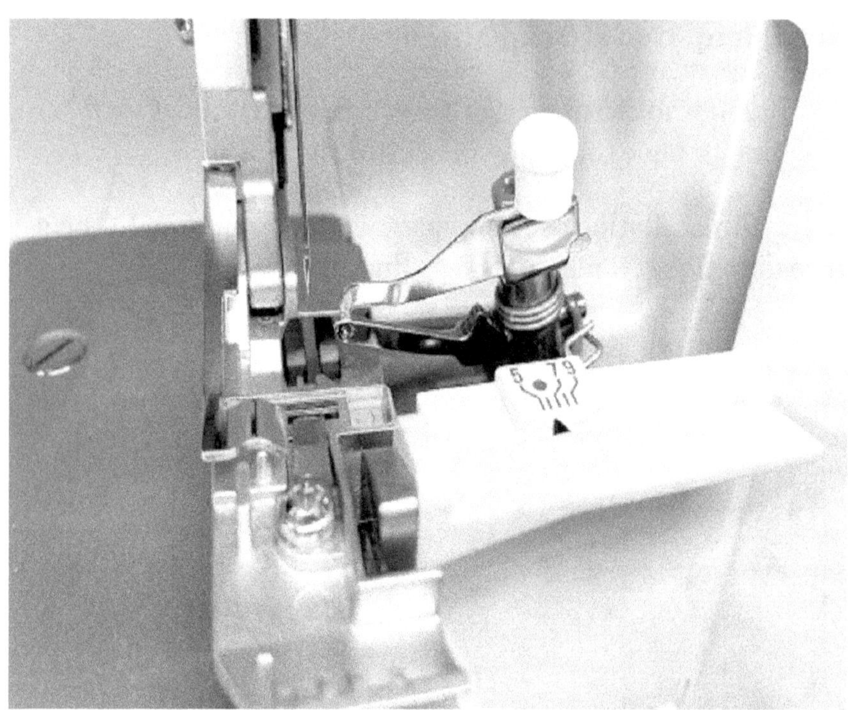

Now stitch the raw edges of the fabric together and then pull the fabric apart to see the difference between your thread-thread stitch and the two-thread stitch. A three-thread stitch adds extra strength to the seam.

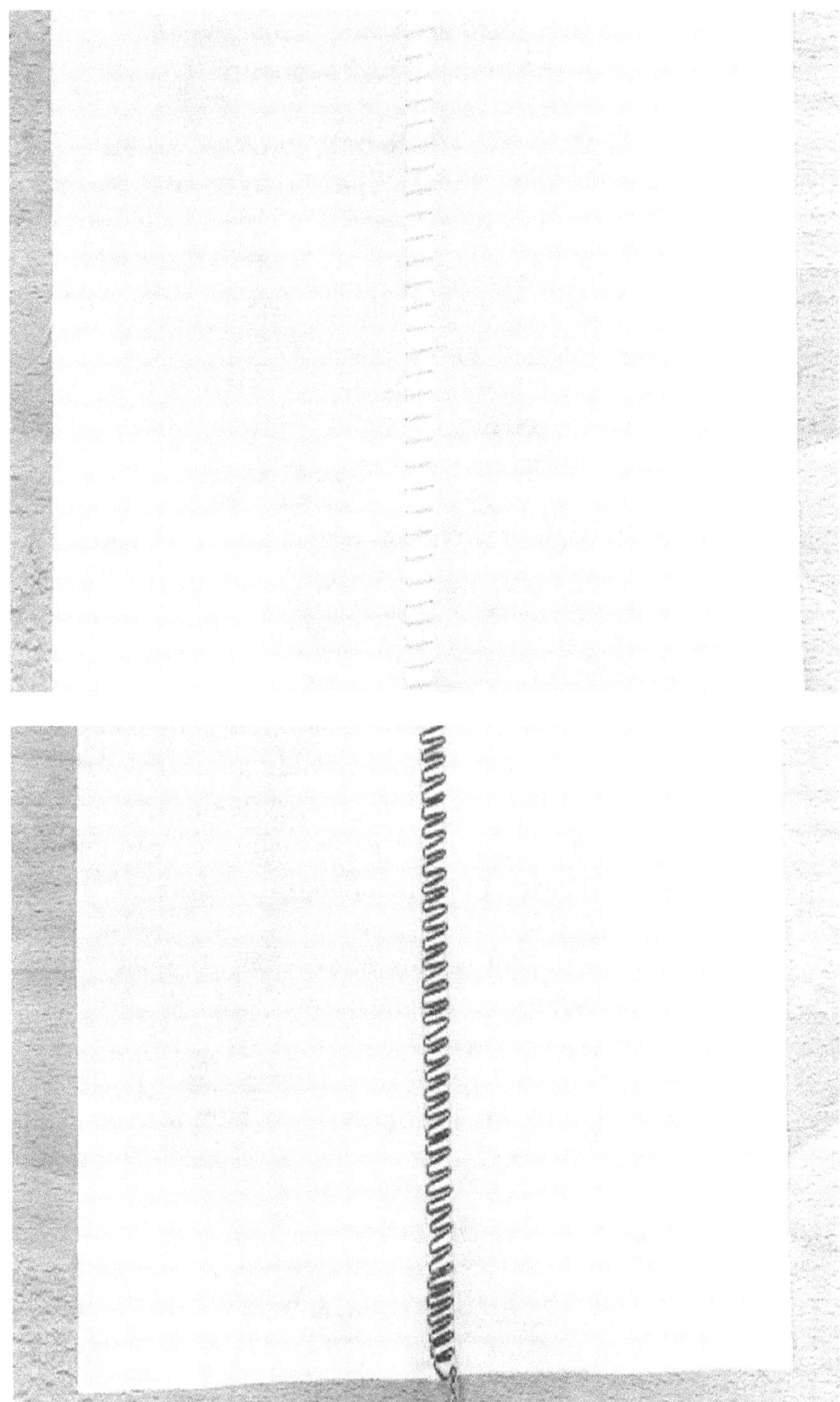

Keep in mind that the ladder side is made using the needle thread while the loop side uses loopers.

A 2-thread flatlock can create both narrow and wide flatlock seams depending on the type of needle you're using.

To get a perfect flatlock seam, you need to test several settings and adjust different controls to give you a perfect stitch. You can practice with a 3-thread flatlock and have a balanced tension setting, and inspect the stitch formation. Change your tension setting and test the stitch. Compare the results of the flatlock seams.

Do that until you come with a perfect stitch for your project.

Hemming with a Flatlock

Another way you can use flatlock stitches is by hemming especially if you want to create an invisible hem. If you use a matching color, the ladder stitch on the right side of the garment will almost disappear. Alternatively, you can use contrasting color threads to form a decorative stitch.

But what is important is how you're going to hem your garment and at the same time, leave it with a professional finishing on the inside.

This can easily be done using the blind hem foot but you can also use your standard foot.

How to create hems with flatlock

1. Fold the fabric with the wrong side to create the hem width and press the fold

2. Fold again and align the folded fabric above the raw edge

3. Serge along the edges using a flatlock stitch. You can use either 2- thread flatlock or 3-thread flatlock.

4. Unfold your fabric and pull it to reveal the set stitches with a lovely inside hem.

If you're using a matching thread, you will have well-blended stitches on the fabric that are almost invisible. But if you're using the contrasting thread color, you will see the threads. Pull the fabric to clearly see the decorative loops.

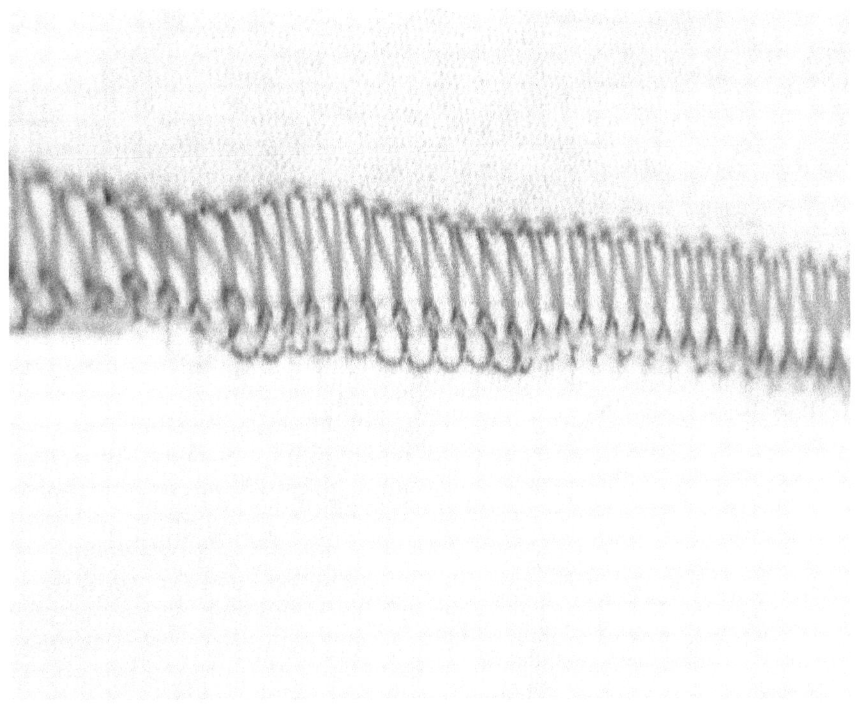

Slightly pulled fabric

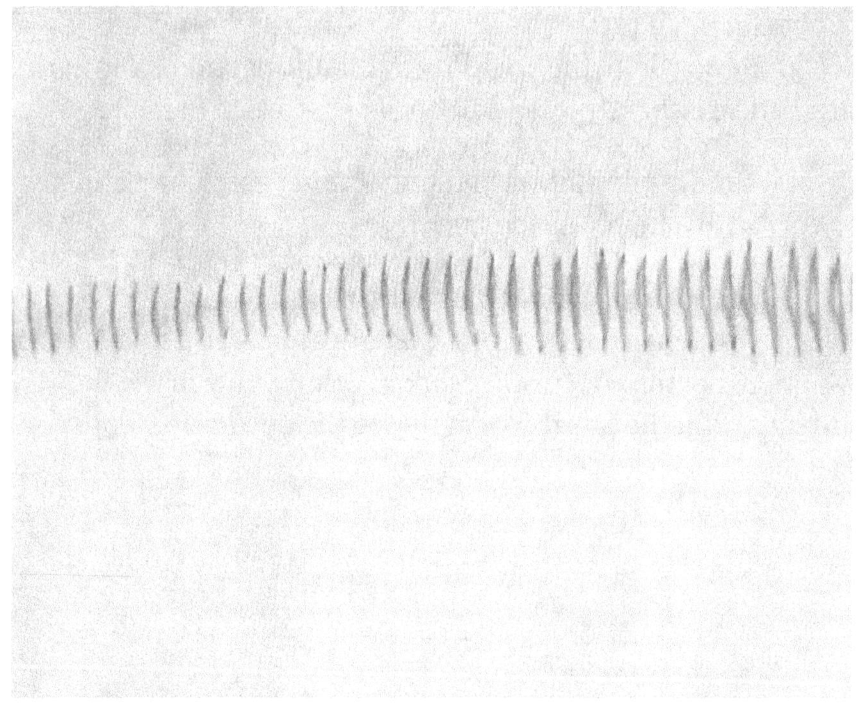

For example, this t-shirt picture below has flatlock seams around the arms that not only adds decorations to the t-shirt it also makes you feel comfortable. The t-shirt also has hems on the sleeve.

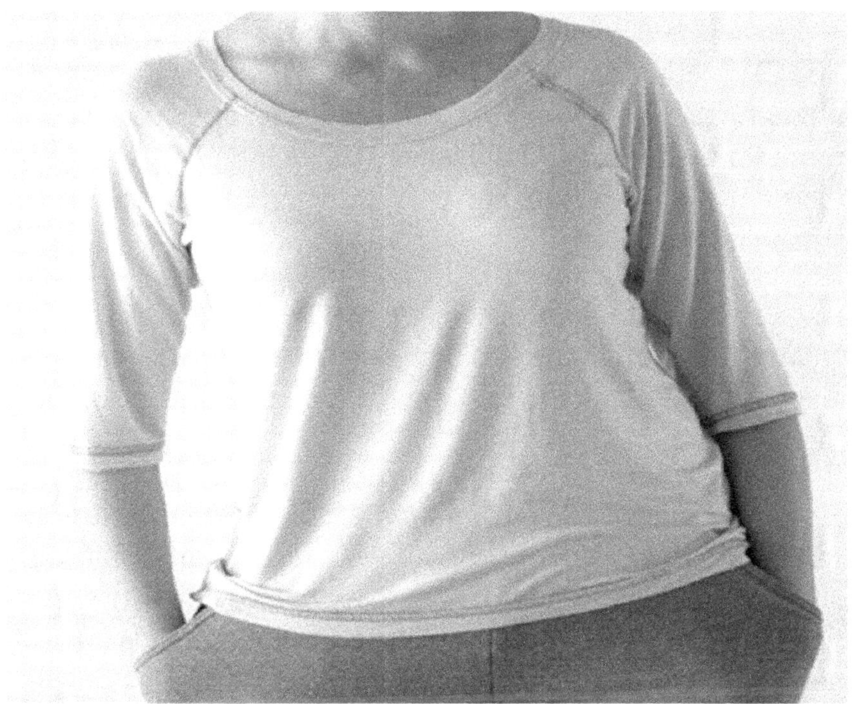

After serging flatlock seams on your garment, you need to secure the ends of the seams. Flatlock seams do get opened up, so it is important to leave at least 3" to 4" thread chain at the start and end of the seam.

You also need to tuck the threads and secure them using a fray blocker.

Troubleshooting Flatlock stitches

When using flatlock stitch, there are few factors you need to consider. For example, the above stitch chart can be found in your serger manual but you can tweak the settings. If the fabric doesn't open up or lay flat, you can reduce the needle tension. As a result, you will have more slacks on the ladders.

In addition, you can adjust the Micro Thread Control (MTC). Increasing the MTC number and moving the stitch finger further away from the fabric helps create an extra room for the seams and the fabric will open up neatly. And at the same time, it will preserve the integrity of the flatlock stitch and tension.

Threads with different weights and textures are great for creating decorative stitches in your garment. The threads give better results when used on the loopers rather than on the threads.

If you use textured nylon threads, you will have extra soft and fluffy seams for your activewear garments. You can also try metallic threads on both loopers to get an extra sparkle seam in your garments. Heavyweight threads form both stitches when used in cotton or wool fabrics.

Chapter Summary

- A flatlock stitch is used on stretching fabrics to create a flat seam on both sides of your garment. It also adds some decorations to your garment when different thread colors are used.

- Flatlock seams are mostly used in activewear, underwear, or use it on t-shirts to make them more comfortable.

- When creating the flatlock stitch, tension adjustment determines the type of seam you will have in your garment. Always confirm with your manual before making the adjustment of the tensions.

- In addition, to get a perfect flatlock stitch, you need to practice with scraps of the fabric and adjust the width and tension appropriately.

In the next chapter, you will learn how to use the yarn application foot.

Chapter Eight: Yarn Application Foot

Yarn application foot is a great presser foot tool that works as an all-purpose narrow cord foot because it can attach any small cord that measures 6 mm wide or less. The foot is mostly used to attach a clear cord to your machine and create a curly finishing line hem.

A yarn application presser foot is also great for attaching a decorative cord, an elastic thread, creating rolled hems, attach beading wire, and also shape the edges of your garment.

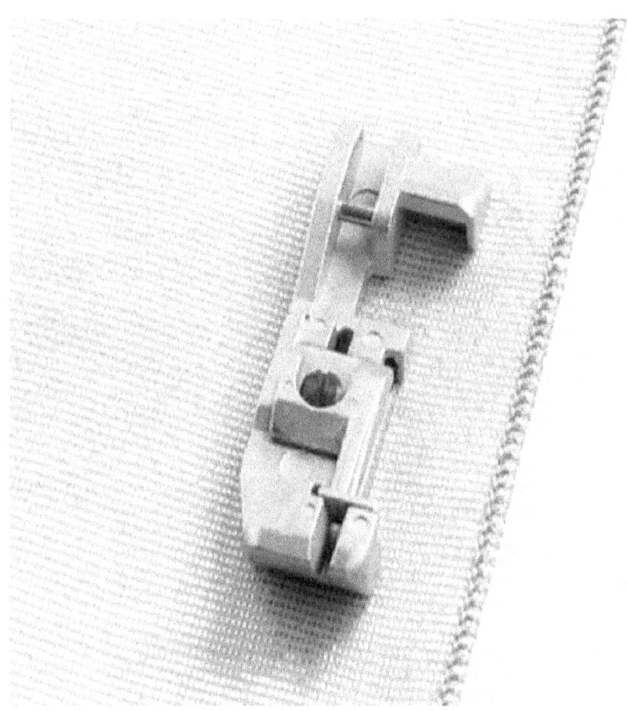

The foot can sew yarns such as cords and nylon gut with a thickness of up to 1.0 mm. The yarn can also create stiffer hems found in a wedding dress or in a valance.

Machine set up

- Set up the right needle in your machine

- You can decide to use any of the two stitch types: Two thread lower looper thread with a wrapped rolled hem or use a three thread upper looper thread with a wrapped rolled hem

- Set the stitch length to 2 mm

- Use normal position for differential feed lever

- Set your upper knife into a working position

Using yarn foot

Remove the standard pre-installed presser foot and replace it with the yarn application foot. Loosen the screw on top of the foot to remove it and screw your yard foot.

The foot applies a narrow cord so well because of the small hole at the front and the little tunnel that feeds through your serger.

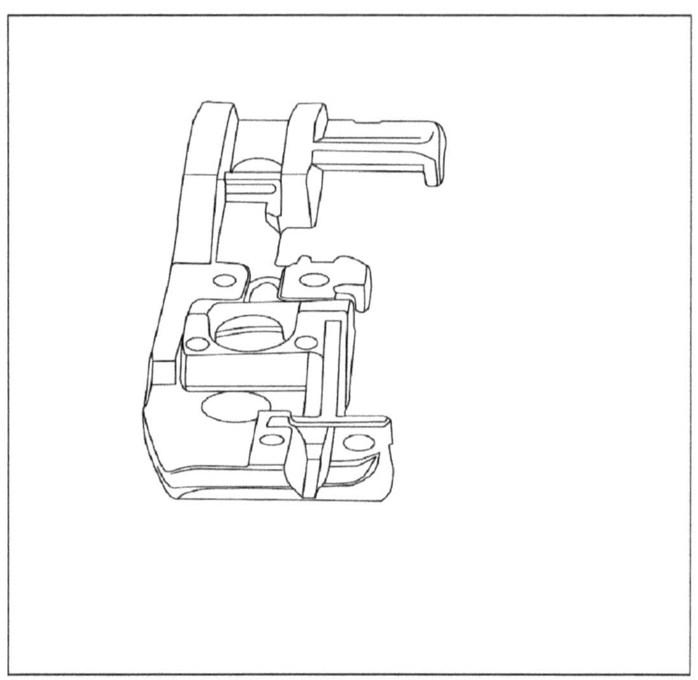

The adjustable screw allows you to adjust the cord. Unscrew it to give you more room to work with.

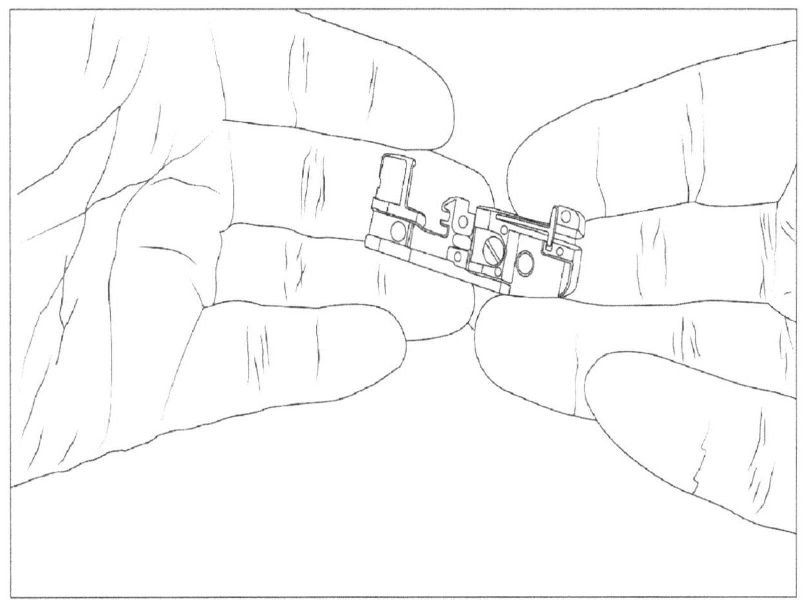

Before you start sewing, you need to thread the cord or your nylon gut. Pass your cord through the front, secure it on the tunnels, and tighten the screw.

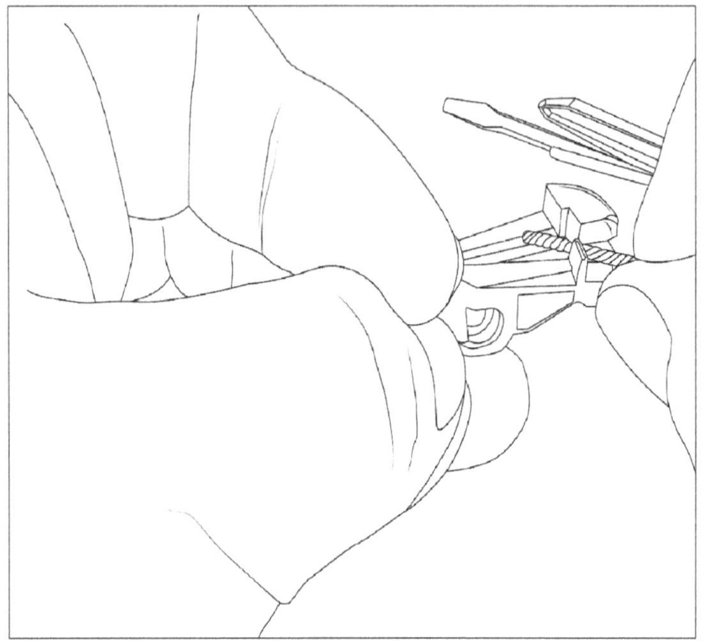

Once you install the yarn foot in your machine, it is very easy to insert a thin clear cord into your machine.

The clear cord can be used to make curly finish lines or bold rolled edge hem to your garments.

For example, let's pick your clear thick finishing line cord that weighs 30" and insert it through the foot and pull the cord to the back.

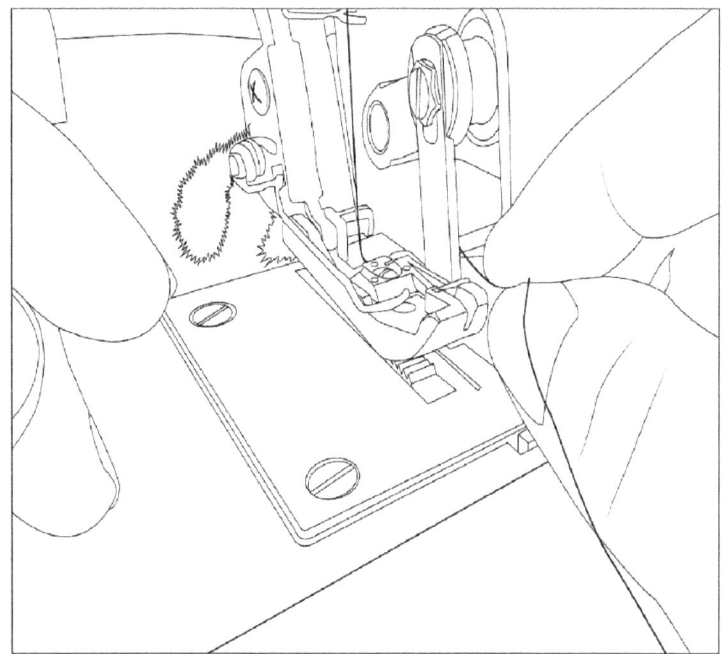

Place a scrap fabric under the presser foot and test the flatlock stitch. If your stitches are perfect, you can now start using your yarn foot.

Start serging a rolled edge chain. Place your fabric underneath the foot and start serging.

When using a thicker cord like the above 30 weight, you have to pull the rolled edge chain at the back to secure the embroidery on your machine and continue serging.

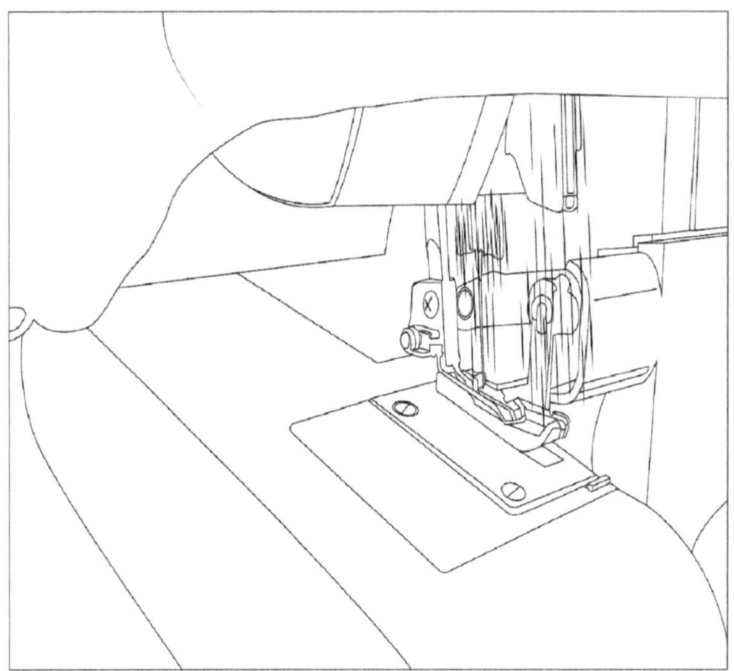

The foot ensures that the cord is stitched at the edge of the fabric and don't have to worry about the cord being pulled by the machine or getting into the knives. It ensures the fabric feeds through well.

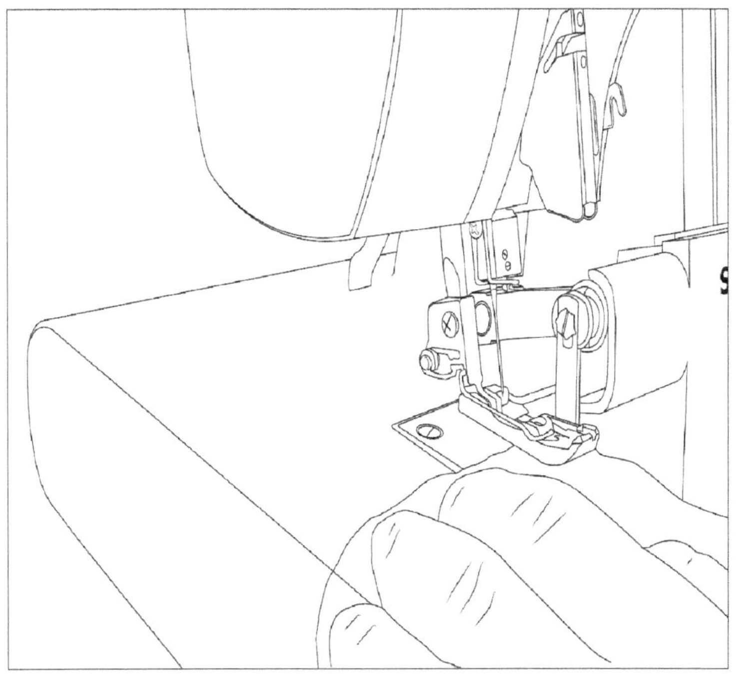

If you need super tight cords in your fabric, wrap the finishing line around a small cylinder and heat it up with your hairdryer or heater.

If you use a nylon thread on the upper looper, you get a super soft finishing.

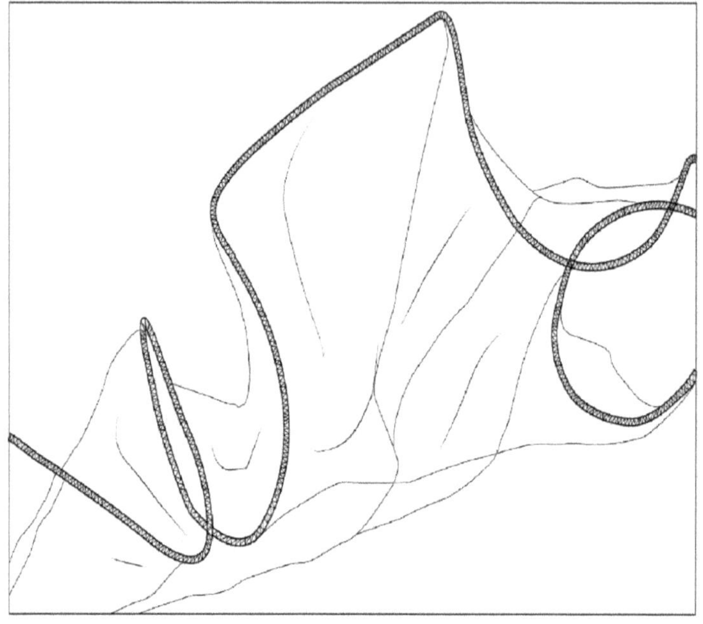

The yarn foot can use any type of nylon cord to give you different sewing effects. For example, you can use a bead stringing wire or jewelry wire to create custom narrow hems to a lightweight fabric.

You can also use a super craft beading cord to give your edges a unique finishing.

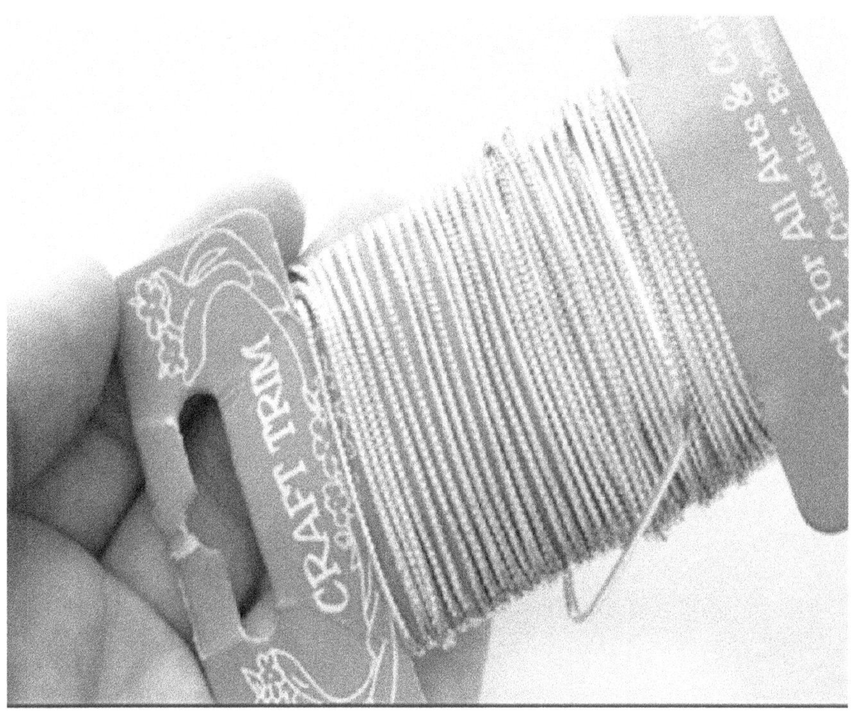

This craft code gives your garments a more decorative look. You only have to thread the metallic thread on the upper looper to get the sparkles on your garment.

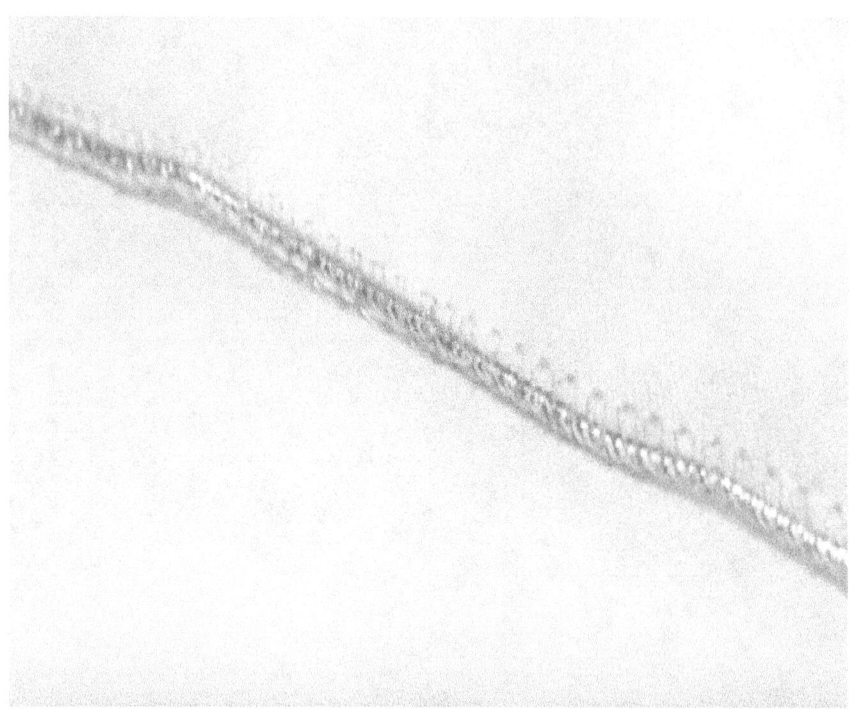

Alternatively, you can use elastic thread to add decorative stitches.

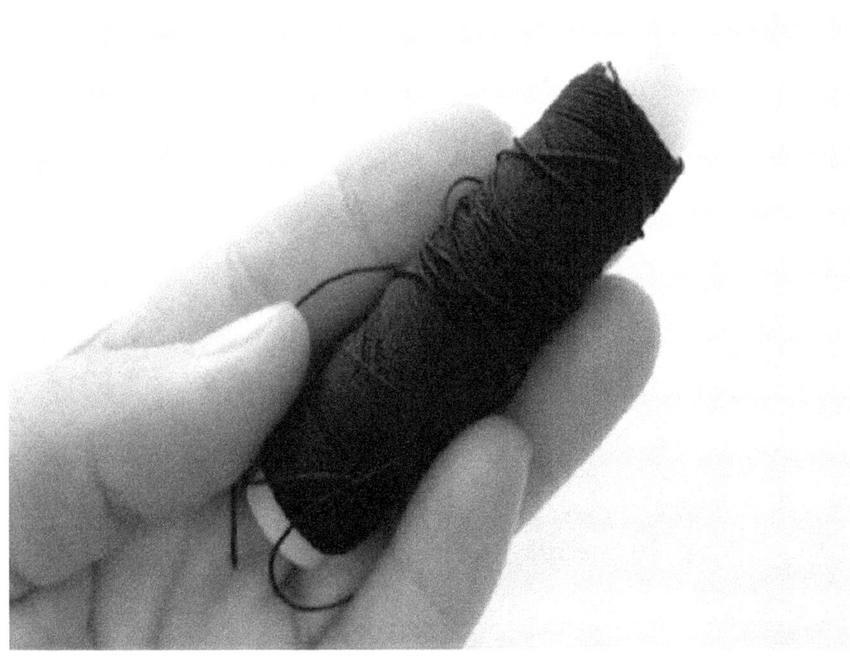

When feeding it through the machine, hold the thread tight with your fingers. This ensures the tension creates a nice gathering on the fabric.

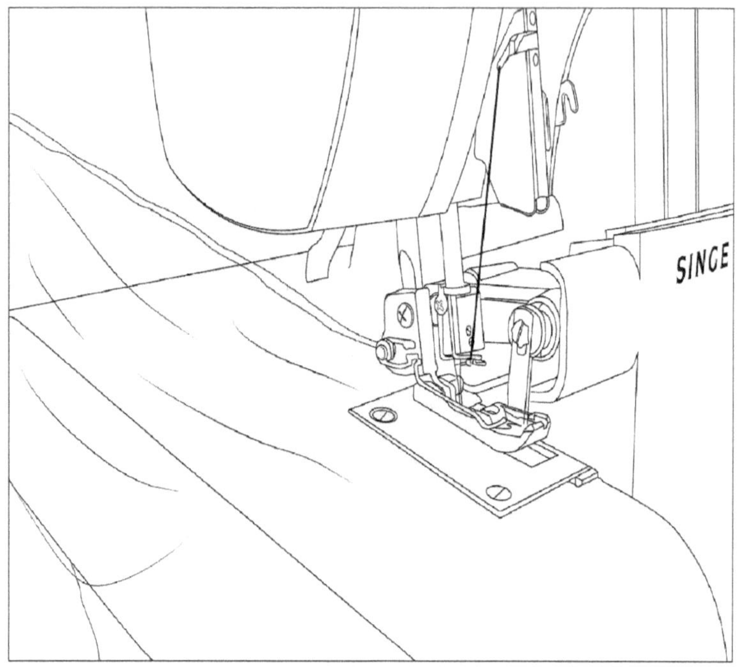

The foot also ensures the fabric feeds well and creates neat gathers for you.

With these easy steps, you can use your yard foot to create decorative stitches with different types of threads. The foot is used to attach a decorative cord, use an elastic thread, or even use a beading wire to make unique curly finishing line hems.

Chapter Summary

- A yard application foot is an all-purpose foot that you can use to apply a small narrow cord with a width of less than 6mm. the foot can be used to insert clear cord, elastic thread, and beading wires.

- With this foot, you can create rolled hems, creating curly finishing lines, adding decorative stitches, and shaping the edges of your garment.

- Change your machine to use the yard foot and adjust the machine setting to the desired stitch length and tension. You can set up your machine to use either the three-thread stitches or use the two-thread stitches. Feed the threads to your loopers and needle then start your sewing project.

- Yard foot allows you to add professional clean and curly finishing to your garments.

In the next chapter, you will learn how to use lace application foot.

Chapter Nine:
Lace Application Foot

A lace application foot is a great tool that allows you to attach lace trims of different sizes to the raw or finished edges of your fabric. This foot uses a protective built-in guide that keeps the knife away from your lace edges.

The foot consistently feeds the fabric such that it doesn't shift out of place when serging.

It also allows you to create lace to lace trims using your flatlock seam. You can also use lace application foot to add decorative stitches to your fabric and ribbons. The foot comes with a screw you can use to adjust your stitches and allow you to work with a variety of trim sizes.

The lace application foot is an exclusive serger foot that helps you serge delicate trims on a piece of fabric without interfering with the header of the trim.

The adjustable foot ensures you have accurate trims and the lace remains intact. In the end, you will have a professional look and with your exact style.

It provides you with better visibility when attaching a ribbon or a lace to your fabric.

Anatomy of lace foot

There are different lace application foot in the market, but they all work the same way. Therefore, make sure you buy lace foot that is compatible with your serger model. You can check your manual to learn more.

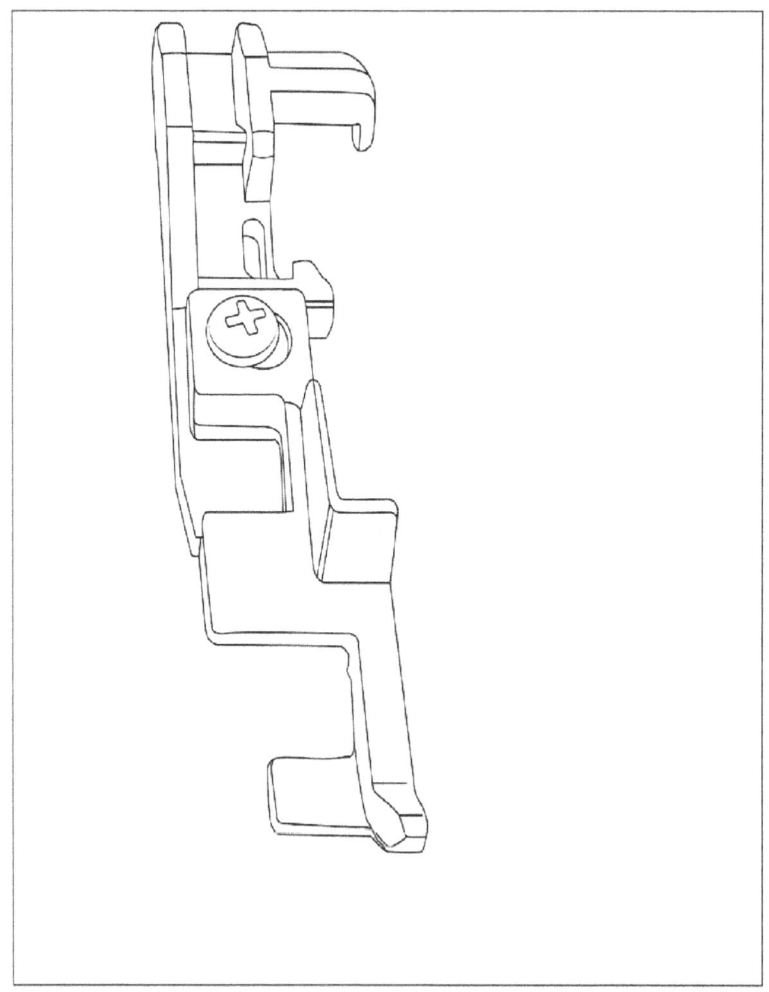

The lace application foot has a long toe that acts as the edge guide for the lace. When you attach the lace to the edge of the fabric, the lace passes through the toe guard at the back of the foot and over to the metal lip.

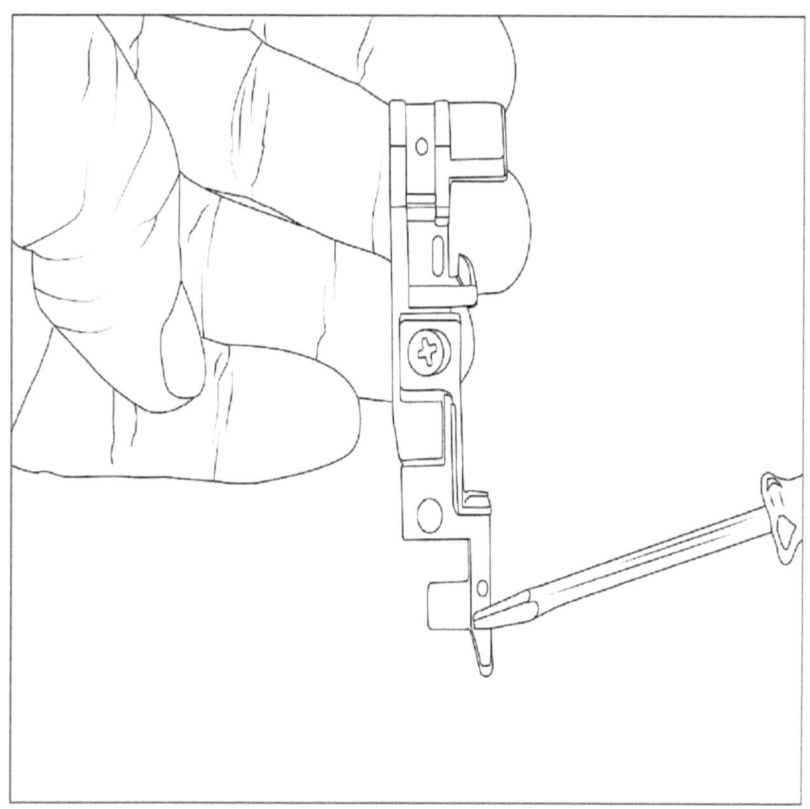

Your fabric will pass through the metal clip unto the front of the lace. This application foot has a screw that you can use to remove the guide but the screw is not adjustable so you shouldn't mess with it.

The lace foot has grooves on the backside that helps feed fabric and lace as you serge and also holds the fabric in place. You don't have to worry about the trim lace shifting or slip off the foot.

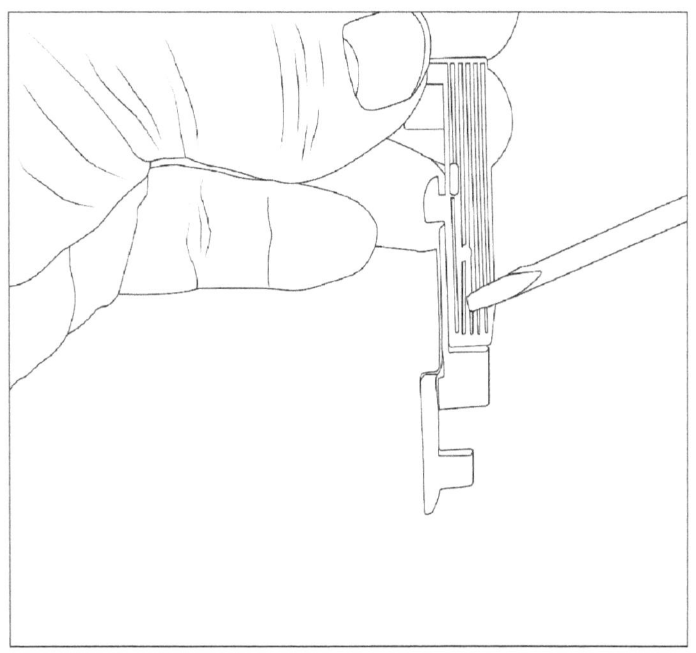

Start serging lace trims

Based on the model of your machine, ensure the machine setting are properly adjusted. In most lace foot applications, needle tension is not required. Although not all serger models have tension control, follow your model manual to know how to adjust the tension if your machine has tension controls.

Depending on the type of model, you can do two-thread flatlock lace or three-thread flatlock lace. In our tutorial, we will focus on three-thread flatlock stitches.

Before you start using the lace foot in your machine, you need to remove the pre-installed presser foot and snap the lace application foot to your machine and start attaching lace.

The lace foot ensures your lace is attached neatly to a raw fabric edge using a three-thread overlock stitch.

Settings

- Left overlock needle: use a color of your choice or a coordinating cone thread

- Upper looper: use a decorative thread (we will use 12" weight thread)

- Lower looper: serger cone thread which doesn't show on your fabrics

- Stitch length: 1.5 although you can use varying stitch length based on your preferences, fabric type, and thread weight.

- Stitch width: choose the widest

- Stitch selector: D

Steps

Take your fabric and place it under the foot.

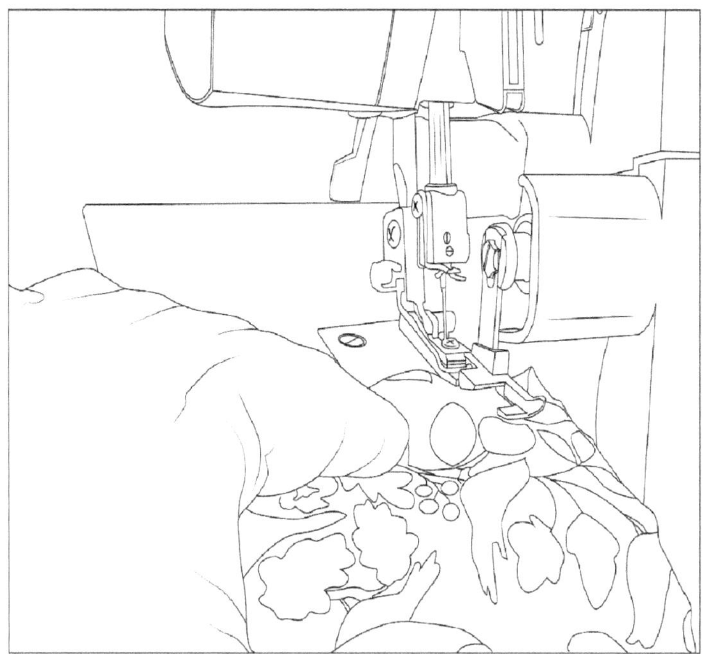

Slide your lace on top of the fabric with the right side down along the guide and start serging.

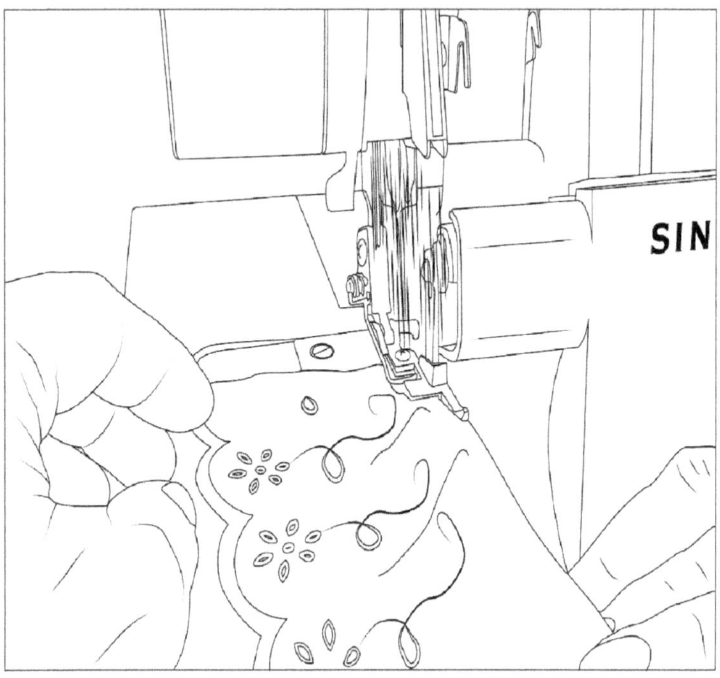

The guide in the metal lip makes your work fast and easier since it makes it easy to control the fabric and the lace from shifting out of place.

It also ensures the lace edges are not cut by the blade as you serge and ensure the fabric feds consistently.

The lace foot ensures your project looks more professional and with neat edges.

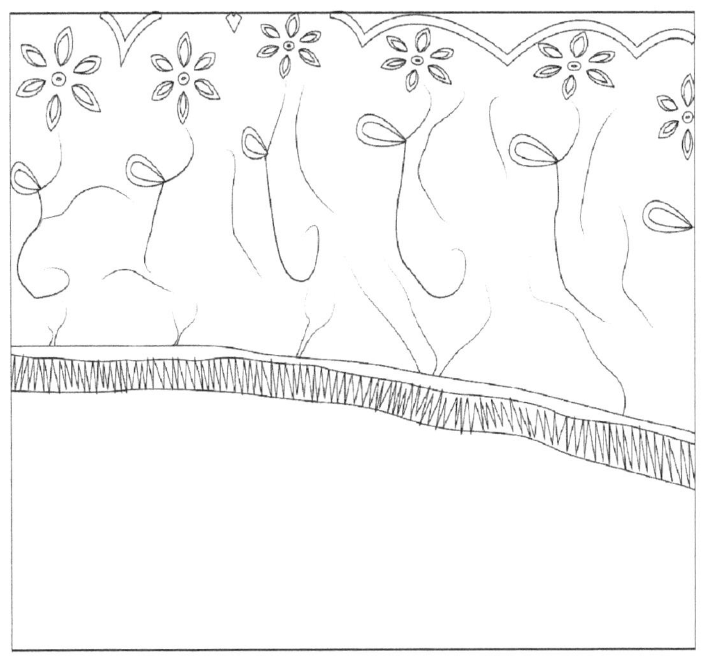

Flatlock stitches with Lace Application Foot

The lace foot is also great for creating flatlock stitches. When you want to join lace to fabrics, you can use flatlock stitches to create unique and decorative stitches on your fabric.

So instead of the fabric passing through the metal lip, insert both fabrics in the lace with the right sides facing each other along with the toe guide and over the metal lip.

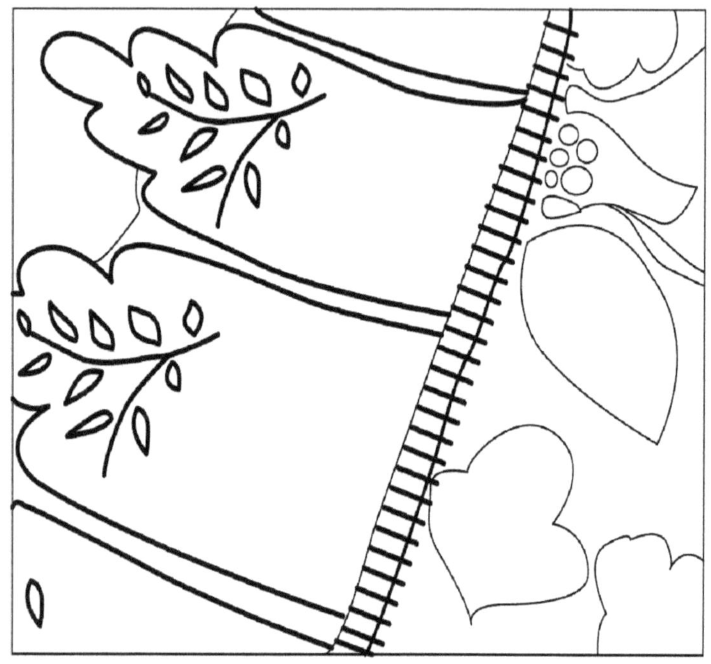

The loops are created over the stitch finger with a seam allowance of about 1/8" off the lacing fabric edge. There is no tension in the needle and sometimes it causes the stitches to appear loose. This is because the upper looper threads are loose while the lower looper thread is tightened. As you serge, the fabric feeds through with ease.

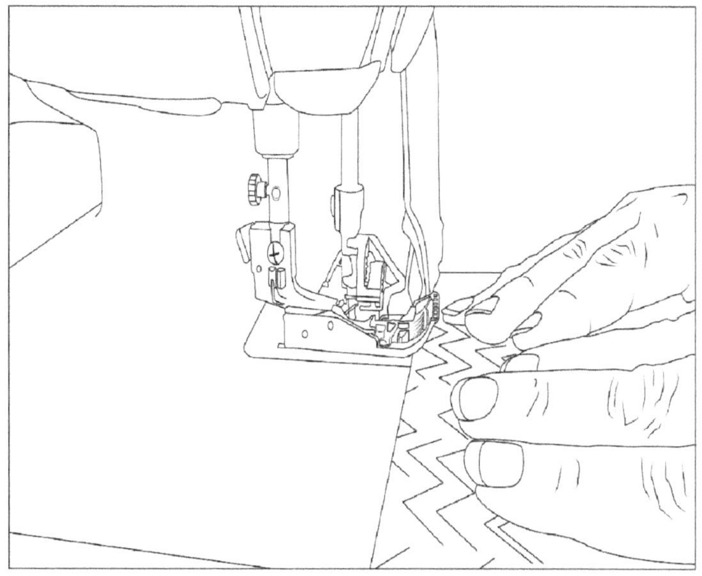

Once your flatlock stitches are formed, you just pull the fabrics, to have a flat and neat finish. Flatlock stitches also appear strong.

The lace foot can help you join two pieces of lace edge together. Place the pieces of fabric through the toe guide and over the metal lip and serge the fabric to the end.

In addition, you can thread your needle with decorative thread and use flatlock stitches on different laces to create a unique finishing to your fabric.

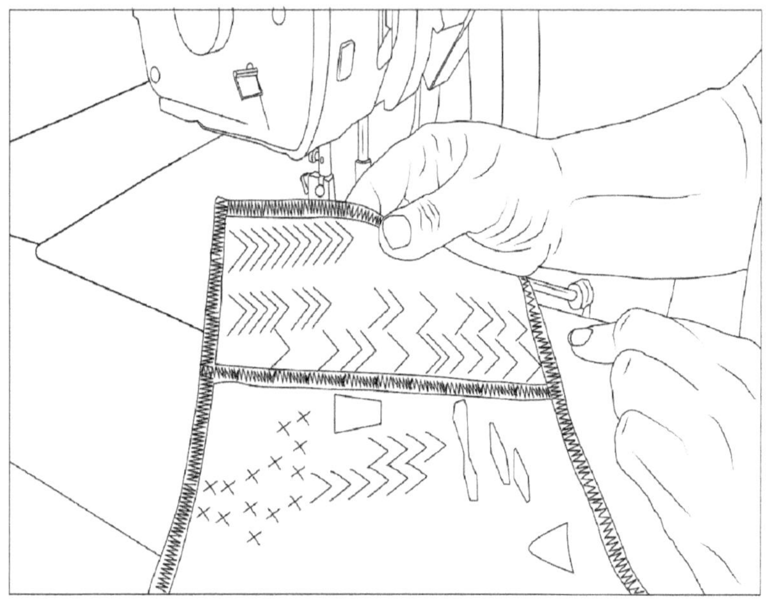

Creating different stitches on your garment makes it look more decorative. You can practice with different types of laces and different threads for your upper and lower looper to make the stitches look unique and neat.

Chapter Summary

Lace application foot is a great tool that allows you to sew flatlock stitches among other decorative stitches in your fabric. The foot has an edge guide that ensures your fabric is put in place as you serge. The guide also prevents the knife from trimming your fabric while stitching.

Align your fabric and the lace with the guide and don't pull it, let the foot feed the fabric through. Depending on the model of your machine, you may have different lace applicator foot but they all serve the same purpose. You only need to master the settings of your lace foot from the instruction manual of that model.

When sewing decorative stitches, you consider having different thread colors and weights. adjust the stitch length based on the fabric and serge your fabric. After serging, pull the pieces of the fabric so that you have a flat seam on your garment. Needle stitches on the right side out should appear clean and neat.

Final Words

This step-by-step instruction guide helps beginners to know how to operate a serger machine. The manual introduces you to different parts of a serger machine and what you need to know about them. If you need to have a professional finishing to your garment, a serger machine will help you achieve that.

In our introduction chapter to sergers, we are able to learn what a serger machine is and what makes it different from a sewing machine. You're also able to learn different parts of the serger machine and their functions.

The serger machine is also known as the overlock machine creates seams to your fabric and at the same time, it trims excess fabric. This makes them faster in sewing garments as well as gives you a clean finishing. The machine performs multiple functions simultaneously to create a strong stitch.

After knowing the different parts and functions, you're also able to learn some of the tools you need in order to get started with your serger machine. These tools are a must-have for you to successfully complete your sewing projects.

These tools enable you to set up your machine and get it running. For example, knowing the needle parts makes it easy to fix the needle in your machine and also how to thread it. In this chapter, you're able to learn how to choose the best serger machine. We are able to evaluate the factors to consider before making your buying decision. In addition, we listed some of the best Serger machines in the market you can choose based on your needs.

In chapter three, we learned how to thread your machine like a pro! With the step-by-step guide, you are able to thread both the left and right needles and both the lower and upper loopers. You are also able to know how to adjust the needle tensions and differential feed for you to have a perfect stitch.

Learning how to customize the serger controls helps you adjust the stitches that give you better results based on the type of fabric you're using. Further, you are also able to know how to troubleshoot any threading issue with your machine and fix it.

Once you have threaded your machine, it becomes very easy to change the threads. With just a few steps, you can easily change the threads to match your fabric. You don't have to follow the long procedure of threading your machine again. Your secret trick is to cut the old thread and replacing it with the new thread. All you need is to tie a knot of the old thread with the new thread.

A serger threading and thread tension differ from that of your regular sewing machine. Thus you need to know how to operate and adjust them. In a serger machine, the knives trim part of the seam allowance as you stitch your fabric. And for that reason, you need to know how to guide your fabric under the presser foot and what to expect while stitching. Once you're comfortable with how your machine operates, you can dive in for your first sewing project.

There are different types of stitches you can create with your serger machine, That is why in chapter 4, you're able to learn how to use different types of stitches to add finishing the raw edges of the fabric, create decorative stitches, blind hem stitches, rolled hemstitches, and other forms of stitches.

You're also able to learn how the stitches are formed and when to use each type of stitch. The type of stitches to use and how to use them depends on the model of the serger machine you have. Some models come with a built-in serger foot that allows you to create different types of stitches while others require you to purchase a particular serger foot designed specifically for doing a particular stitch. Read your serger manual to know more about what type of stitches you can do with your machine.

When you choose a particular stitch for your fabric, you have to determine the number of threads to use (1- thread, 2- thread, 3-thread, or 4-thread), whether to use the left or the right needle and how to set up the loopers.

Sometimes, depending on the stitch you choose, you have to change the presser foot, change the needle position, adjust the tension dials, and disengage the blades. Learning how to create a balance between the loopers and the needle threads helps create a perfect stitch. Confirm with your manual before making any changes to your serger controls.

The fabric type affects how the stitches are formed and that's why we have learned how to adjust the tension dials and stitch length to have a clean stitch. However, there are instances where adjusting the tension can not balance your stitches. In such instances, you need stabilization of seams so as to improve the quality and strength of your seams. In this tutorial, you're able to learn how to stabilize your stitches using stay tape, ribbons, binding, and using clear elastic.

Stabilization of seams helps reinforce stitches in some of the high-stress areas like your shoulders or when sewing a stretchy fabric and don't want it to warp out of shape. The above simple steps will help you employ different techniques to stabilize your stitches.

In chapter 6, you're able to learn how to serger around corners, and curves. Know how to stitch rounded corners, and other forms of curves make it easy to create projects that have pockets, collars, straps, bows, bag flap, clutches, and other decorative shapes. You are also able to know how to clip the corners and curves to give your garment a professional look.

Further, you're to know how to create rolled edges and flatlock stitches on the raw edges of the fabric and give your projects a neat finishing. Flatlock seams allow you to sew raw edges of two pieces of fabric side-by-side. It is a great stitch for joining fabrics together and leave you with a flat decorative stitch. If you want to create an invisible stitch, you can use the hemming technique with a flatlock.

In addition, we have different thread choices for serging, if you want to make decorative stitches, you have to delve into the world of decorative threading, use yarns, fine ribbons, and beading wires. Different threads are made using a variety of fibers that make them look beautiful and sparkle when used on garments. Using different tools like yarn application foot, lace application foot, and gathering foot among others makes your serging better.

Threading a nylon thread on your upper loopers will give you a super soft finishing on your garment. You can also use bead stringing wire to create custom narrow hems in your garment. A lace foot allows you to attach different lace trims to the raw edges of your fabric. The foot provides better visibility when attaching ribbons or lace into fabrics.

A narrow clear elastic adds stability to your knit seams. If you're using lightweight fabrics or stretchy fabric, then a clear elastic thread will be of great use. Continue practicing with different stitches and make professional custom-made projects.

Image Credit: Shutterstock.com

Intermediate Guide to Serger

Alter and Redesign Your Favourite Loose-fitting Garment

Introduction

In this intermediate guide to serging, you will learn advanced techniques that you can use to make several knit garments. Most of the DIY projects are much easier to do with a serger machine.

One of the greatest benefits of the serger machine is to learn how to make blind hems. In most of your garments, you want to create an invisible stitch from the outside. In this tutorial, you will learn how to use the blind hem technique to create a deep hem for your pants, skirts, and unlined jackets.

You will also learn how to install the blind hem foot, adjust the tension, and needle threads for you to create a perfect stitch for joining two folded edges of the fabric.

Another important foot for any serger is the gathering foot. If you love to create a lot of gathers in your garment Projects, you will be able to learn how to use the gathering foot and an example Project you can work out with to make gathers. Depending on the task you want to do, you can invest in an appropriate foot and make garments that have a professional look.

You will also learn how to take care of your overlock machine and extend its lifetime. Regular maintenance of the machine is very important to keep your machine clean and improve its performance. An accumulation of dust and fill up of threads and trims inside the machine can lower the performance of your machine. This manual will teach you to regularly clean and oil the different parts of the machine.

You will also know how to make simple DIY projects using different stitches and features in your machine. Some of the simple DIY projects you will learn to make at the end of this tutorial include: sewing a personalized baby blanket, sewing a pillow cover, serging a drawstring bag, sewing a dust cover for your overlock machine, sewing a Christmas stocking, sewing a holiday napkin tree, and sewing your own face mask.

These are personalized serging projects you can do with your machine. You will learn the step-by-step procedures on how to sew each of the projects. Some of them are very easy and they will not take you a lot of time to sew them. These projects are also budget-friendly since you can make some of them from scrap fabrics.

You will also be able to add your personal touch to the projects. Once you learn how to sew these different DIY garment projects, you can give them a gift to your friends and loved ones.

Get ready to learn on your next serging project!

Chapter One:
Blind Hem Serging Technique

Did you know you can make super clean hems with your serger machine? Although you can make blind hem with your sewing machine, the serger sewing technique is a super-fast and easy way to hem your fabrics and give your hems a clean finish. For this reason, a serger machine dominates the regular sewing machine making it the most preferred for excellent sewing projects.

A blind hem is a technique used to create a blind stitch on a cloth with little visible threads on the front side of the cloth. A blind stitch helps create an invisible stitch thread by joining two pieces of fabric together. These invisible stitches are hidden under the folded edges of the fabric.

When you use blind hem stitches, the thread is invisible at the front of your garment and almost hidden on the inside of the garment. This sewing technique ensures the stitches remain hidden inside the fabric hem.

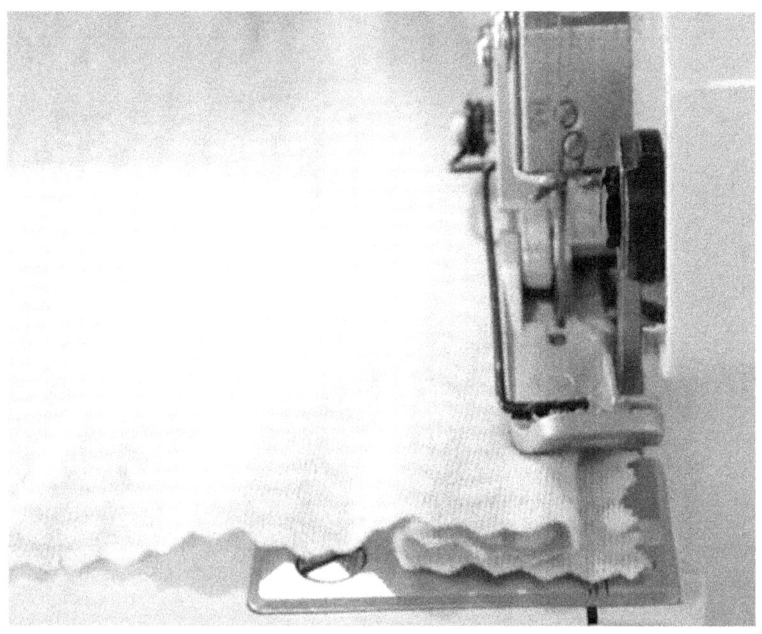

When using a serger machine to create invisible hems, ensure the fabric stretch remains natural.

You can use this technique to attach pockets and trimmings to your garment.

If you're using a regular sewing machine to create a blind hem, you need a presser foot and then select the stitch pattern suitable for sewing blind hems. A zigzag stitch can be used to create a blind stitch using the sewing machine.

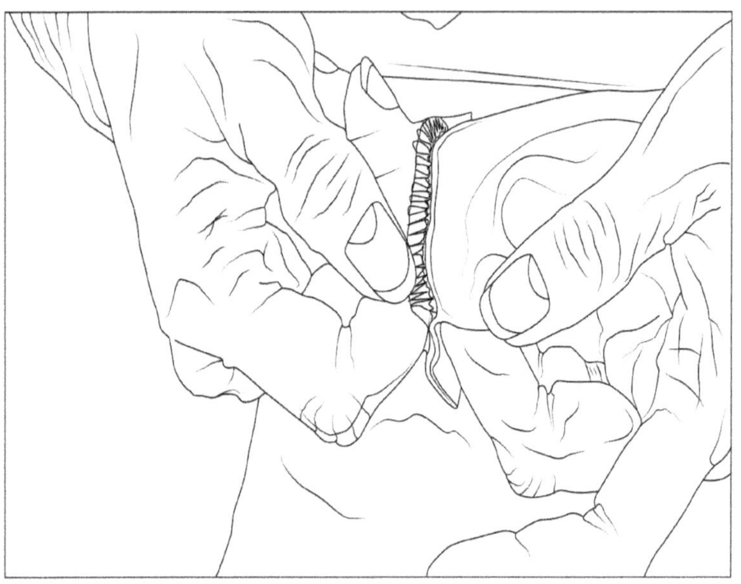

How to use a Serger machine to create a blind hem

In just one move, you can serge the edges of the fabric, trim, and stitch it at the same time! Your serger machine allows you to do that all in one easy step.

Requirements:

1. Thick threads for your looper

2. Ballpoint needles

3. Blind Hem foot presser

4. Fabric you want to do serging on

Blind hem foot

This universal adjustable blind hem foot is designed to fit in most overlock models. It helps you sew neat and professional looking stitches. This foot is suitable for creating blind stitches on your skirts, trousers, and jackets.

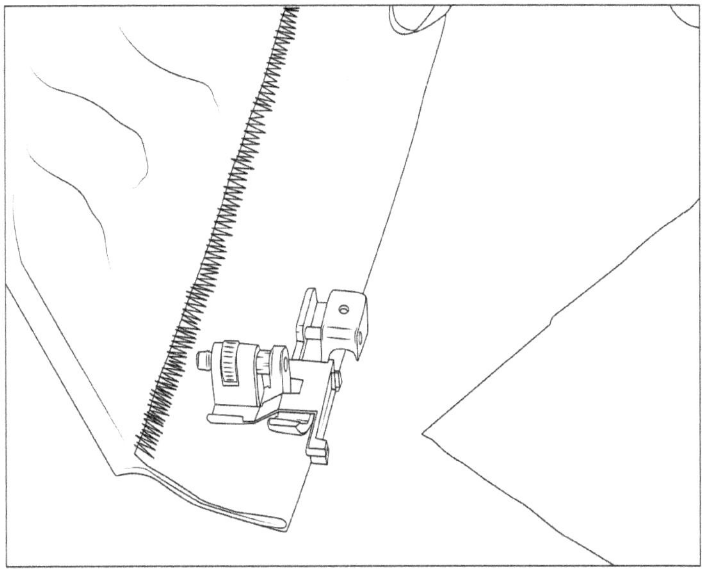

When stitching, the bulk stitches are sewn on the hem while the larger jump stitch moves across to attach to the hem of the fabric on the wrong side up.

Before you begin to use the foot, you should match the stitch position with the available hem fabric in three ways:

- Adjust the foot using the metal screw and move the plastic plate to the left and right.

- Adjust the stitch width

- Adjust the needle position (although this applics to selected serger machines)

The foot has a metal guide at the center and three grooves located on the underside. When blind hemming, the fold of your garment snugly fits against the metal guide in the foot. This maintains the accuracy of the stitch on the edges while the underneath grooves prevent slipping of the garment.

The needle will swing over the metal guide in order to create slack in the upper looper tension and as a result, you create an invisible stitch on your garment.

Match the folded fabric with the plastic guide. You can also adjust jump stitch nibbles to feed on a small amount of the fabric. If you set a larger nibble, you will have a larger stitch on the right side of the hem.

Blind hem foot not only creates blind hemstitches at the bottom of your skirts and jackets, you can also use it to make a perfect topstitch on garments. If you're using it to add a topstitch, ensure the guide is up and lined with the outside edges of the fabric.

You can also use this foot when creating seams around the neckline, the arm cycles, or creating a bodice on your skirt using a topstitch.

Steps to create a blind hem stitch

Step 1

Insert a ballpoint needle for sewing knits into your fabric. A ballpoint needle is used for sewing special fabrics. Insert the needle in the needle bar clamp and fasten the screws. Ensure the long groove faces the side where you thread the needle.

Step 2

Take your blind Hem Foot presser and attach it to the stock foot presser of your machine. Put the top thread underneath and pull both threads to the back. Adjust the screw on your blind hem foot presser to adjust the stitch width according to your need.

This can be done by moving the gauge either left or right. You can also test it first to ensure you have moved it to a good position.

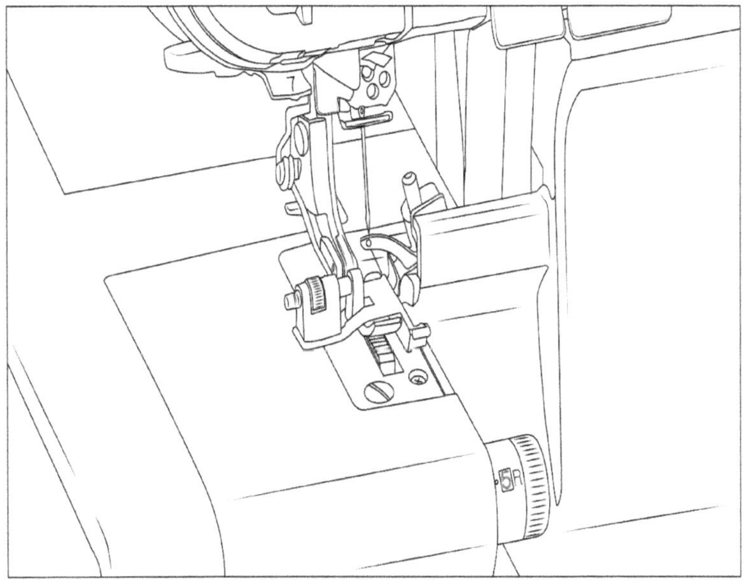

Step 3

Adjust your needle settings based on the type of fabric you're using or when you want a different stitch length. In this example, we are going to adjust the settings to sew a narrow hem in our fabric.

This is just a standard serging process so we will not adjust the stitch length or do anything to the differential feed. To start with, we are using the left needle so we need to lower your left needle to position 1. You can even set it to zero based on how tight you need the stitches but the best setting is usually 0 to 2. We are not going to use the right needle.

Make sure to thread the needle with a color that matches the fabric you're sewing. This ensures the little stitches that appear at the front (right side) of the fabric are hardly visible.

You can also use different colors for the looper thread because the stitches usually show on the inside.

Strengthen or tighten the upper looper by increasing the tension to 6 and then decrease the tension of the lower looper by 3.

Step 4

Take your fabric and double-fold it. You will sew on the wrong side of the fabric.

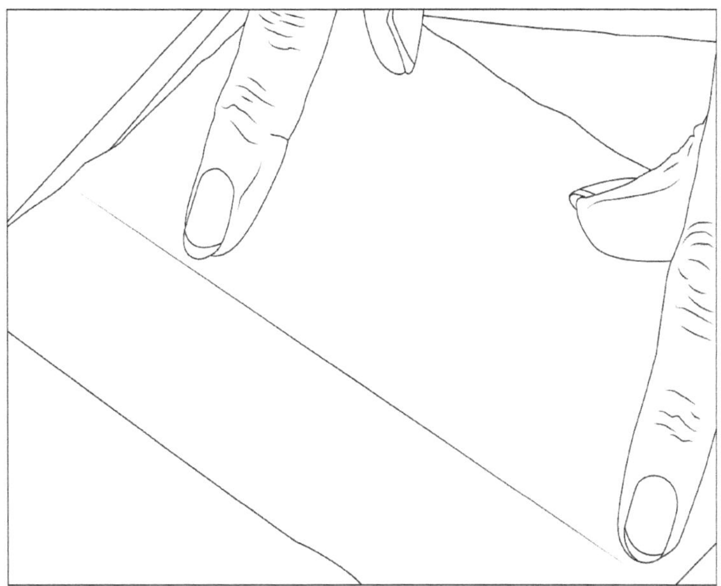

Step 5

Flip the fabric and get ready to feed it to the serger machine.

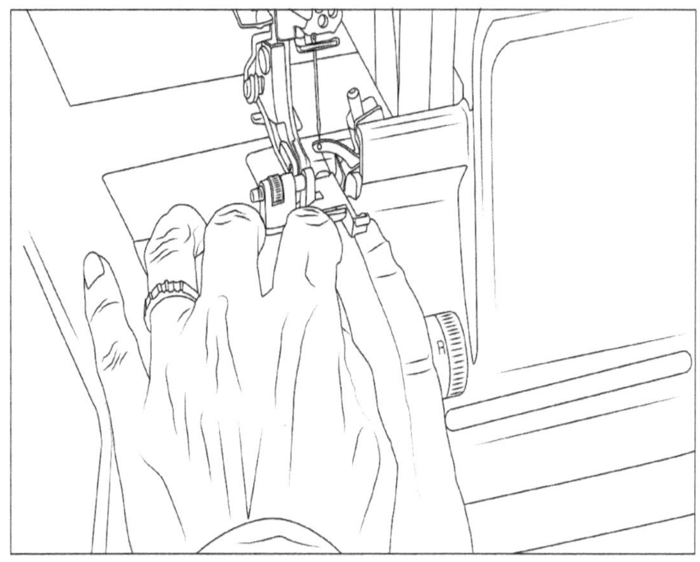

Step 6

Place the wrong side of the fabric facing up. Then, feed the fabric such that the folded edge is on the left.

Position your presser foot on the hem so that the needle stitches right at the edges of the fold while the blade cuts the excess fabric. The blind hem presser foot has a metal guide at the center of the presser foot and three grooves underneath. The metal guide ensures you accurately feed the fabric underneath the presser foot while the groove prevents the fabric from slipping.

The closer the needle pierce to the edge of the fabric, the smaller the stitch on the right side of the fabric.

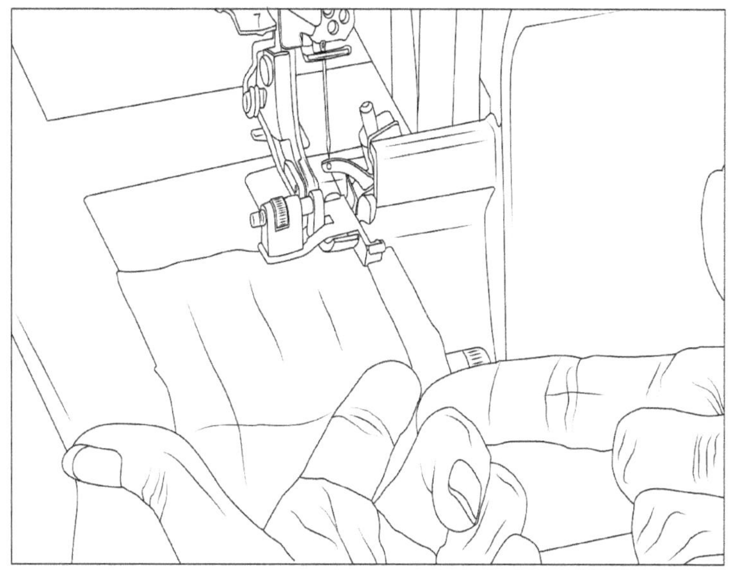

Step 7

You can set the serger speed to medium and start to stitch! While stitching, don't pull the fabric or stretch it. Leave it to feed through!

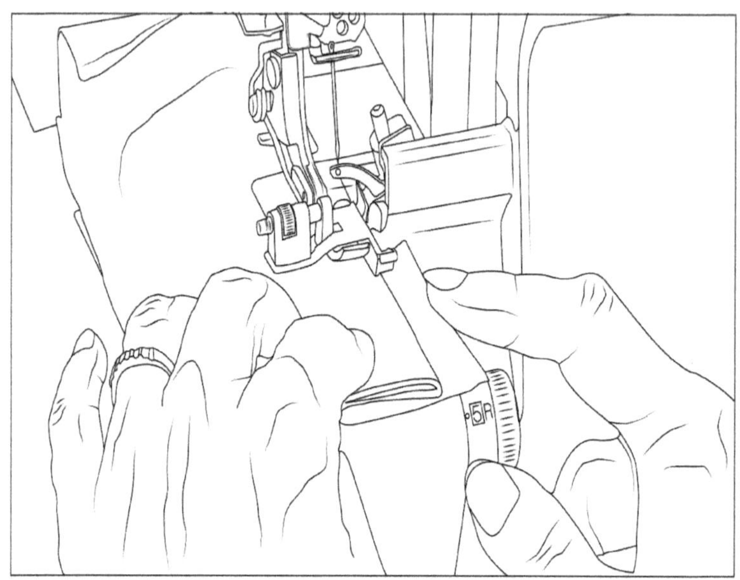

Step 8

After stitching, leave a long chain so that your machine does not come undone.

With these simple steps, you can sew a blind hem to your fabric.

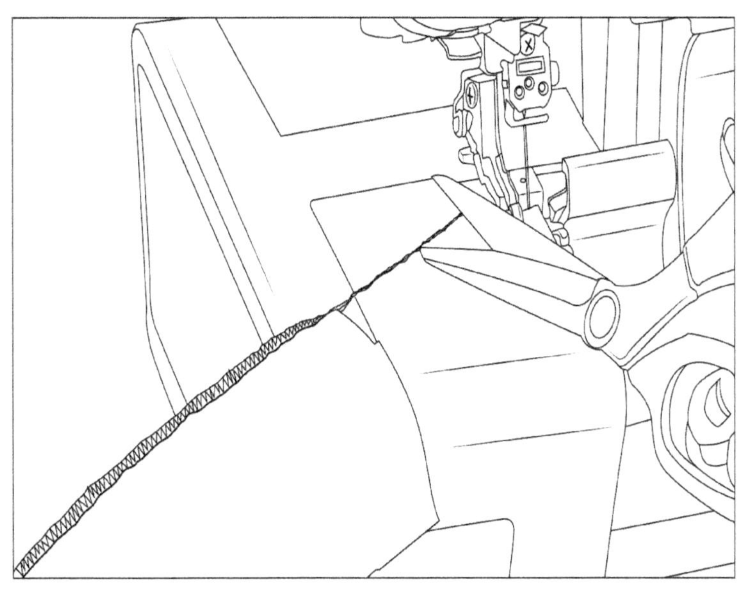

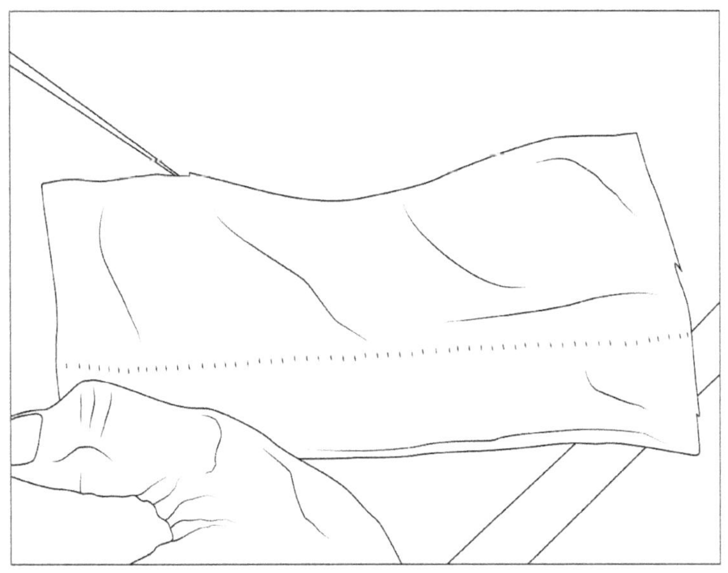

Chapter Summary

- The blind hem serging technique is a great way of creating hidden stitches. These stitches can be used when creating pockets or when you want to add decorative stitches to a piece of garment.

- Based on the type of serging machine you're using, you can change the settings to have blind hem stitch, choose your stitch length and then go ahead to stitch.

- When stitching the garment, avoid pulling it or stretching it because this can result in irregular stitches. Just let it feed through.

- Make sure to use a thread that matches your fabric color so that the stitches remain invisible.

- In the next chapter, you will learn how to use a gathering tool.

Chapter Two:
How To Use A Gathering Foot

If you have been sewing ruffles and gathers a lot then a gathering foot will be a great accessory to your sewing.

A gathering foot will make your work easier and give you excellent results. No one can say no to sewing on a perfectly gathered skirt! The art of making gathers evenly makes your project look awesome.

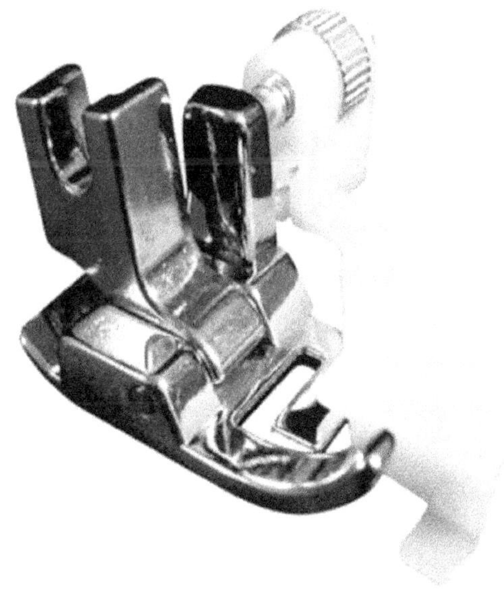

In this chapter, I will show you how to use a gathering tool to create gathers on your project. Regular sewing machines can also use gathering tools to create gathers or fabric ruffles. Whether using your sewing machine or serger machine, it works the same.

What is a gathering foot?

A gathering foot is a great sewing tool that allows you to automatically create a gathered ruffle. It looks like the regular presser foot but due to the shape of the foot, it gathers as you sew the fabric.

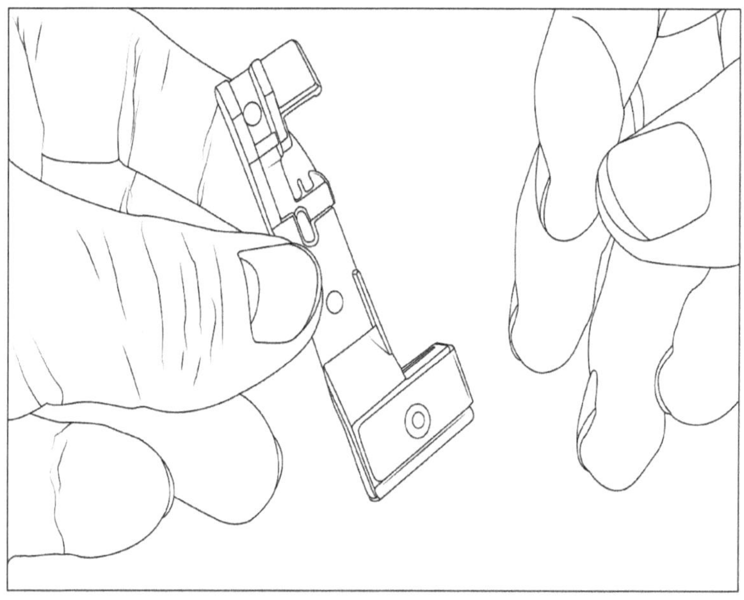

A gathering foot works well with finer fabrics otherwise it will not work well with thick fabrics.

If you love creating gathers on your project, invest in this gathering tool, and get ready to produce fine and soft even gathers.

In addition, you don't have to worry about sliding up and down the stitch line as you sew gathers. You can even sew gathers on the second layer of fabric with just a single pass.

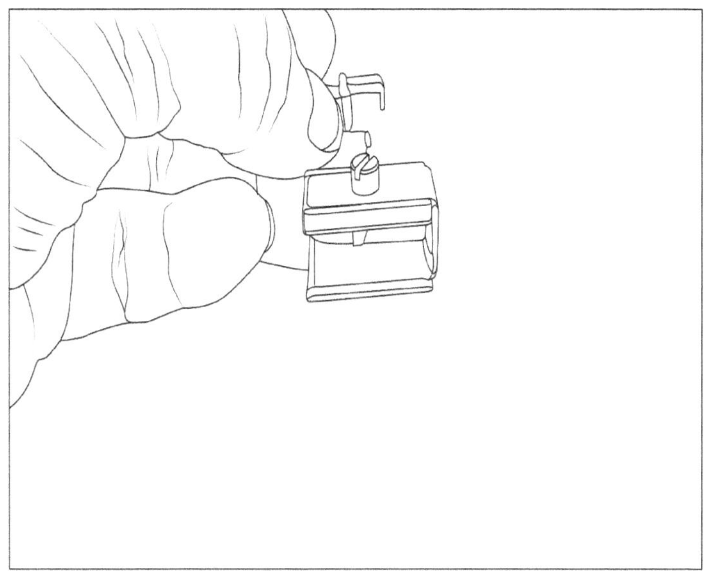

A gathering tool can gather stitches in a piece of fabric alone or it can gather while attaching the gathers to a flat piece of fabric (non-ruffled fabric).

You can use a gathering foot in three ways:

- To gather/ruffle fabric alone

- To gather/ruffle fabric and at the same time sew it on a piece of non-ruffled fabric

- To shirr using elastic thread

How to gather the fabric alone

Step 1

Remove the presser foot and replace it with the gathering foot in your machine

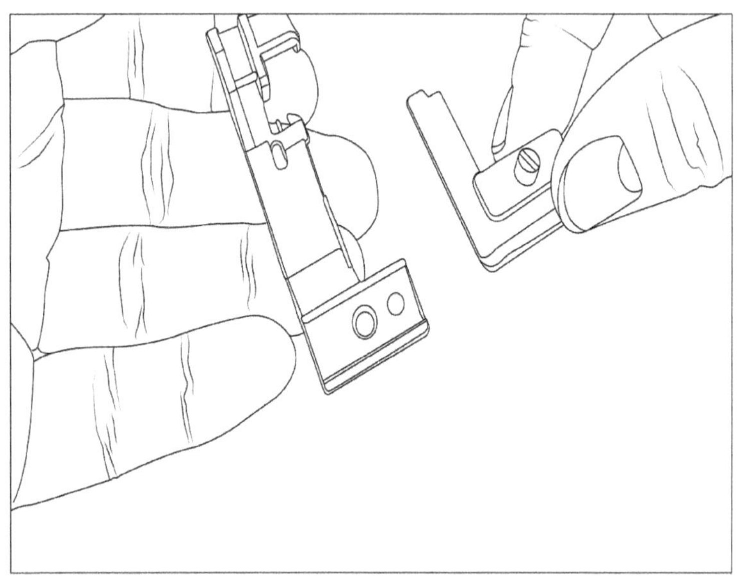

Step 2

Adjust your stitch length. If you want to have more gathers in your garment, you have to increase the stitch length. You can practice with different stitch lengths before you settle on your perfect stitch length for your gathers.

You can also adjust the tension dials for better results. Increasing the tension will enable you to gather more tightly.

Hold the thread tails before you start sewing to prevent them from being caught underneath.

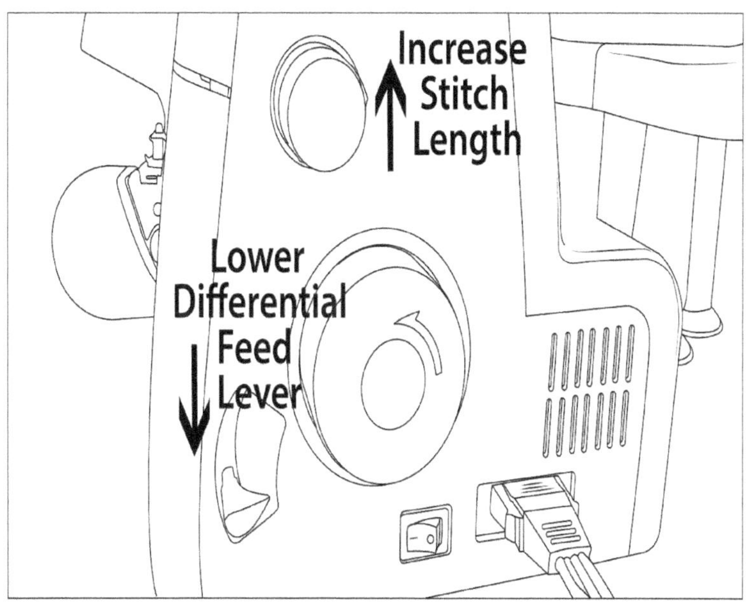

Step 3

Place your piece of fabric underneath the foot and lower the foot down. Go ahead and sew gathers on the fabric. Do not pull the fabric or push it while sewing, let it feed through.

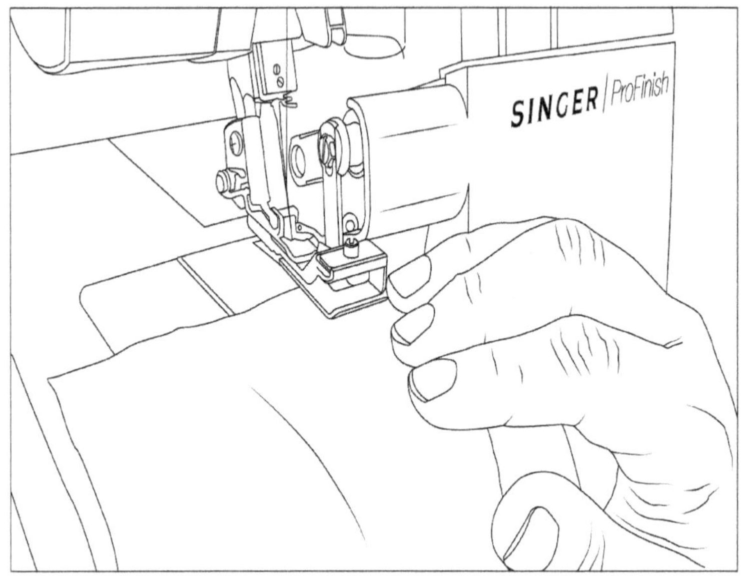

Based on the stitch length you will notice neat and even gathers. You can trim the fabric to have your desired size.

Unlike traditional methods of sewing gathers, a gathering foot allows you to stitch just one line and you don't have to pull the threads once you have finished sewing.

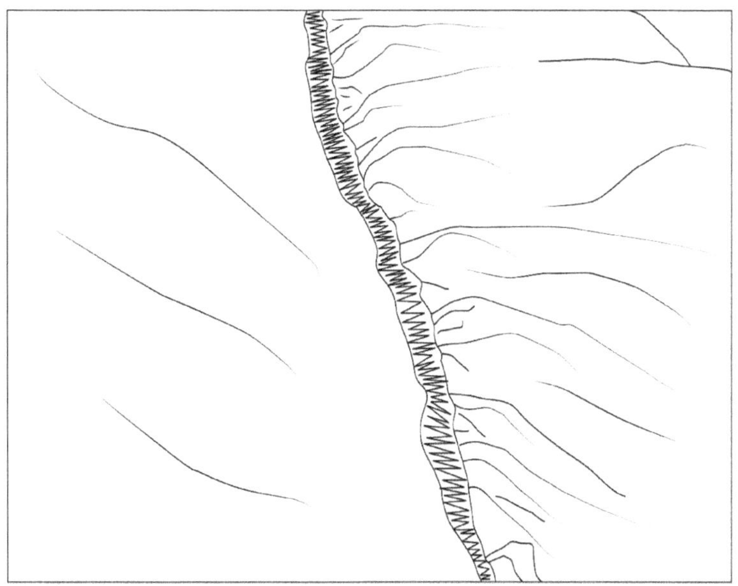

Note: The thickness of the fabric affects the distribution of gathers on the fabric. Heavy fabrics are very difficult to gather with gathering feet but you can easily do them using the ruffler foot. Gathering feet are suitable for fine fabrics.

How to gather fabric and at the same time sew it to a non-gathered fabric

Step 1

Replace the standard presser foot with the gathering foot tool.

Step 2

Set your stitch length very high. You can set it to the maximum level of your machine and tighten the upper tension looper for you to obtain fuller gathers.

Step 3

Place the fabric that needs to be gathered underneath the foot and then lower the gathering foot. Place the fabric that is to be unruffled at the center slot of the gathering foot. The right side of the fabric should face down.

Go ahead and create gathers at the same time sewing unruffled fabric. Hold the unruffled fabric when sewing and pull it slightly to the right to prevent it from slipping out.

This results in evenly distributed gathers attached to a non-gathered fabric. You can trim any excess gathered fabric on the sides giving your garment a great finish.

How to shirr using gathering foot

A gathering foot can also be used as a shirring foot because it can be used to make shirred effects using an elastic thread on your bobbin. The shirring effect improves the texture of your fabric and makes it look more beautiful.

You can create puckered shirred effects by sewing several rows of gathering stitches.

You need to hand wind your bobbin using a loosely thin elastic thread. Don't stretch the thread. Insert the top thread in your sewing needle and bring up the elastic thread. Push the threads to the back and start sewing.

If you want to sew small gathers then make the stitch length short but if you need full gathers, make the stitch length long.

After adding gathering stitches on several rows, you can use a steam iron on the stitched rows. Just place the iron with the steam over your fabric and the shirring will shrink up to create a good shirr effect.

You can practice this on a piece of fabric scrap before you sew these shirring gatherings on your final fabric. This will help you determine how much fabric you need for you to create the desired shirring and gathers. It will also help you know how tight you need to adjust the tension and how long the stitch length is.

Gathering using a Serger machine

Gathering with a serger machine is much faster and easier. Once you know how to gather using your serger, you will never go back to using your normal sewing machine to create gathers.

When gathering using a serger machine, you don't need a special foot tool or any attachments. All you have to do is adjust the stitch length and change the setting to the differential feeding system.

Step 1

Set your serger to have 4 thread serging.

Step 2

Increase differential feed to the highest number. In this case, we will use 2. Increase your stitch length to have the highest number. Some sergers have up to number 5.

Step 3

Start to stitch along the raw edge of the fabric. You will notice some gatherings on your fabric as you continue to serge.

Step 4

Near the edge of the fabric, put your needle underneath the two parallel needle threads. Do not touch the looper threads otherwise, they will knot if you touch them.

Step 5

Pull the needle threads from the chain of threads. Make sure the threads don't get tangled. If done correctly, it will be easy to slip out.

Then pull the two-needle threads in order to start gathering your fabric.

Step 6

Now you can go ahead and make gathers to your fabric. You will not have any stray threads that end up on the outside of your ruffled or gathered fabric.

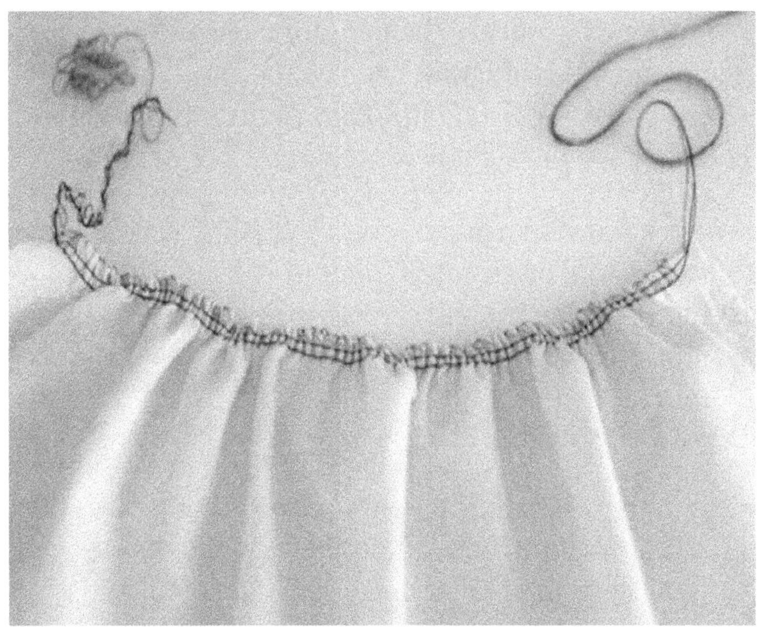

With these easy steps, you can easily serge your way to a great gathered project!

Tips for using a gathering foot

When using a gathering foot, it is difficult to control the length of the finished fabric unlike when using traditional gathering methods. You can solve this by cutting the fabric longer than the required size then trims the excess fabric after gathering. With this, you don't have to worry about how to get the perfect stitch length and tension.

Alternatively, you can use a test strip about 10 inches and then sew gathering stitches on it. Measure your new fabric length after the stitch. If the remaining length is 5 inches then you have 2:1 gather. Continue to adjust the stitch length and tension until you obtain the perfect ratio.

When sewing, ensure the flat fabric has the right side facing up and the fabric that needs to be gathered should have the wrong side facing up. That is, the garment and the ruffle must have the right sides together.

When gathering using a serger machine, you don't need a special foot tool or any attachments. All you have to do is adjust the stitch length and change the setting to a differential feeding system.

Chapter Summary

- A gathering foot can help you to gather a piece of cloth or allow you to join a flat piece of cloth on the gathered fabric all at once. This saves you and gives you neat gathers.

- With a perfect stitch length to tension ratio, you will be able to create gathers on your garment. A tight stitch is a result of having a long stitch length and a higher tension.

- You can also create shirr gathers using an elastic thread to create rows of stitches. Although you can use a shirring foot, gathering foot also helps you create great projects with shirring effects.

- Alternatively, you can use a serger machine to create your gathers. The serger is faster than the sewing machine. Once you know to use the serger, you will never go back to your normal sewing machine.

In the next chapter, you will learn about serger maintenance.

Chapter Three: Maintenance of Serger Machine

Maintenance of your serger machine is the most important thing you can do to extend the lifetime of your machine. Cleaning and oiling your serger sewing machine makes it run smoothly.

Like any other mechanical equipment, the quality of your serger performance is greatly influenced by regular care and maintenance. After every sewing project, you should remove any lint and bits of fabric remaining on the machine.

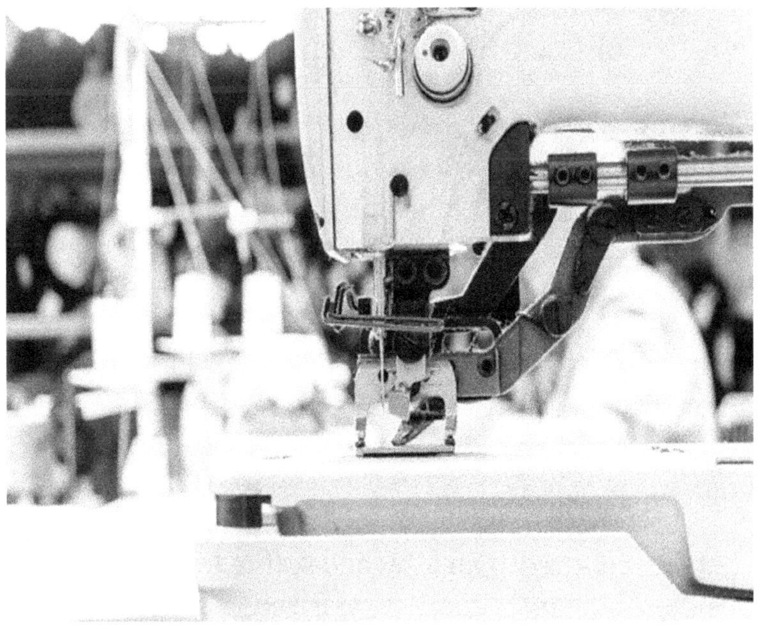

Image source: Evgeny Haritonov/Shutterstock

The lubricated area of the machine acts as a magnet that draws lint into the inside parts of your serger machine. The lint absorbs the oil leaving the moving parts to dry out. This affects the functioning of your machine and can shorten the machine life cycle.

Therefore, proper care will extend the lifetime of the machine as well as ensure your projects are perfectly made. For the sewing machine to function properly, it needs basic maintenance like cleaning, oiling, and lubricating it.

Serger requires a little bit of extra care because of its higher number of movable parts and serging speed.

All serger models come with a manual on how to clean them. You should go through the manual to learn how to clean and maintain your machine.

Having trouble with your machine?

When you're facing challenges with your serger machine, the general rule is to *clean it first*. Most of the problems you may be facing with your machine may be due to dust, lint, or pieces of threads that have collected from the working parts of your machine.

Leaving dust and lint to accumulate for long may affect the functioning of your machine. Simply brush them off after every use and you will have your machine run for a long time without any problems.

Sergers come with an attached soft nylon brush to clean the insides of the machine. Alternatively, you can use a narrow paintbrush to remove tint in the bobbin case, in the feed dog, and under the needle plate.

If there are pieces of thread or tint that you can't remove with the brush, then you can use tweezers to remove them.

If you leave lint to accumulate for a long time, it can be soaked with the oil or the lubricant and this will affect the operation of the machine. Once you remove this dirt you may notice the machine works properly and no further adjustments are needed.

Some of these instructions do not apply to all serger machines. Therefore, it is important to compare this guide with the specific procedures recommended to clean your machine by the manufacturer. For instance, a chain stitch machine or an electric machine that uses bearings packed with grease has specific instructions on how to clean, oil, and lubricate them.

Equipment and supplies

You need the following equipment and supplies to properly maintain your serger sewing machine.

- Small and a large screwdriver

- Small adjustable wrench

- Tweezers

- Needle holders

- Cake pan to soak parts in a cleaning fluid

- Small oil can for cleaning the fluid

- Paring knife/ pocket knife

- Cleaning brush (either nylon or narrow)

- Recommended sewing machine oil

- Small crochet hook

- Cleaning cloth

- Fabric to test stitches

- Sewing machine lubricant

- Can of cleaning solvent

- Flashlight

- Rubber gloves

- Old Newspapers

- Magnifying glass (optional)

Always check the machine's instruction manual of the recommended lubricant, cleaning solvent, and sewing machine oil. Use a cleaning solvent that doesn't flash a flame if temperatures go below 120° F. Carbon tetrachloride shouldn't be used because it is highly poisonous. You should never use gasoline because it is highly flammable.

Place newspapers on the floor or on the tabletop where you place your machine. You also need a flashlight for hard-to-see areas although this is optional.

General cleaning

Before you start cleaning your serger machine, you should assemble all the supplies and equipment you need. Unplug your machine and bring it to a well-lit room where you will do the cleaning.

If you want to do a full cleaning, unthread the machine, remove the needles, slide plate, and the presser foot. Some serger models allow you to remove the throat plate. Put all of them in a pan and add cleaning fluid to cover them. Leave them to soak and proceed with cleaning the other parts.

Make sure you note the position of each of the parts you remove and which side is supposed to be on the top. When unscrewing, make sure you put more pressure on the push and not on the twist. If a particular screw doesn't loosen up, then soak it with the cleaning fluid for a few minutes. The screwdriver blade size should be proportional to the slot in the screw. You should also use a wrench on the bolts and not pliers.

Open the serger doors to have access to the loopers. Take the soft nylon brush or the paintbrush and start cleaning the inside. Brush the area around the loopers and the feed dog to remove all the lint in the area. You can also use a brush that has some stiff bristles to push all the lint out. If there are threads sticking in some areas where the brush cannot reach, you can use tweezers to pull the threads.

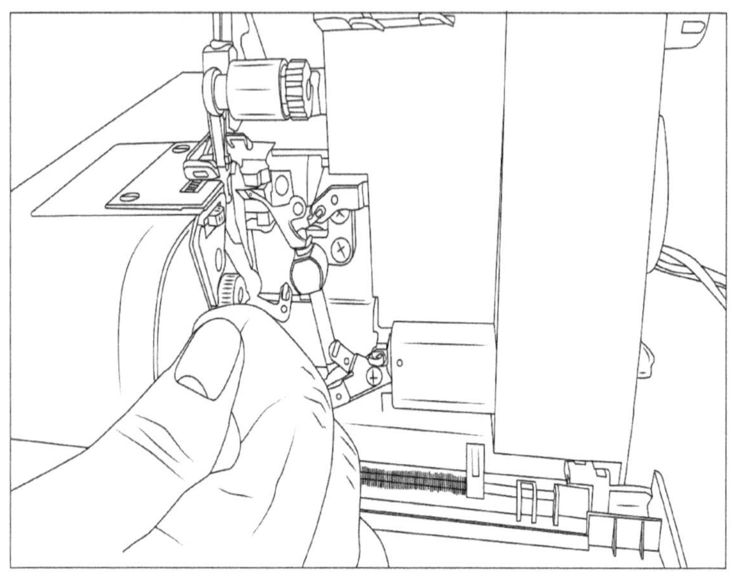

After cleaning the looper, apply oil around that area using the manufacturer's recommended oil. In most cases, apply oil on the moving parts of the metal. One or two drops of oil are enough.

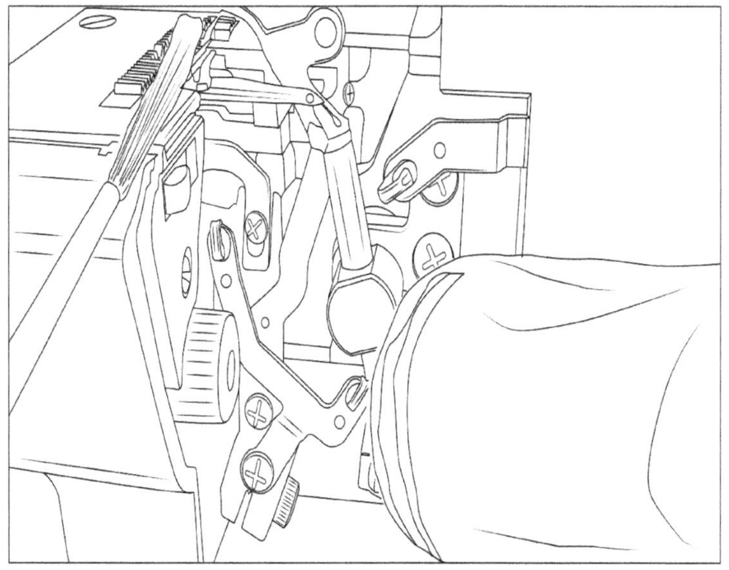

Clean the tension dials using a Perle cotton or a piece of embroidery floss. This will remove lint and threads left in the tension dial. If lint builds up around the tension dials, it will affect the accuracy of tension dial settings as well as interfere with stitch length and formation.

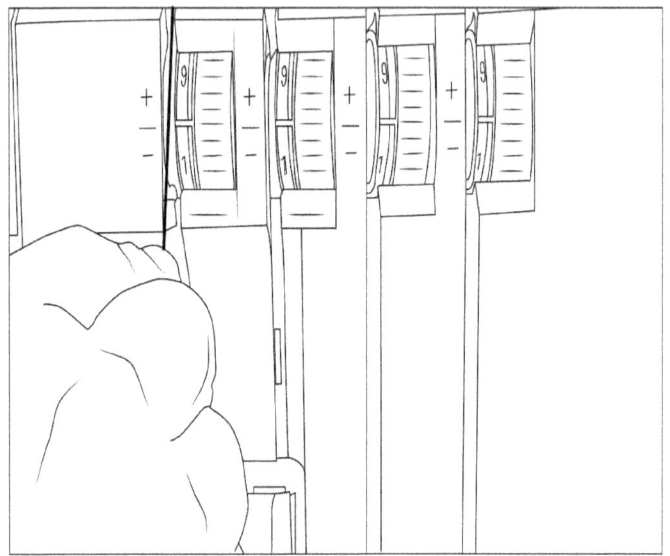

If your knife cut chewed edges instead of a clean-cut, then it is time to replace them. There are sergers that have only one blade while others have two: the upper blade and lower blade. Depending on the type of your machine, you can easily replace your knives. Make sure you return the knife to the precise position for it to work correctly. Alternatively, you can look for a serger technician to replace the knife for you.

After you're done cleaning and oiling the machine, screw back the presser foot, the stitch plate, and any other plate you removed. Replace the needle with a new one. You should always insert a new needle into your machine after cleaning it.

Wipe clean the outside of the serger to remove any fingerprints and thread your machine.

Oiling

Not all sergers require oiling so check the model manual to know whether to oil and after how long. The manual also has information on where to apply the oil and how often you should apply.

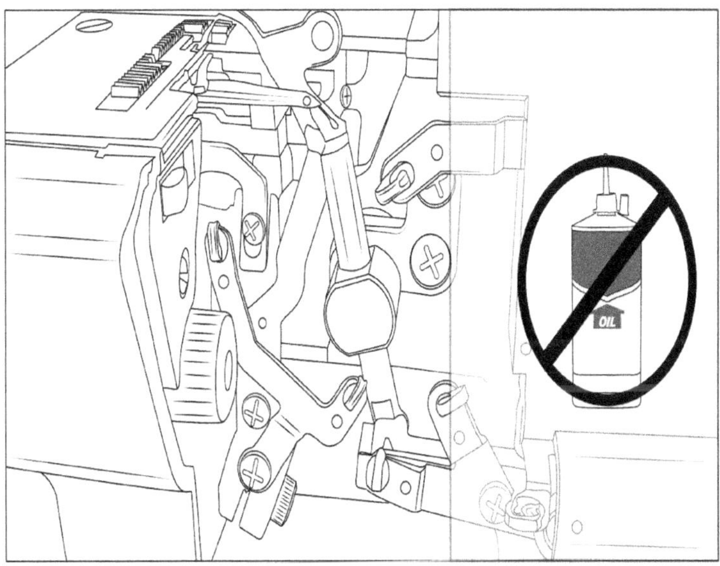

If your machines require oiling, there is a standard rule that states that the machine should be oiled after 8-10 hours of serging. You should also oil it whenever you hear a metallic scraping sound.

Changing needles

If you have bent or nicked a needle it may end up breaking or skipping some stitches while sewing. Bent needles can also cause the serger timing to go off, so you should change your needles more often.

Some manufacturers recommend changing the needles after every 8-10 hours of serging. Following some of these simple steps to keep your serger machine clean will increase the lifetime of your machine. You will never have any issues with the machine!

Chapter Summary

- Maintenance of your serger machine is very important. Cleaning and lubricating the machine extends the machine's life and boosts the performance of your serger.

- Different manufacturers have specific recommendations on how to take care of a particular model of the serger. Make sure to look at the recommendation before putting the above steps into practice.

- Each model of the machine does recommend the type of oil to use while other brands don't need oiling. Therefore, read the instruction manual on what type of oil to use for each model of machine.

In the next chapter, you will learn how to make a baby blanket.

Chapter Four:
How To Make Baby Blanket

Learning how to make a baby blanket will give you great satisfaction. Baby Blankets are a more personal gift for the baby and the parent. It is the best gift any parent can give or receive. Making your own baby blankets is what makes them more special.

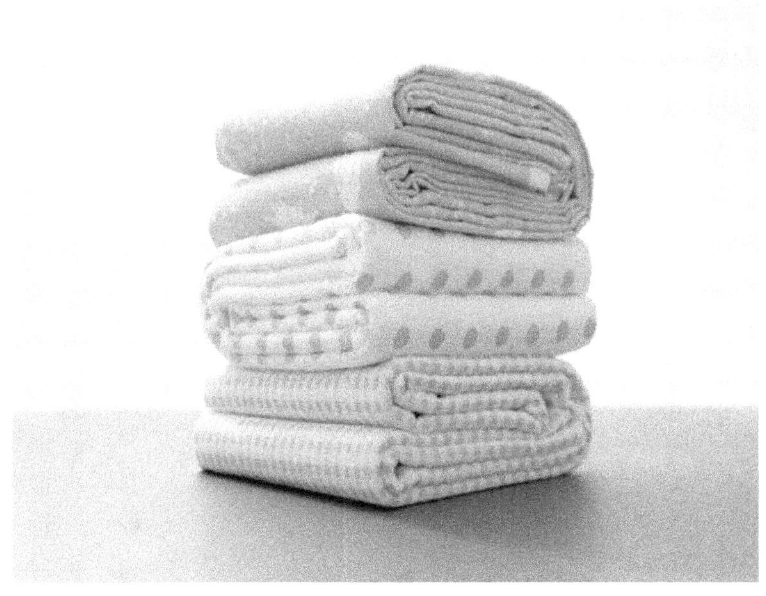

Image source: Kitch Bain/Shutterstock

Making a blanket to keep your little one warm gives you some sense of satisfaction. It is also a great gift to your loved ones!

Learning how to make baby blankets is a simple serging project for a beginner and it prepares you for making more basic serging projects.

There are various designs for homemade sewn baby blankets you can make for your loved ones. Some of these designs are simple and easy to use. Choose the design of your choice and make a great blanket for your baby.

If you're expecting your baby very soon, or someone you love is, then this simple project for making a baby blanket is for you. Let's get started.

Tools required

- 2 pieces of cloth

- Cutting mat

- Rotary cutter/ scissors

- Pins

- Thread

- Serger machine

Make sure to purchase fabrics designed specifically for baby clothing. In this project, we will use flannelette fabric. You can choose any other soft fabric but make sure it is made of breathable natural fiber and soft on the baby's skin.

In this tutorial, we are going to make a light baby blanket. If you want to make a heavyweight blanket, you can add an extra layer of flannel inside the blanket.

You can also wash the fabric before you start sewing. This will remove any chemical finishing left on the fabric that might irritate the baby. Some natural fabrics do shrink after washing them, so washing the fabric before sewing helps prevent further shrinkage.

Steps to follow

- Cut fabric to your desired size

- Pin the two pieces of the fabric together

- Sew stitches all around the blanket and leave an open space at the corner of the blanket.

- Turn the right way out

- Sew the open space

The beauty of making your own DIY project is to choose the features and details you want to be incorporated into your project. When it comes to choosing the size for your blanket, you can go for a size that suits you.

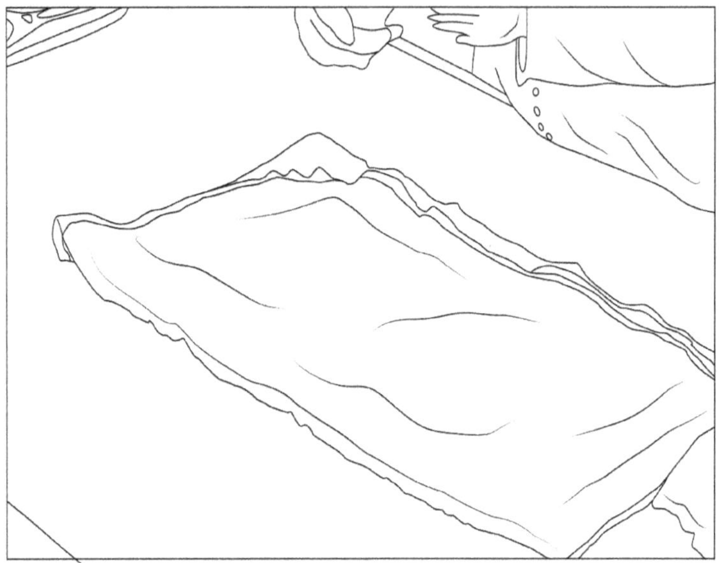

Step 1

Cut the two pieces of fabric based on your desired size. One-piece will be used for the front while the other piece will be for the back. You can sew round corners that look more professional than square corners. It is also easy to sew rounded corners.

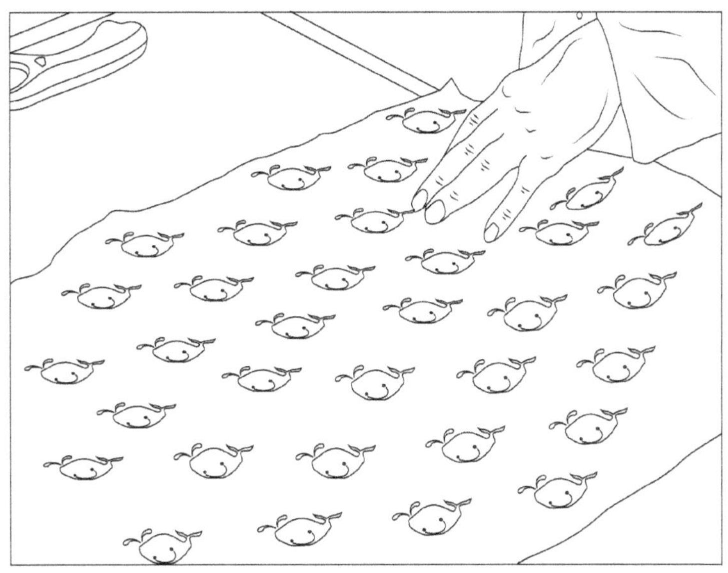

You can use tins or other kitchen equipment to make round corners. Avoid using plates because they are too large.

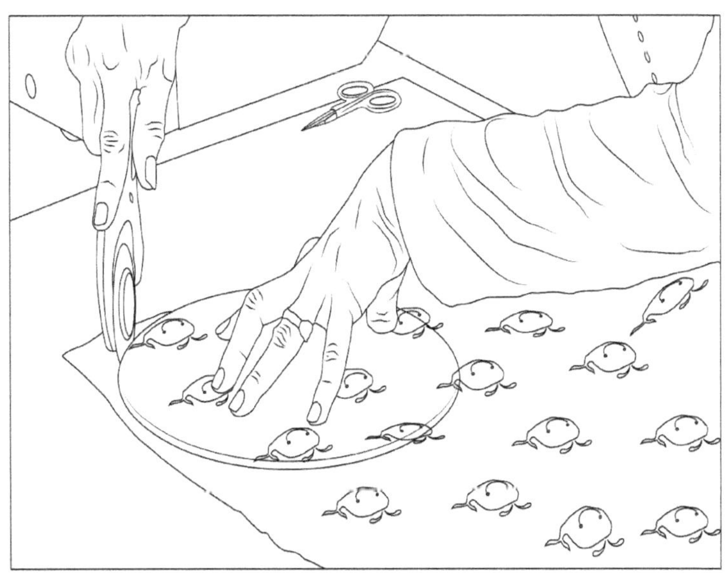

Fold your fabric into quarters then cut the four-round corners at once. This ensures you have even corners. If you have a thick fabric, you can cut two layers at a time instead of 4 layers.

Step 2: Optional

Add embroidery to the top fabric. If you want to personalize the baby blanket, then you can do that at the front fabric. Make sure any stitching you're going to add or the trims are safe for your baby. You can also add applique, adorable little characters, and other patterns to make the blanket more attractive.

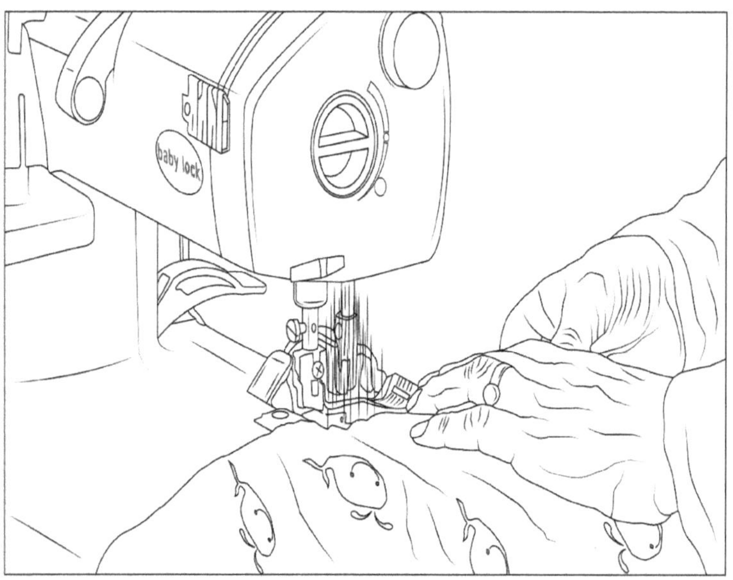

Step 3

Pin the two pieces of the fabric together and ensure the right sides face each other. Go ahead and stitch all four edges of the fabric using a 12mm seam allowance. Leave at least a 3-inch opening (7.5 cm) on one side of the fabric.

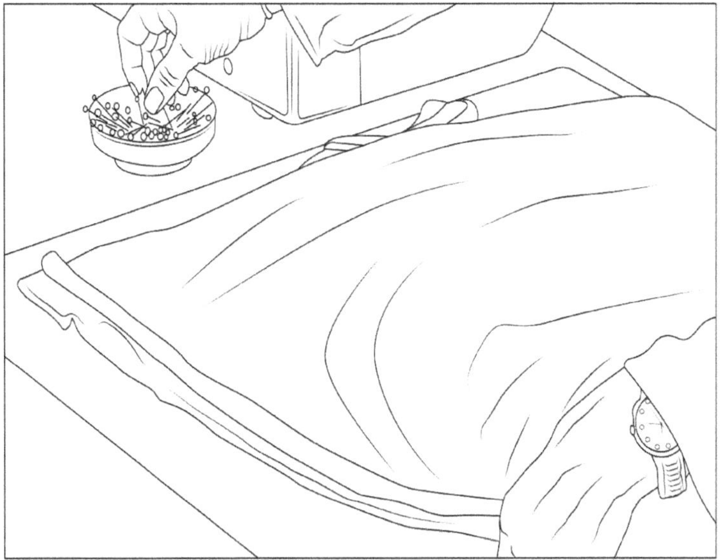

If you're using the square corners, then you will have to stop at every corner, lift the presser foot, and pivot to sew stitches on the next side. But if you're using rounded corners, the sewing will be continuous. No stopping and turning the fabric to sew the other side.

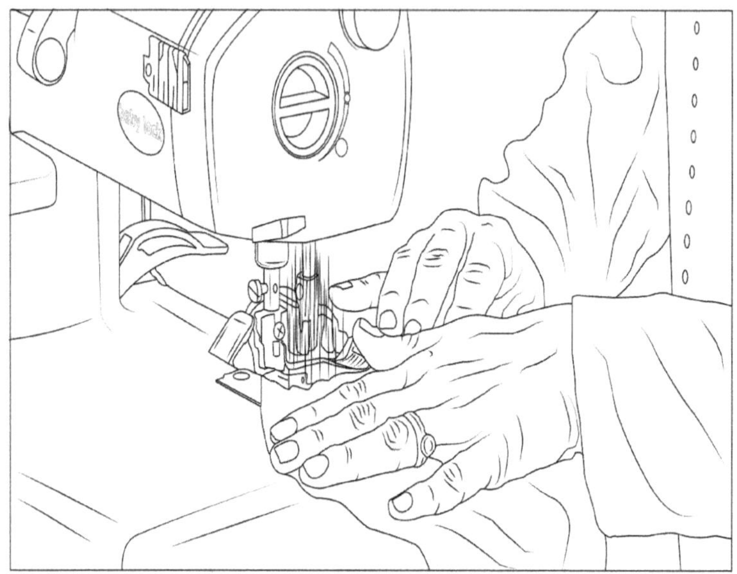

You can add more than one row of stitch to your blanket, you can have more rows to decorate the blanket. Alternatively, you can use different stitch options instead of using the regular straight stitch.

Step 4

Clip the curves of your blanket to reduce bulkiness and ensure you have a flat seam. Clipping ensures corners look neat and more professional when turned to the right side.

After clipping the blanket, it is time to turn the right way out via the 3-inch gap you left. Poke the corners of the blanket out. Do not use any sharp object to poke the corners.

Press the blanket to give it a great look and ensure the seams appear flat. Use an up and down motion when pressing rather than using the sliding method. Press also the seam allowance at the gap area.

Step 5

Topstitch around the edges of your baby blanket in order to close the gap. If different fabrics are used for both top and bottom, then you need to use matching colors for your top and bobbin.

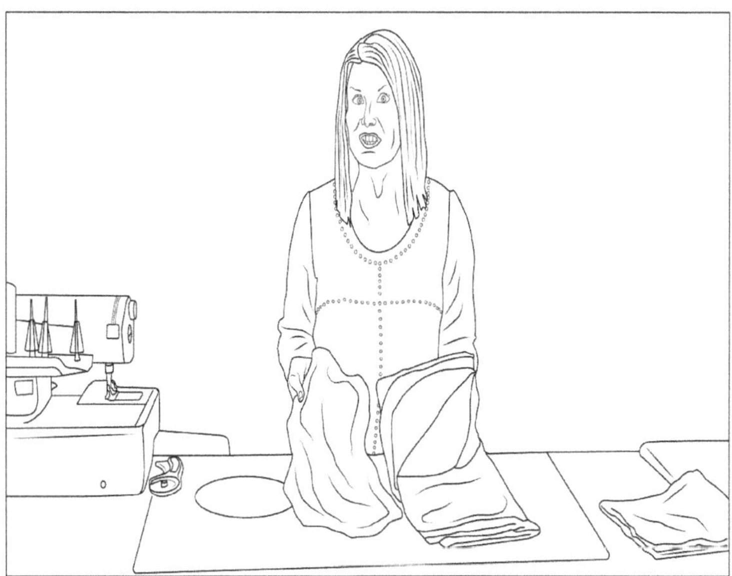

Chapter Summary

- Making a blanket for your baby doesn't have to take more than 20 minutes. With these few steps, you can easily make one for the new member of your family. Once you know how to make them, I am sure you would want to make them a gift too!

- You can personalize the blanket by adding embroidery letters and other patterns of your choice. Make sure any additional embroidery you do on the blanket is safe for your baby.

- Baby items use a small amount of fabric, so you can keep practicing by coming up with different designs like the colorful bunny blanket, adding patchwork pieces like you would on a quilt and a lovely binding border.

- There are different options to choose from, keep practicing and you will be able to make more DIY projects.

In the next chapter, you will learn how to make your own pillow covers.

Chapter Five:
How To Make Your Own Pillow Covers

Pillow covers are a great accessory to add glam to your home. They are easy to make and any beginner can make one in less than ten minutes.

You can also make zippered pillow covers instead of using hem tape that will leave the pillows with a bulging seam.

Do not be afraid to take the challenge and make your own pillow covers. Some people are also afraid of sewing zippers in their projects. With this tutorial, you will find it is much easier than you think. So adding zippers doesn't have to be scary anymore.

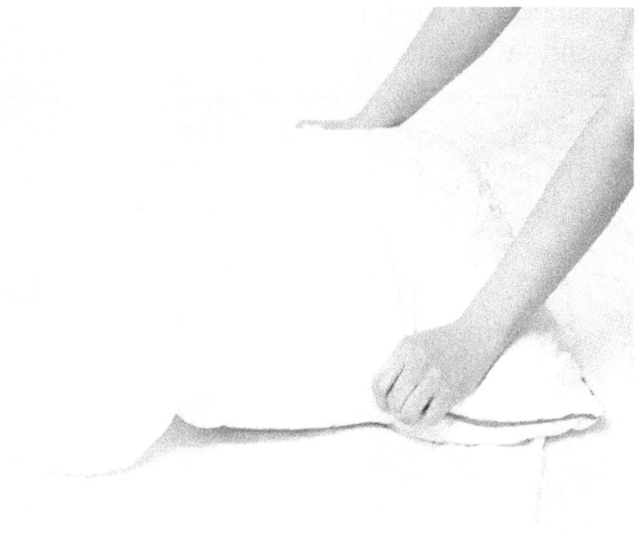

It's time to learn how to make your own pillow covers, you can even personalize them based on your preferences. After learning these simple steps, you will never spend money again buying pillow covers.

Choosing your own fabric that freshens up your living space is something you're going to do more often. Once you learn how to make one, you will keep making more pillow covers with different colors and patterns for your home.

So how do you make the pillow covers? Follow these step-by-step guides to make your own.

Required materials

- Half yard of fabric: Home décor fabric is the best for making the pillow covers because the material is thicker and it holds its shape nicely. You will need two pillow cut pieces of the same dimensions as that of the pillow insert.

- Invisible zip: Make it to be about 4 to 5 inches. Always make sure the zipper is shorter than the bottom edge of your pillow.

- Pillow insert: You can have 16-inch pillows that will look good on your sofa.

- Matching thread: Same color with the fabric you're sewing.

- Scissors or rotary cutter to make cuts perfect.

- Pins: To hold the pieces together.

- Tailor's chalk: To mark the areas where you want to cut the fabric.

- Measuring tape: To measure the accurate size required to make the pillow covers.

Steps to make pillow covers

Step 1

Fold the fabric into half and lay the fabric on a flat surface. Use the measuring tape to mark 8 inches and 16-inch wide fabric. Cut the two pieces of fabric.

The size of the fabric to cut depends on the size of the pillow inserts. Make sure to cut the same size for the pillow cover to make the cushion look fuller.

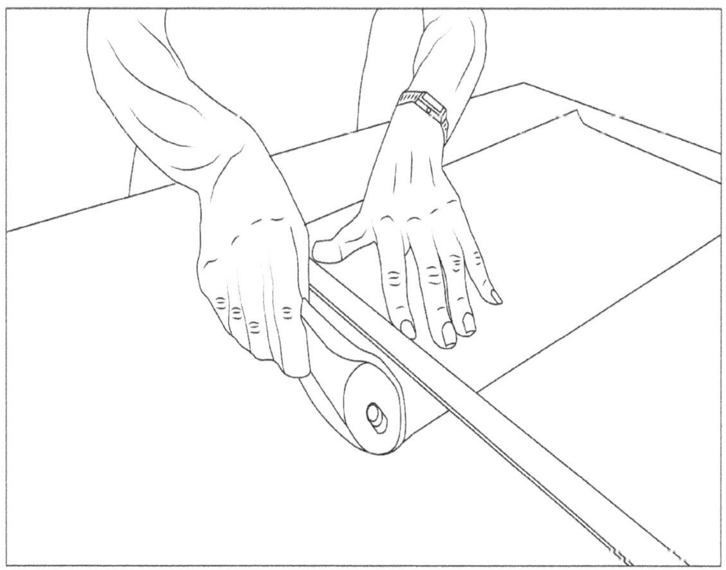

Step 2

Stitch the zip by folding one side of the 8-inch fabric and pin the zip on the underside of the fabric. Place the fabric under the presser foot and remove the pin and start serging. If you have more than one pin, you can remove them as you continue serging.

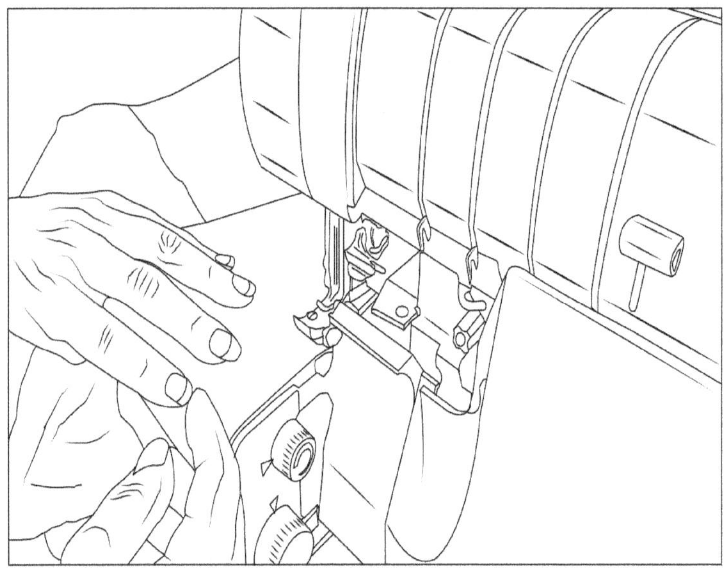

If you cannot control the serging speed, you can use masking tape to hold the zip in place while serging instead of the pins.

Once you have stitched the zip on one piece of the fabric, do the same to the remaining piece of the fabric and ensure the zip is closed.

Trim any excess fabric and sewing the zippers.

Step 3

Stitch the other sides of the pillow covers. Once you have stitched the zip on both sides of the fabric, put the perpendicular sides together with the right side face each other and pin the seam line.

Place the fabric underneath the presser foot and start stitching following the seam line. Remove the pins as you continue stitching. Do the same to the other perpendicular side.

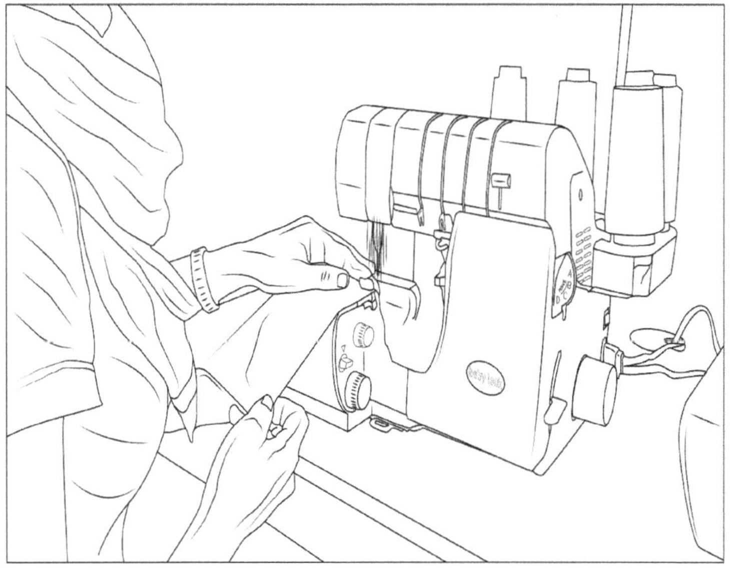

Step 4

Pin the remaining bottom side of the fabric. Open the zip then stitch the bottom side following the seam line. Remove the pin as you continue stitching to avoid breaking the needles or creating another problem for the machine.

Step 5

Serge the edges of the pillow to avoid coming off although you have zippered pillow covers that make it possible to take them off and wash. So if you need them to last, you have to finish the edges of the pillow cover.

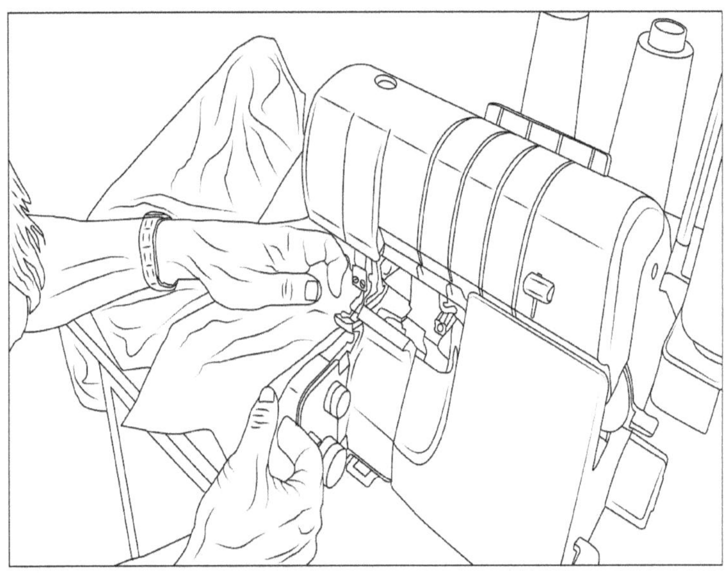

Serge all the edges and trim any excess fabric using your serger machine. Adding finishing to the edges prevents them from fraying and you can wash the pillow covers as many times as you want without any worry.

Step 6

Turn the pillow cover with the right side out and press the edges to make the pillow cover look neat. Now you can add the pillow insert and zip up to enjoy your new pillow.

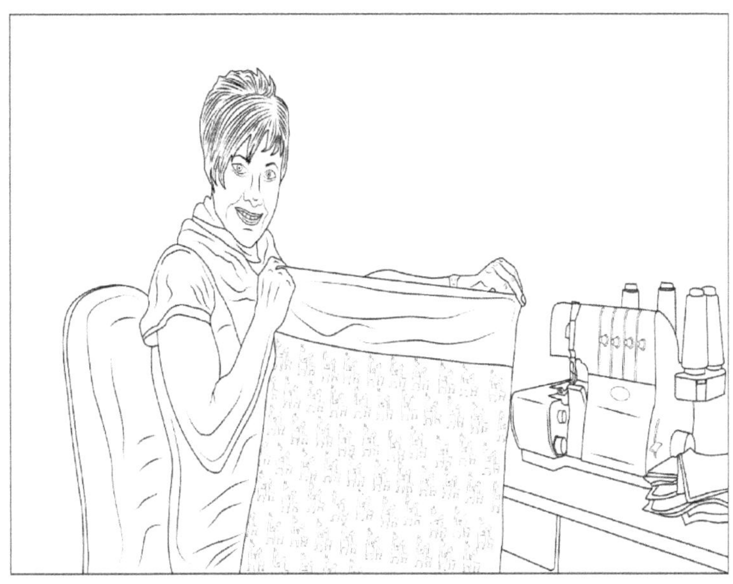

Chapter Summary

- Making your zippered pillow covers doesn't have to be scary. With these few steps, you can make your own pillow cover. You can be more creative and add more decorative designs to the pillow covers to glam your sofa.

- You can also make pillow covers with different colors to match your home color theme. Personalizing these pillow covers for your home will bring you the greatest satisfaction.

- So go ahead and practice more and become a pro in making the pillow covers. You can also make them as a gift to your loved ones.

In the next chapter, you will learn how to make a drawstring bag using a serger machine.

Chapter Six:
How to Make Drawstring Bag Using Serger Machine

Drawstring bags are a great accessory and they are easy to make. A drawstring bag can be used for holding small items together, separating your clothes and shoes in a suitcase while traveling, carrying it as a picnic bag, etc. You can customize the size of the drawstring based on your personal preferences.

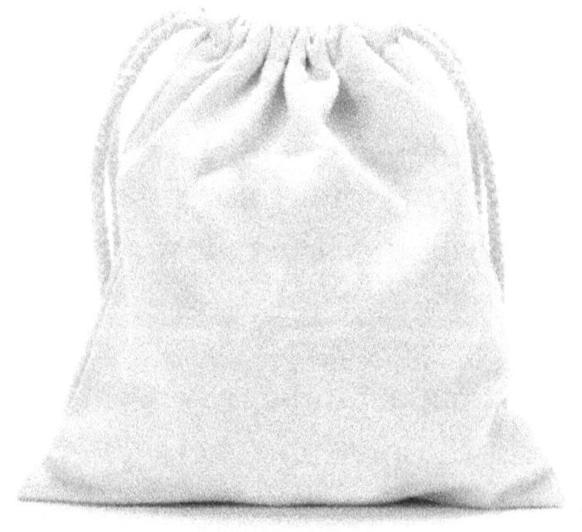

Image source: xiaorui/Shutterstock

If you have some scraps left, you can cut enough material and make a drawstring bag for yourself.

They are very easy to make and can act as a perfect size for a little gift bag. You will find it much faster to sew these little bags using your overlock machine. Learning to make these drawstring bags can help organize all your smaller tools in a simple manner. You can also give them as a gift during baby showers or birthday parties.

What are drawstring bags?

A drawstring is an open-top bag secured with a drawstring closure that runs around the top of the bag. The drawstring closure acts as the handle to carry the bag by your hands or use it as a shoulder sling to carry the bag as a backpack.

These bags have easy accessibility and are lightweight making them suitable for carrying a small number of supplies. They are mainly designed for your daily use and can help you organize with ease.

You can bring them with you when going to parties, games, the beach, or the gym. Its unique designs allow you to bring them with you on a wide range of occasions. Some of the classy designs serve as a trendy fashion accessory for the younger generation.

Let's learn how you can make one for yourself.

Materials required

- Cotton fabric, at least10-inch squares

- 2 strips of material, the same width as your bag

- 1 yard of ⅛ inch ribbon cut into half

- 3 spools of matching serger thread

- Large-eye needle or bodkin to thread ribbon

- Serger machine with a standard Presser foot

Steps to make the drawstring bag

Step 1

Prepare the fabric

Cut two strips of the fabric with the same width as your bag and 2 inches/50mm tall to make the bag casing. Fold the ends of the two casing pieces at ½ inch/10mm.

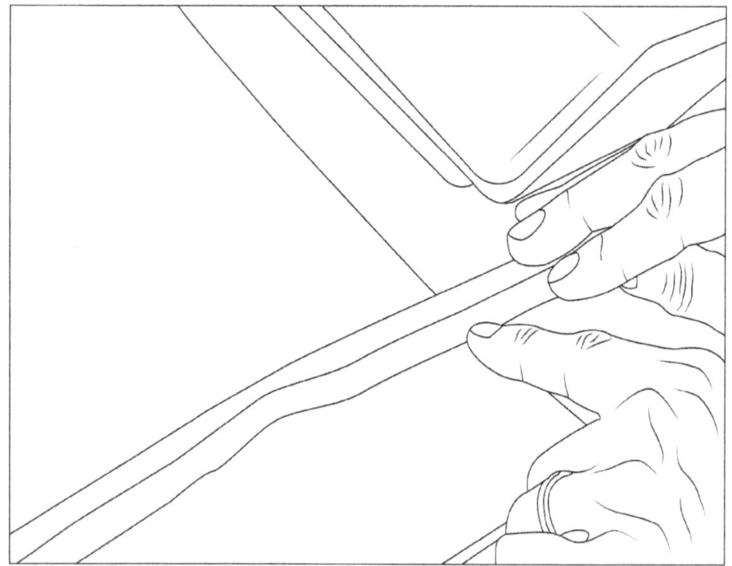

Step 2

Fold the raw edge again under itself and press the fold. Do the same on the other piece of casing. Serge the folded edges of the casing and make sure you serge on all the layers to prevent fraying of the edges.

Step 3

Fold the strips into half and press them hard enough to leave a crease.

Step 4

Fold a piece of the casing strip and one piece of cotton fabric into half and press hard enough to leave a crease.

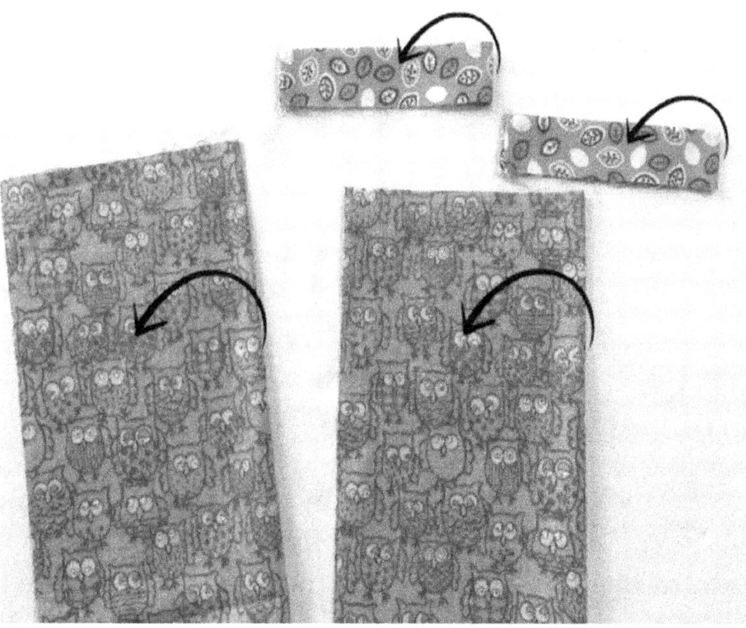

Step 5

Place the raw edges of the casing strip on the right side of one piece of the cotton fabric. Line the casing strip at the top edge of the bag fabric. Pin the pieces together to keep them in place. Do the same to the other piece of fabric and casing strip.

Lift your presser foot and place the attached piece of fabric underneath it to serge. Lower the foot and start serging the bag and the strip together. Reduce your serging speed so that you can remove the pins holding the fabric as you continue serging using a 6mm seam allowance.

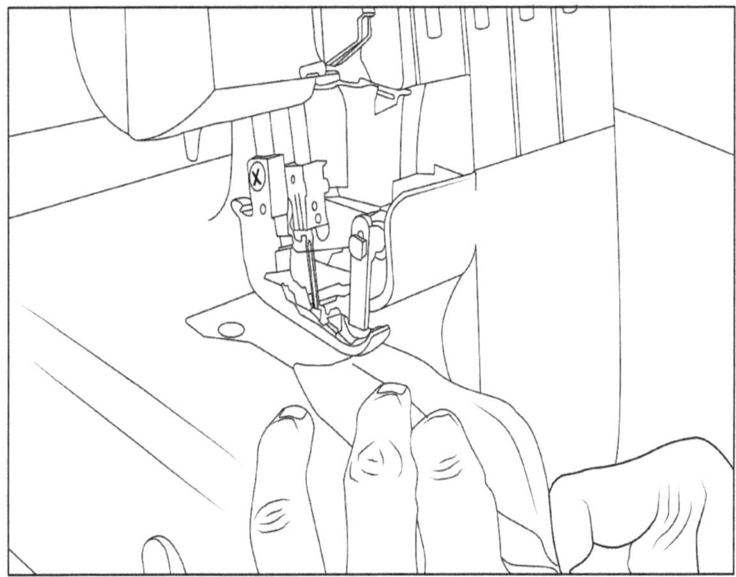

Step 6

Press the casing strip and seam allowance to make the seams neat. Add a topstitch at the front to strengthen your bag and at the same time to catch the seam allowance on the underside.

Step 7

Place the two bag pieces together with the right sides facing each other. Serge around the two sides of the bag and the bottom side using a 6mm seam allowance. You can

choose a different seam size, you don't have to stick to a
6mm seam.

Step 8

Turn right side out and press the edges.

Now you can feed the ribbon into the casing of the bag.
Use the large needle or the bodkin to insert the ribbon in the
casing. You can start inserting the bodkin on any side. You
can start on the right side.

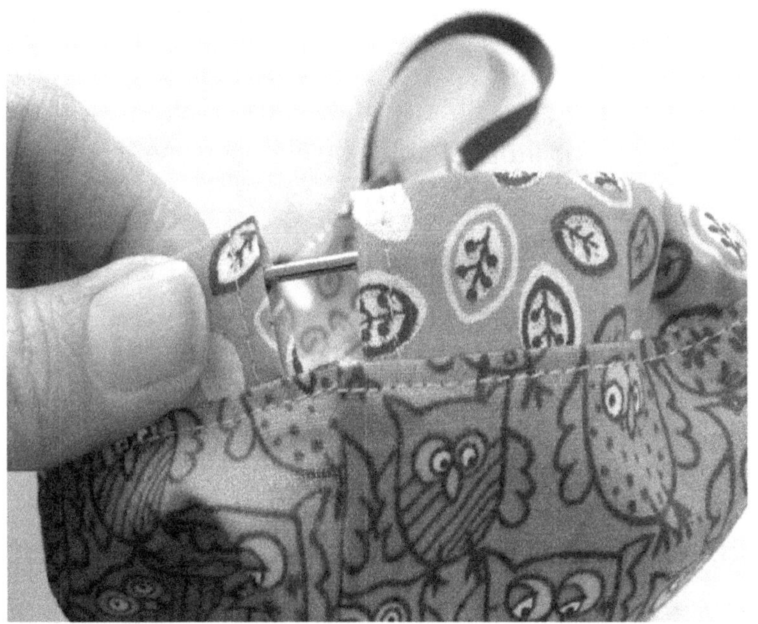

Step 9

When you get into the gap in the casing, jump it and
continue to insert the bodkin into the other casing piece.
Bring out the bodkin at the end of your bottom casing. Tie
both ends of the ribbon together.

Use the same step to feed the second ribbon into the casing starting in the opposite direction of the first ribbon (left side).

Step 10

Tie the two ribbon pieces together. To prevent unraveling on the cut ends of the ribbon, you can apply a fray check.

Now your drawstring bag is ready for your use. Once you put your items in the bag, you can pull the ribbons on both sides to close it.

When making the ribbon, make sure to choose a thread that matches your fabric color. You can also use the same fabric for the casing and the bag.

If you want to make your drawstring bag more attractive, you can use a box for the bottom corner or add patch pockets to the bag to hold a few more items. There are different ways you can make your drawstring bag. You can choose among different designs that appeal to your eyes and go ahead to make the drawstring.

Making box bottom drawstring bag

A box bottom drawstring bag is a type of string bag that sits up on its own. If you want to package a gift, using a drawstring with a box bottom will look classy and esthetically appealing.

You can easily customize a drawstring based on shape, design, size, and even height. The best drawstring is one with a stable bottom to allow you to place it on any flat surface.

Let's see how you can make your own packaging gift with a stable bottom!

Requirements

- Two pieces of fabric each measuring 10 inches * 9 inches

- Two pieces of the lining, 10 inches * 9 inches

- Two pieces of ribbon or string 28 inches

- Matching thread

- Safety Pin

Step 1

Hold the two pieces together with the right sides facing each other and serge around the fabric edges within a 0.25 inch seam allowance. Leave the top side open and a gap on either of the sides to add the drawstring.

A gap approximately 1-inch wide is enough and should be 2.5 inch from the top. Since you're going to use the drawstring more often, it's good to backstitch the gap area. If your fabric has some stripes, consider lining them up to give a cleaner look.

Step 2

Put the two pieces of lining together with the right side facing each other. Stitch around the sides of the lining including the bottom but leave the top open. No need to leave gaps on the lining.

Press the seams.

Step 3

After serging around on the main fabric and lining, you're ready to make the box corners. To do this, a special stitch is required on the left corner and right corner of your bag.

Let's start with the left corner. You can decide which corner you want to start with.

Start by lining up the bottom seam together with the side seam and hard press such that the material appears flat and at 90 degrees.

Use a ruler to draw a straight line, using the tailor's chalk or fabric pencil, where the legs of the triangles are at 3 inches.

Step 4

The line drawn is the hypotenuse of the triangle. Draw the line on both sides of the bag and on top of the line, sew a straight stitch.

Step 5

Cut the corners of the fabric while leaving at least 1.8 inches of the seam allowance.

Repeat the same process on the right corner of the bag. Draw the line, stitch, and clip both sides of the fabric

Step 6

Turn the main fabric to have the right side while the lining should have the right side out and put the lining inside of the main fabric.

Step 7

Ensure the side seams on both fabrics match and pin them in place.

Step 8

Leave a gap about 2 inches wide so that you can turn the main fabric right side out.

Step 9

Stitch on top of your bag leaving 0.25 inch seam allowance

Now turn the main fabric right side out via the gap. This will leave the main fabric and the lining facing out.

Step 10

Now push the lining inside your main fabric and hard press at the top where the main fabric meets the lining so as to have a smooth and clean edge.

Step 11

Use a ⅛ inch seam allowance to stitch around your bag and close up the gap.

Step 12

Use your drawing chalk to draw two lines above and below the drawstring gap on the sides of the bag to create a casing.

Stitch at the top of the lines all around the bag. If you want a cleaner start and finish of the stitches, you can start stitching at the seam.

Step 13

Now it's time to add the ribbon or a piece of twine to make your drawstring. Take one piece of twine and loosely tie it to a safety pin. You can use a large needle or bodkin to do this.

Step 14

Feed the safety pin through one of the drawstring gaps and feed it through the casing. When you reach the gap on the other side, skip it and continue to feed the safety pin to the casing. The twine/ribbon should enter and exit out of the gap on the same side.

Step 15

Tie a knot on the two ends of the twine. Repeat the same process to the second gap on the other side of the bag. When the twine comes out at the other end, take the two ends and tie them together.

You can now pull your strings to form your drawstring bag.

Your bottom looks stable and you can place the bag on any flat surface after filling your goodies inside.

In our second example, we have created the casing in the main fabric compared to having an extra fabric for the casing. Therefore, you don't have to limit yourself. You can go for a simple drawstring bag or go for classy designs with box bottoms. There's no excuse not to make your own drawstring bag.

You can also make a drawstring bag to carry on your back. Once, you have been able to successfully do the two examples, you can make a drawstring of any shape.

Chapter Summary

- Drawstrings bags have become very popular due to their weight-bearing capacity. Depending on the design and size, they have a wide array of uses. The younger generation use them as trendy fashion bags to carry around or use them to sort out and store various accessories at home.

- Depending on the uses of the bag, you can make a size suitable for your needs. With the above simple steps, you can make a drawstring for any occasion and use. They don't require a large amount of fabric so if you have some fabric left after a sewing project, you can use the remaining to make the drawstring bag.

- You can make a smaller size drawstring with a box bottom to use as a packaging gift.

In the next chapter, you will learn how to make a dust cover for your serger machine.

Chapter Seven:
Dust Cover For A Serger Machine

A dust cover for your serger machine is essential. If you are in an environment with a lot of dust, you need to get a dust cover for your serger machine to extend its lifetime. When not using the machine you should cover it. This not only keeps your machine free from dust, it adds some color to the sewing room!

If you have children, I am sure you don't want any needle-related accidents on their little fingers. Sometimes children can mess up the threading and settings of your machine especially if you have taken a break from your sewing project. In such situations, I'm sure you don't want to come right back to a total mess. A simple cover goes a long way to shield from dust and little fingers away.

Sergers come in different shapes and designs, therefore, having a custom made dust cover gives you more satisfaction compared to ready-made dust covers available on the market.

In this tutorial, you will learn step-by-step procedures on how to make your own dust cover. It is easy, quick, and more functional than some dust covers in the market. To make it more unique, we will add a pocket to store notions and other serger accessories.

Let's have some fun making a dust cover for your machine.

Requirements

- 1 yard of outer fabric 1

- 1 yard of fabric 2

- Pencil

- Scissors

- Matching thread

- Pins

- 1 yard of folded Bias tape

- Fusible fleece

- Tape measure

- Iron and ironing board

- Serger machine

If you need a quilted dust cover that covers your machine from front to back using two side pieces, you have to measure your machine to get the right dimensions.

How to make a dust cover

Step 1: Taking measurements

Measure the front of your machine in the base area. That is the widest part of the machine. If your machine has a wheel, you need to add that to your measurement. Then add an extra 1 inch to 1.5 inch for seam allowance.

It is better to have a loose dust cover than a tight one that is hard to fit your machine in. The extra inches will give you plenty of room.

The next measurement you should take is across the front going all the way to the back. Start from the table and go up the front of your machine up to the thread tree and across the back to the table at the back.

You will notice the measurements are in a slanting position. Depending on the type of machine, you can adjust your tape measure to have straight measurements.

Measure the width of your machine. You need to measure the height of the machine. Do that from the table to the top.

If you use estimates, the cover may turn out extra-large. Don't worry, if the cover turns out to be too big, you can always trim it to get the right size for your machine.

Based on your measurements, you can cut the fabric into squares, rectangles, or rectangles with rounded top corners.

Step 2: Creating pattern pieces

After taking the measurements, the first pattern piece you're going to make is the giant rectangle from the two measurements you took on your machine. That is the base length at the front and the measure from the front going across the back.

The next pattern piece will be for the sides of the machine (width*height). Curve the edges at the top of the fabric.

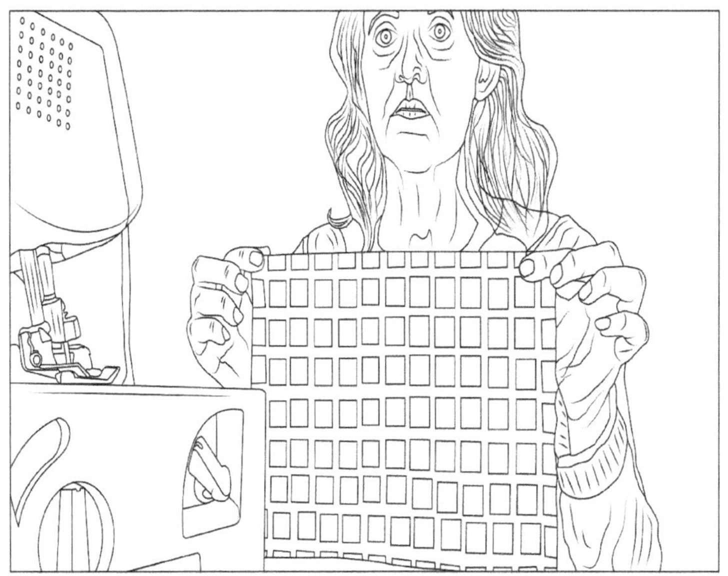

Now you have two patterns created: The main pattern and the side pattern.

You can add a pocket to your dust cover, although this is an option. Use the same width of the main pattern to make a pocket pattern. You only need to decide how high you need the pocket to be on the front of the machine. In this case, I used 5 inches. After cutting the pattern, you'll see it has a rectangle shape.

Step 3: Cutting the fabric

Now we have three patterns we're going to use to cut the fabric. On the main pattern, we will use the pattern to cut 1 piece from the outer fabric 1, 1 piece from fabric 2, and 1 piece from fusible fleece.

Using the side pattern, cut 2 pieces from the outer fabric 1, 2 pieces from fabric 2, and 2 pieces from fusible fleece.

Using the pocket pattern, cut the fabric you want to use for your pocket. You can decide to use the outer fabric 1 or fabric 2. Let's use fabric 2 to make the pockets.

Step 4

Apply the fusible fleece to the wrong side of the main fabric and on the two pieces of the side fabric. Press the two pieces together using your iron.

For better results, you can cover the fabrics with a piece of light material and spray it with your spray bottle. Then place the iron on top of the material to press them together.

Do not iron, only place your iron on top of the fabric at different spots to make sure the fleece doesn't come out of the attached fabric.

Be careful not to shift the fleece when covering with the piece of material.

Do the same to all three pieces of fabric. Make sure the fleece is applied on the wrong side of the fabrics.

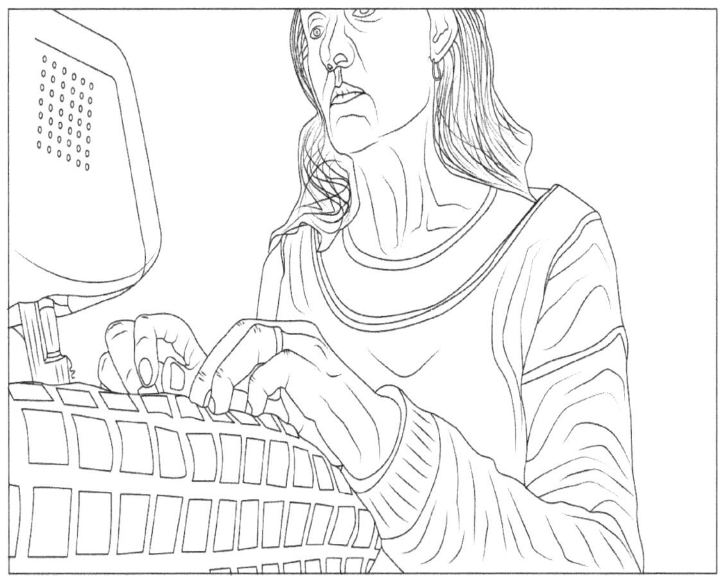

Step 5

Pin the two side pieces of fabric 2 into the long edge of the main fabric. Place the main fabric with the right side up such that it faces the right side of the side fabric.

Line the width of the main fabric with the width of the side fabric and pin the two fabrics on the edges.

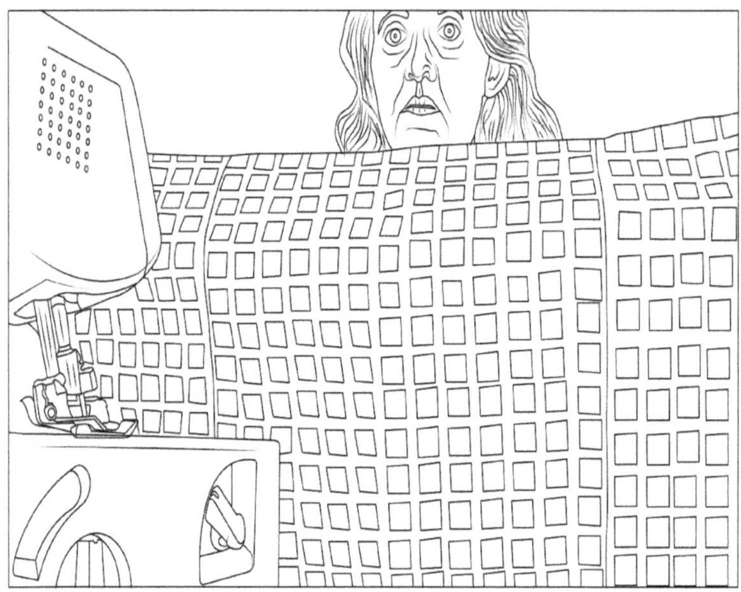

Step 6

The curve length should line up with the length of the main fabric. When you get to the curve area, lift the fabric, and continue pinning the curve at the straight long edge of the main fabric going up to the other side.

Step 7

After pinning, you will have rectangle shaped pieces together.

Step 8

Now pin the remaining piece of side fabric 2 on the other side of the main fabric using the same process.

Step 9

Stitching your fabrics together. Use ¼ inch seam allowance to stitch the pieces together. When you get around the curves slow your sewing speed and smoothen the fabric to avoid any wrinkles. Put the needle down and then lift the presser foot, adjust the fabric, and bring the presser foot down.

Continue stitching around the curve and then adjust the fabric again to have a smooth finished stitch. Be careful not to stitch on the pins, you can remove the pins as you continue stitching.

Stitch the other piece of side fabric on the other side of the main fabric.

Step 10

Stitch the side pocket to the fabric. Take the cut fabric and fold it into half width-wise. Press at the center to have a crease.

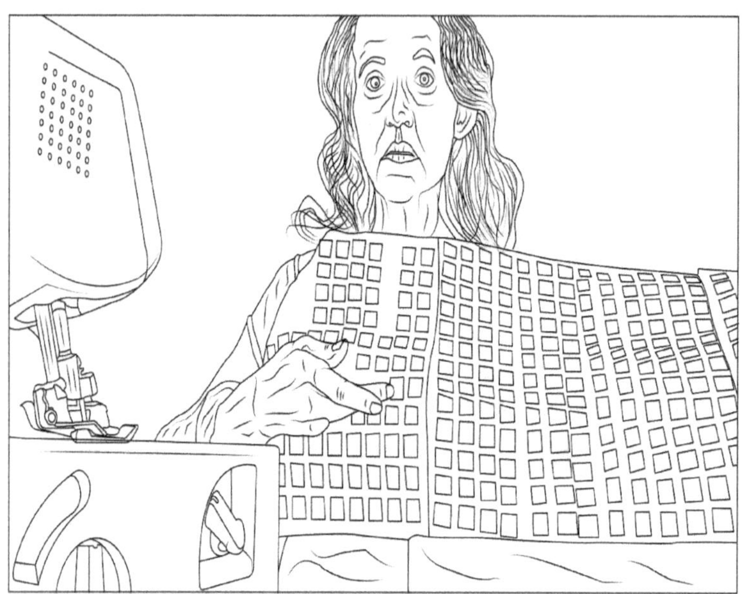

Step 11

Place the bias tape on the side with the crease. Pin it up to the end of the fabric. Since both sides are the same, it doesn't matter which side you pin the bias tape on.

Step 12

At your machine, sew right at the edges of the crease. Use a regular stitch for this and don't forget to backstitch at both ends.

Step 13

Now take the bias tape and fold it over to the other side.

The edges of bias tape should cover the stitches you have made. Then sew the topstitch on the bias tape that catches the bias on the backside. Sew the stitch around the edges of the bias tape. Make sure you're using a matching color.

Step 14

Take your main piece of fabric 1 with the right side up so that you have your width on the downside and then take your pocket fabric and place it on top so the edges match up.

Step 15

Pin the fabric together and stitch a temporary base stitch on all the sides. If you need an individual compartment on the fabric, use the fabric marker to draw separating straight lines on the pockets and then stitch them.

Step 16

Just like we did with fabric two, take the individual side pieces and pin them to the main fabric with the right side facing each other.

Lift the fabric and pin on the curves along the length of fabric 1.

Flip the curves and pin around the full length. Do that for both sides of the fabric and stitch around the edges of both fabrics.

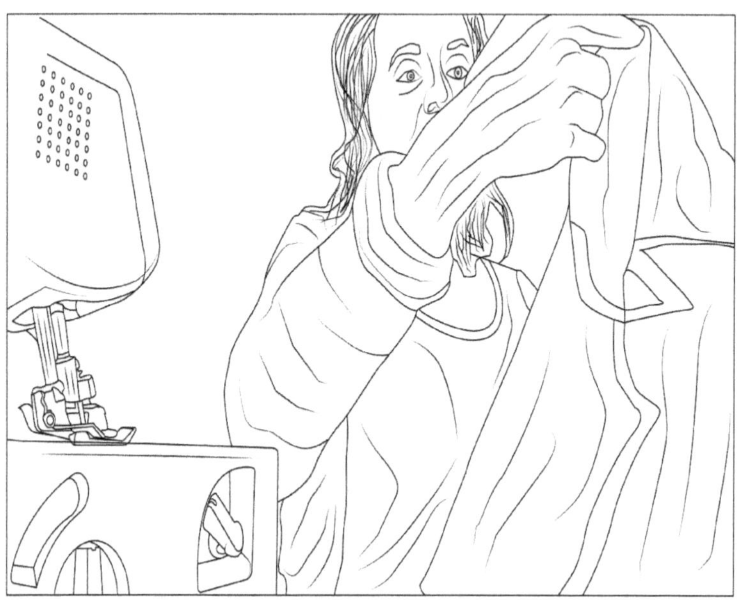

Step 17

Once you're done stitching fabric 1 and 2, try to press the seams open. Flip fabric 1 cover over fabric 2 covers so that the wrong sides are together. Match all the seams together and pin the raw edges together.

Use a bottom stitch to sew along all the bottom edges.

Step 18

Add the bias tape to finish the raw edges at the bottom. Take your bias tape and line it with the bottom raw edges of fabric 1. Fold the tape at the beginning of the fabric and pin it. When you flip it over, you will have a folded edge. Pin all the way around until you get to the other fabric.

Step 19

After pinning, you have to stitch on the crease. When you're done stitching, fold and flip the tap over to the wrong side of the fabric. Add a topstitch that catches the bias tape at the backside.

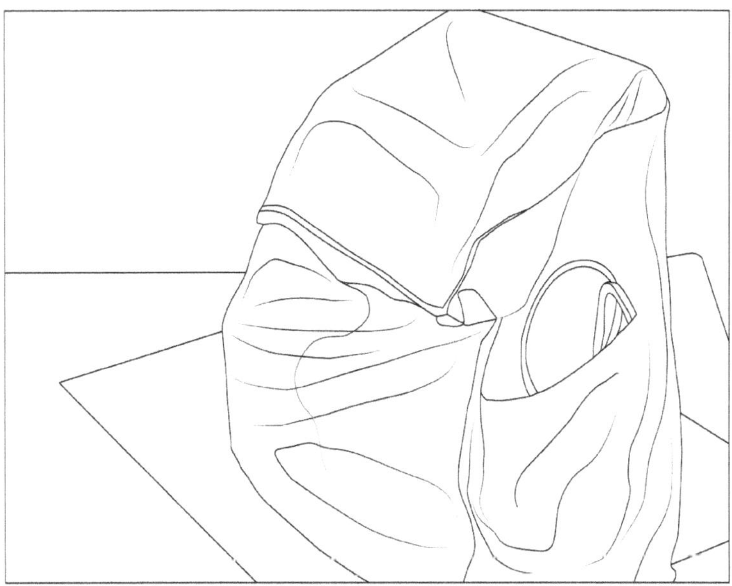

Now you have your dust cover for your serger machine. With this cover, there are no raw edges exposed and you can enjoy putting it on your machine. Now go ahead and make a dust cover for your machine.

Chapter Summary

- Serger machines collect a lot of dust when not being used. Therefore, you need a dust cover to prevent dust from accumulating in your machine since it will have a negative impact on the long-run and functioning of the machine.

- Keeping dust away ensures your machine operates smoothly. Some machines come with a plastic cover that isn't aesthetically pleasing although it does serve its purpose. Instead of buying a dust cover, use these steps to make a simple dust cover for your machine.

- Your preparation for the size, fabric, and all other requirements you need determines the success of your project. Get the fabric of your choice and practice making a dust cover for your machine.

In the next chapter, you will learn how to make Christmas stocking.

Chapter Eight:
Christmas Stocking

Christmas is here and it's a good opportunity to make stockings for your children. Christmas stocking resembles a sock-shaped bag that is usually hung during Christmas Eve and Saint Nicholas day so that either Saint Nicholas, Santa Claus, or Father Christmas can fill them with gifts.

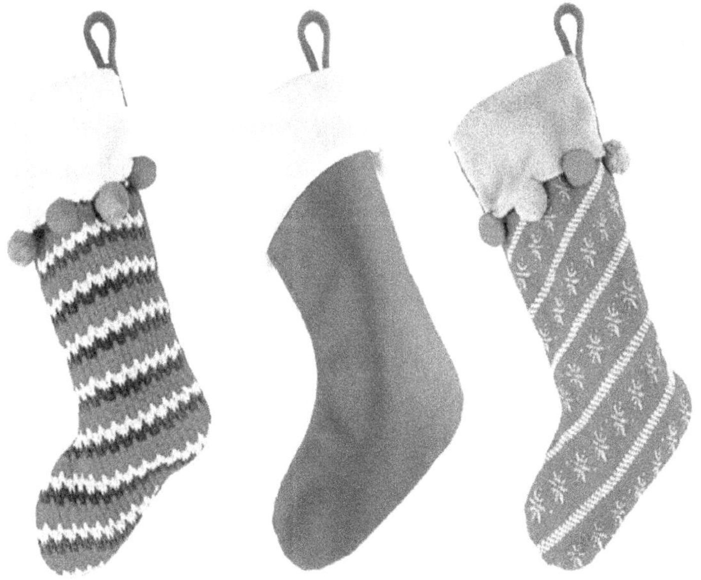

Image source: Valentina Proskurina/Shutterstock

These gifts are toys, coins, fruits, candy or other small items and they are usually referred to as stocking stuffers.

According to some traditions, especially in Western culture, children who behave badly will only receive a single piece of coal in their stocking. Children hang up Christmas stockings around their home because they believe that Father Christmas will fill it with gifts.

This is actually a tradition that originated from the life of Saint Nicholas who put gold coins in the stockings of three poor sisters. One night, the girls had hung their stockings over the fireplace to dry. Saint Nicholas knew their father wouldn't accept the gifts, so he secretly threw three bags of gold coins through the window. One bag landed on the stockings. Since then, children have been hanging up their stockings on Christmas Eve with the hope that they will find them filled with gifts when they wake up.

There are a lot of stores that sell a variety of Christmas stockings made of different sizes and styles. Today, there are a lot of homemade Christmas stockings. Creating your own Christmas stocking allows you to customize it for your family and friends. You can have the names of the family members sewn on the stocking so that Santa or Father Christmas will know who it belongs to.

So how do you make a Christmas stocking? Keep reading to learn the step-by-step procedure on how to create Christmas stockings for your loved ones. You can also give it as a gift to your friends and extended family.

Making your own custom made stocking is very easy and cheap. Following these easy steps, you can make as many stockings as you want.

Requirements

- Fabric of your choice. For example, Comfy Flannel, fleece, or cotton.

- Lining material

- Matching thread

- Scissors/ Rotary cutter or cutting mat

- Pins or clips

- Tailor's chalk or Pencil

- Iron and ironing board

- Serger machine

Step 1

Cut the fabric to make your stocking. Make sure you have enough fabric to cut two pieces for the front and back and another fabric to cut the two linings pieces. Cut the front and back pieces of 13 inch *15 inch.

If you're using an old Christmas stocking to create your pattern for the new one, you can lay the old stocking on newspaper or brown paper. With your pencil or chalk trace all around the stocking leaving about ½ inch spacing. Remove the stocking and cut the pattern out.

Use the cut pattern to cut the outer fabric and lining for your new stocking, both the front and back fabrics.

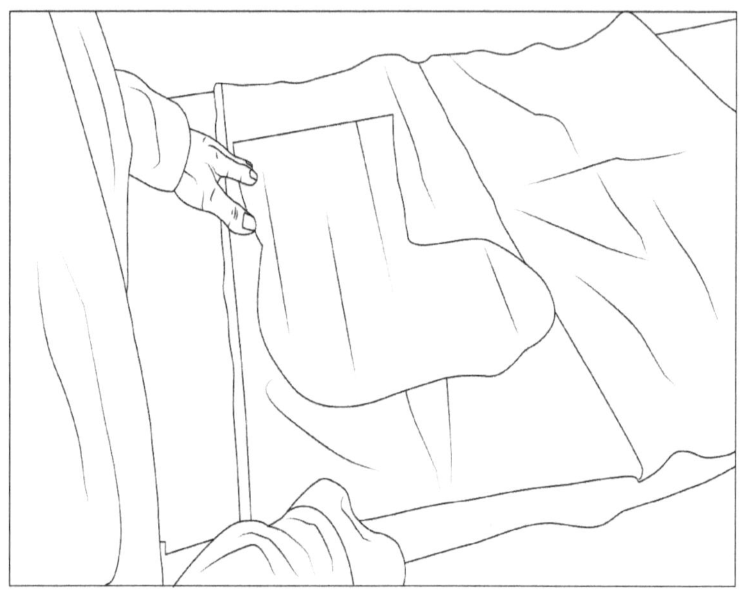

Step 2

Hold the two pieces together with the wrong sides facing each other. Pin the pieces together and cut the stocking shape.

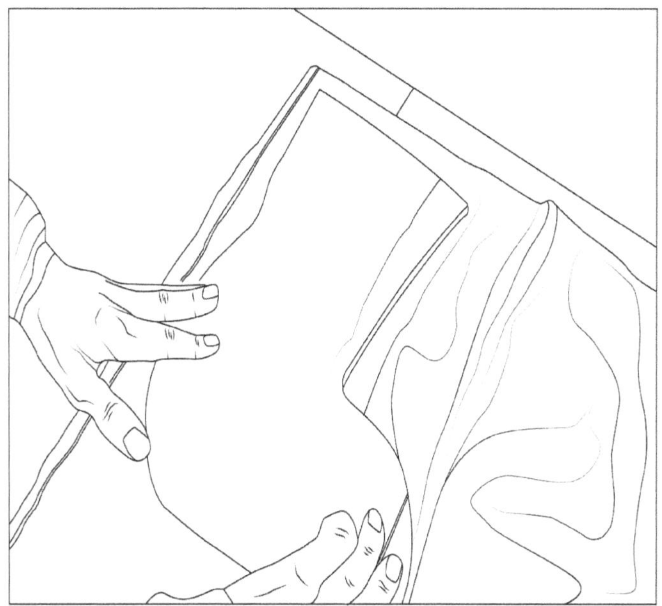

Step 3

Put the wrong sides together then cut the two pieces of stocking shapes for your outer fabric and the inner lining pieces. Ensure the toes are in the same direction as you cut the fabric. Matching the fabric on the wrong sides together ensures you cut stocking pieces that face both directions.

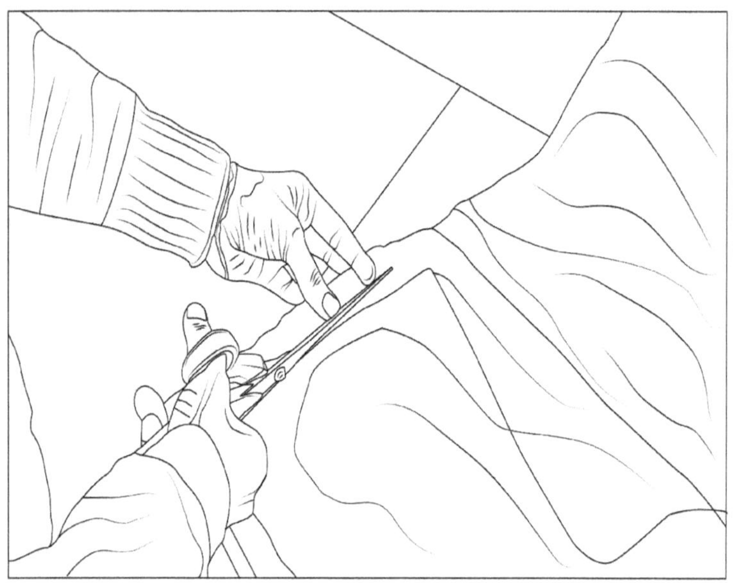

Step 4

Line one piece of the outer fabric with one piece of lining fabric and toes facing the same direction. With the right sides of both the outer and inner lining facing each other, stitch the two pieces with a ¼ inch seam and leave some gap on the stocking to help you turn the right side out after you're done with sewing.

After sewing, open the two pieces and press the seams for both the front piece and the backside. You can also use the iron to smoothen the seams.

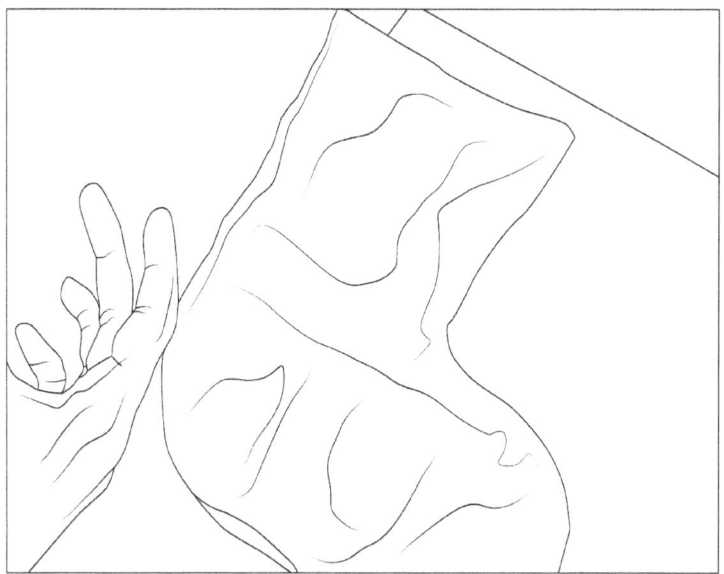

Step 5

Do the same to the other piece of the stocking. The right side out should face each other. The lining fabric should have the right side facing each other. Sew around the sides and leave a gap in the lining to turn the right side out. Ensure the center seams match each other.

You can use a ¼ inch seam allowance on the outside fabric and ⅜ inch lining on the lining fabric. This will make it easy to remove bulkiness on the seams of the lining fabric. Alternatively, you can use ¼ inch seams for both the outside fabric and the lining.

Step 6

Cut some notch curves around the toe curves. This will ensure your stocking looks neat when turned. Do not clip on the seam.

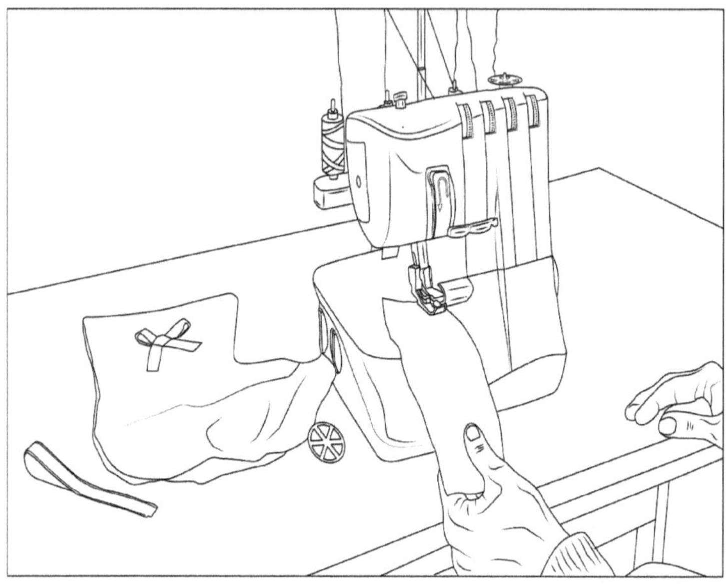

Step 7

Clip the lining fabric with the clips close to the seams to help remove bulkiness. Now turn the right side out and add topstitch to the stocking to close the gaps.

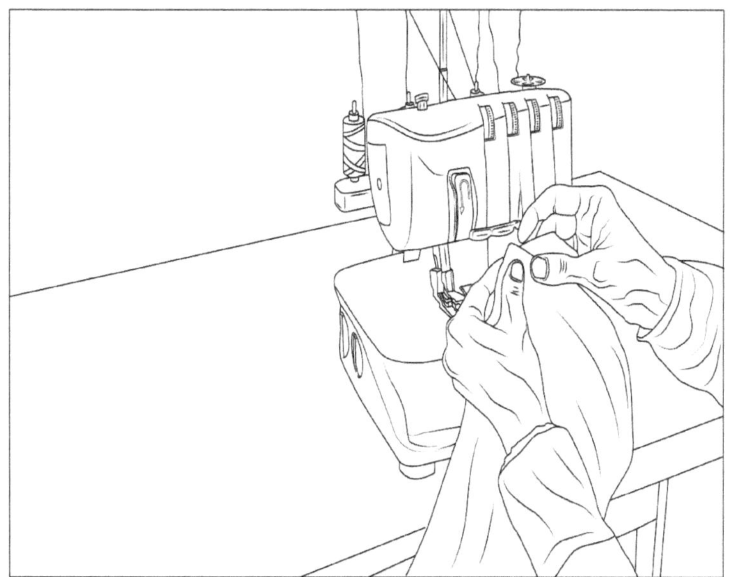

Step 8

Press the seams to make the curves look neat. Tuck in the lining into the stocking and sew a top stitch around the edges of the opening to give it a more finished look.

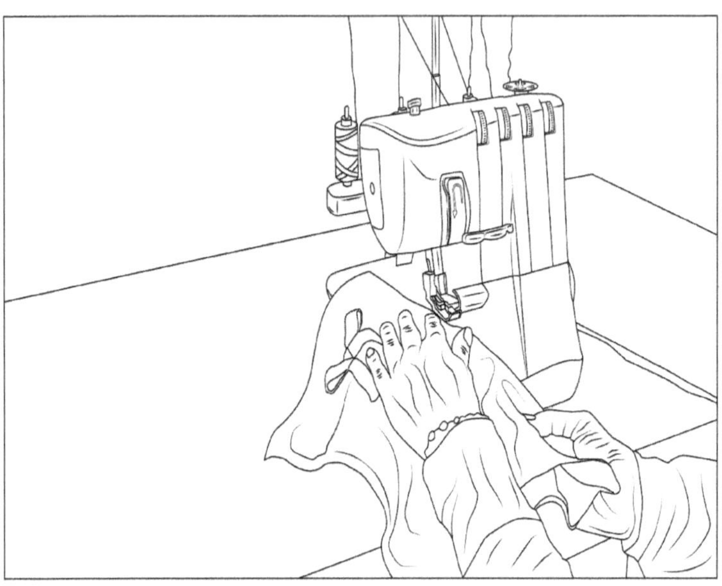

Step 9

Fold the cuff down and add a decorative seam to make your stocking look more attractive. Although, this is optional. You can even use craft glue to add ric racks.

Step 10

Make a hanger for your Christmas stocking. Cut a rectangle piece of fabric and fold it in half to make the long sides touch each other. Press at the center of the fabric to create a middle crease.

Open the rectangle. Make a fold at the raw edges of the fabric so as to meet the freshly created middle crease and press the fold.

Do the same on the lower opposite raw edge.

Step 11

Fold the rectangle into half again so that your folded raw edges will touch each other. Press. You can also use an iron box to press the fabric. Pin the rectangle to keep the folds together.

Step 12

Add stitches to the open edges of the rectangle strip and use ⅛ inch seam allowance. Now you have made the hanger for your stocking.

Now insert the hanger at the raw edges on the top opening of your stocking. Fold the hanger into U-shape and insert and insert the hanger between the stocking fabric and stitch it.

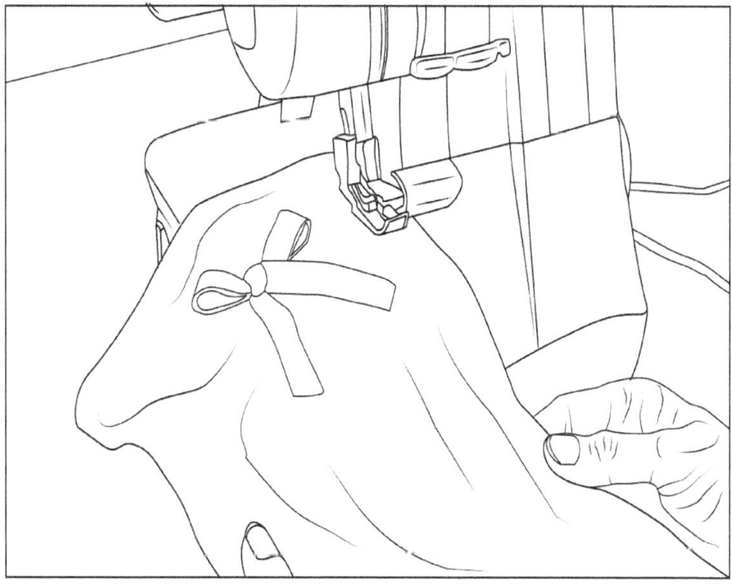

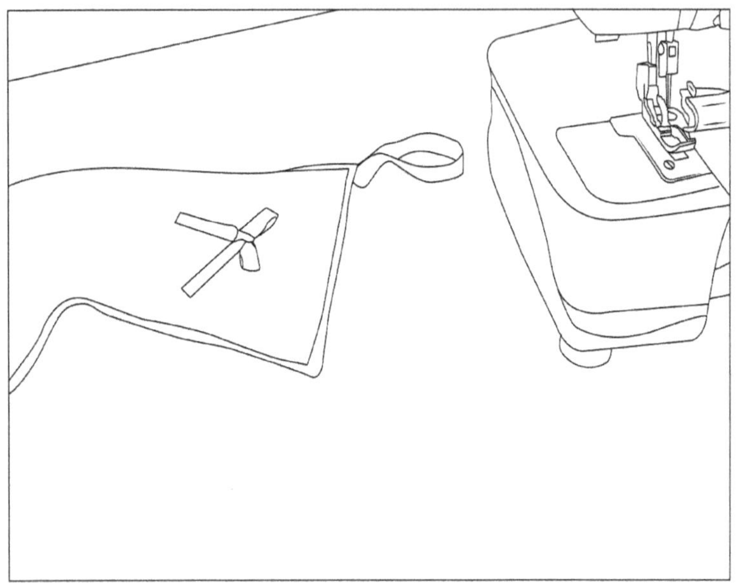

If you had already sewn the topstitch to the edges like in our case above, you can add finishing trims to the edges of the U-shaped hanger and then stitch it on the side of your stocking. You can add a decorative stitch on the outside to make it look even more beautiful.

With these simple steps, you can make your own Christmas stocking. Do more practice with different patterns for your family. If you want better results, you can pre-prep the fabrics by washing, drying, and pressing the seams. You can always customize the fabric based on your preferences and sew your Christmas stocking.

Chapter Summary

- You can easily make your own Christmas stocking in simple steps. After learning these steps, you will never buy a Christmas stocking again. You can use an old stocking to measure the measurements of your new

Christmas stocking or you can decide to make large size stockings.

- There are different patterns you can choose to make your Christmas stockings. You can make different patterns for yourself or for your loved ones. Your family can choose a fabric of their choice for you to go ahead to make a Christmas stocking for them.

- You can use the same fabric for both the outer layer and the lining or choose a different fabric.

- Celebrate this Christmas with your own homemade Christmas stocking!

In the next chapter, you will learn how to make snack bags.

Chapter Nine: Snack Bags

Snack bags are a great accessory for your home. They are perfect for keeping your snacks fresh.

More people are now investing in eco-friendly and reusable snack bags to cut down on the use of plastic. Switching to the use of reusable snack bags will not only help in reducing environmental pollution but also prevent the plastics from ending up in oceans or landfills thus affecting wildlife.

Snack bags are often made of either silicon material or cloth. Some of these bags are microwave safe and you can dish-wash them, making them easy to clean and re-heat.

Image source: Alex Lab/ Shutterstock

Snack bags come in different sizes, making them great for every type of lunch or snack. The smaller size snack bags are ideal for dividing your snacks into smaller portions, for example, into portions that are 100 calories per serving. Extra smaller bags are great for storing your nuts so you can bring them with you.

These bags are also good for packaging pizza slices, sandwiches, cookies, chips, vegetables, fruits, etc. Just grab your favorite bag and go snacking!

Since you can bring them with you, you can create your own custom made plastic bags for food storage. Making your own snack bag is wallet-friendly, all you need is to invest in a durable material and make a variety of sizes at home.

If you have school-aged kids, you may find it more taxing to look for containers with matching tops each morning five days a week. A reusable snack and sandwich bag can come to your rescue.

How to make your own snack bag

It is super-fast to make your snack bag at home. You can also choose your favorite fabric and add decorative finishing to make it more attractive.

Materials needed

- Woven cotton fabric (12 inches * 7 inches)

- Ripstop nylon lining or laminated fabric(12 inches * 7 inches)

- All-purpose serger thread

- Scissors

- Rotary cutter or cutting mat

- Pins or clips

- Fray check

- Serger machine

Step 1

Align the woven fabric and the lining together with the right sides facing each other. Pin the fabrics together. Sew the short edges of the fabric together with ¼ inch seam allowance.

Step 2

Turn the right side out and press the seam although it is impossible for the Ripstop nylon to hold the press. It will make the seam look neat.

Step 3

Fold the edges on the left short end with the right sides together and clip.

Step 4

Fold the other short end with the right sides facing each other and line the ends of the short edges together.

Clip the sides of the folded fabric.

Step 5

Serge both sides with a seam allowance of ¼ inch using overlock stitch. Use a tapestry needle to tuck in the extra thread chain.

Alternatively, you can cut the excess thread chain and apply fray check on the thread chain to lock the stitches.

Step 6

You can decide to box the corners of your snack bag or just leave it as it is. If you don't want box corners for your snack bag, just turn it right side out and you're good to go.

Step 7

If you want to add box corners on the bag, turn the wrong side out and put your fingers inside the bag to flatten the bottom side, and press. You can also use a small awl to pull the corners. Avoid using any sharp object or scissors that can make a hole at the corners.

Clip around ½ inch and serger the bottom. At the same time, trim the excess fabric.

Draw a triangle around the corner edger and stitch the bag with an overlock stitch. Do the same to the other bottom end of the bag.

Step 8

Turn your snack bag with the right side out, use a blunt object or your fingers to push the triangle flap up the side of the seam. Tack in the triangle on the side of the snack bag by stitching a ditch from the outside of the bag. Do the same to create a box corner on the other side.

Step 9

Pack your snacks and turn the folded-down piece (folded pocket with the lining) over the open edge of the bag to enclose your snacks inside as shown on the left image.

Now your snack bag is ready to go! Pack your cookies or sandwich and bring them to the picnic or carry your lunch snacks.

Creating a snack bag with rectangle corners

It is advisable to wash and press your fabric before you begin any project, especially if you're working with cotton fabrics. You can start by washing both the cotton fabric and lining. Press the cotton fabric, do not press the nylon lining.

Step 1

Cut the cotton fabric and nylon lining of the same size (12 inches * 7 inches). You can even create a paper template to help you in measuring accurate fabric size. Place the fabric in a cutting mat and use an acrylic ruler to make your work easier with the rotary blade.

Step 2

Line the cut cotton fabric and a ripstop nylon lining together such that the right sides face each other. Make sure the edges match each other and pin around the bounders.

Step 3

Start sewing one of the long sides of the fabric with ¼ inch seam allowance and leave about a half gap at the beginning of your stitch. Remove the pins as you continue sewing to avoid damaging your machine or breaking needles when you sew over them.

Sew all around all sides of the fabric leaving a gap of around 2 inches between the start and end of your stitch. The gap will enable you to turn the right side out.

Step 4

Trim the corners and be careful not to cut the seams. This will ensure the corners of your bag are not bulky and look good when you turn right side out.

Step 5

Use the gap to turn right side out and use a small awl or your pinky finger to push the corner of the fabric and make them pointy.

Step 6

Press the corners of the two pieces, or iron around the corners to remove any wrinkles. Only iron the cotton fabric and not the ripstop nylon lining. Ironing the seams will make the fabric look nice and flat.

The seam allowance around the gap should be folded in.

Step 7

Turn the fabric with the wrong side out (ripstop nylon side up) and place it on a flat surface. Fold the left short end towards the other short end, but leave 2 inches at the top.

Step 8

Fold the remaining 2 inches down to create a flap. This will leave you with the envelope-like shape of your rectangle. Put a pin around the flap and then sew the sides.

Step 9

Serge along the edges of the short ends of the fabric. Make sure your needle stitches around the corners and edges of the fabric. You can reverse the stitch at the start to secure your stitches. Stitch all the way down until the flap and entire short end is sewn.

Repeat the same process on the other side of the short end.

Now your snack bag is ready for use. Just push up the flap and push the corners with your hands. Put your favorite snacks inside and you're good to go!

Once you add your food inside the bag, you can fold the long edge into the bag. Do not overpack your food in the bag, otherwise some of it will fall out. Instead, make a bigger size snack bag to accommodate more snacks.

You can also add a decorative stitch at the folded-down pocket of the bag to make it more beautiful. If you're making the snack bag for your kids, a decorative stitch using elastic thread or a beaded cord will contribute to the beauty of the snack bag.

If you have any scrap fabrics, you will never throw them away again. With these simple steps, you can create a snack bag for your family use. You can make various sizes of snack bags and use them to store your foodstuffs and snacks.

The snack bags are budget-friendly and easy to clean. You only need to turn them inside out and wash them. If you're stuffing in dry foodstuff, you can pack up the bag several times before you can wash it with your regular laundry.

Chapter Summary

- Snack bags are very essential in a modern home: you can use them to store foodstuffs around your home or pack cookies and sandwiches for your children when going to school. These bags have multiple uses and they are easy to make.

- It won't take you more than ten minutes to make a snack bag. You can make different sizes for your family based on the width of the fabric. They don't have to be only one size if you're making them for your family.

- You can include different designs and let your kids choose the fabric and design they love.

- These reusable snack bags are easy to make and you can wash them with your regular laundry. Grab any scrap fabric and make your own reusable snack bag!

In the next chapter, you will learn how to make a holiday tree napkin.

Chapter Ten:
Holiday Tree Napkin

It is almost December and friends and family will start to flock to your home. You'll want to start shopping for the perfect gift for your friends and loved ones. Or you're planning to cook delicious meals and set up a perfect Christmas table for your family.

Regarding setting up your table, there is so much you can do! Converting your napkins to an adorable tree will make a perfect addition to your dining table. No matter the design scheme you're using, your table will look lively.

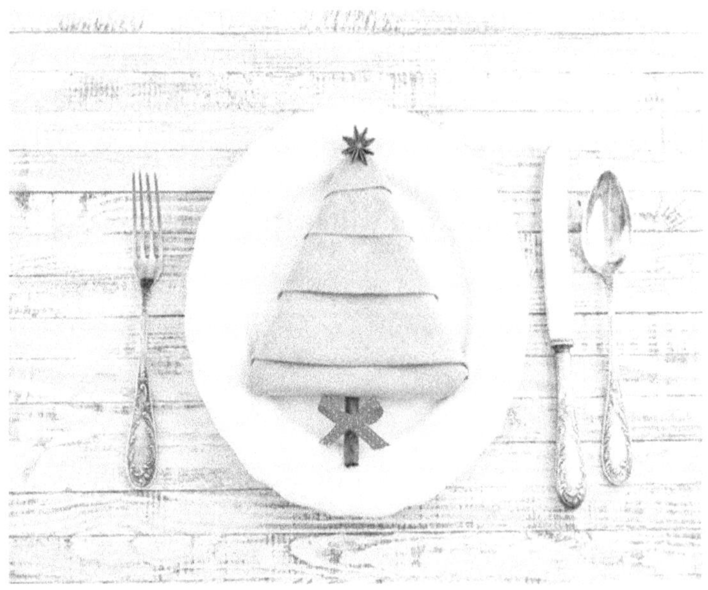

Image source: Mama_Mia/Shutterstock

To add a personal touch to the designs, you can make your own tree napkins for your table. Learning how to make

the Christmas tree napkin will up your holiday table setting
game.

Making napkins for your holiday tree

You can make your own classy modern napkins and
transform them into a Christmas tree in simple steps.
Creating your own custom made napkins for setting up the
Christmas tree not only impress your guests but also leaves
your dining setting looking more elegant.

How to create napkins

You can make your napkins in two ways:

- Reversible napkins: These are easy to make napkins
  and suitable for beginners. They are two-sided and
  reversible making them great for adding some color to
  your table.

- Mitered corners: This type of napkins has hemmed
  edges and usually made of linen material and they're
  unlined. These are the most common traditional
  napkins in every household.

Although this tutorial is going to concentrate on how to
make mitered corner napkins and fold them to form a
Christmas tree, I will briefly show you how to make
reversible napkins.

Reversible napkins

The best fabrics to use in making napkins are pure
cotton and linen since they can absorb any mess and they're
easy to fold.

To make your napkin, you need:

- Fine linen

- Quilting cotton (good if you want to make napkins with patterns)

- Drill

- Cotton duck

Cut and iron the fabric

Cut two pieces of fabric based on your size and add 6 mm seam allowance. In our case, let's cut two equal pieces that measure 16 inches * 16 inches with ¼ inch seam allowance. Iron the fabric to remove any creases.

Step 1

Match the two cut pieces together with the right sides together and pin all around the fabric.

Step 2

Stitch all around the fabric with ¼ inch seam allowance and leave a gap of 2inch on one side to allow you to turn the napkin right side out.

Step 3

Clip the corners of the fabric to avoid any bulkiness around the corners of the napkin.

Step 4

Turn the right side out via the gap. Use the awl or back of your pencil to poke out the corners and press the seams. Press inside the seam allowance at the gap and add a top stitch all around the napkin. Ensure your stitch is around ⅛ inch from the edges of the napkin. This will close the gap as well.

Step 5

Give your napkin a final press using the iron to make the napkin look neat and flat. Your napkin is ready for setting your dinner table.

Making mitered napkins

Mitered napkins are great if you want to decorate them later like making a Christmas tree. To make your napkin, you can use linen material or any other material that is highly absorbent and is made of natural fibers such as cotton.

Step 1

Cut the fabric into a square that measures 16 inches * 16 inches. If you have a plain fabric with no wrong or right side, it will be great for making the napkin holiday tree.

Step 2

On the wrong side, fold the edges with ¼ inch and another ½ inch on one end of the fabric and press the folds.

Step 3

On the next edge, fold the edges by the same amounts of ¼ inch followed by ½ inch. Press the folds. Thick will create a thick fabric at the corners making it look bulk when you stitch the napkin that's why you have to clip the corners to remove the bulkiness.

Step 4

Open the folds, you will notice that the presses have created some creases on the fabric. You can make the creases with your tailor's chalk or drawing pencil to make it easy to know where to clip.

Step 5

Mark a diagonal line touching the corners of the center square.

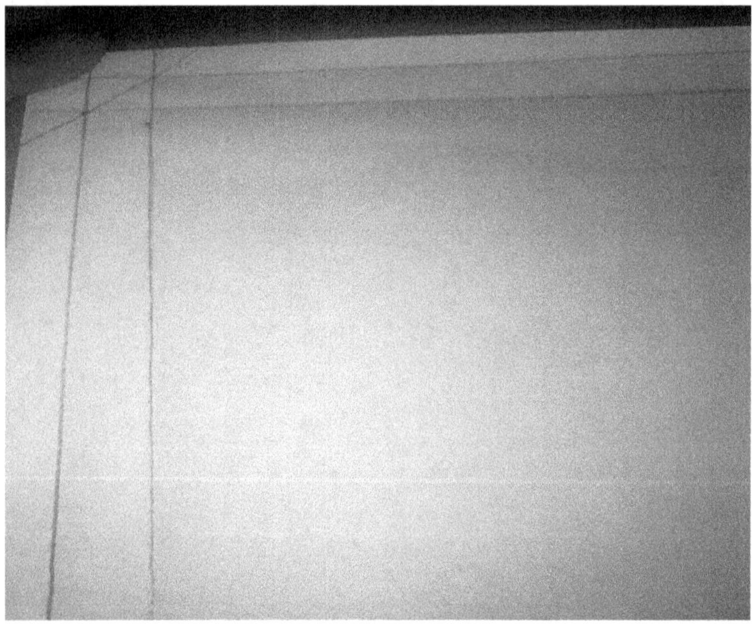

Step 6

Cut the fabric across the marked area.

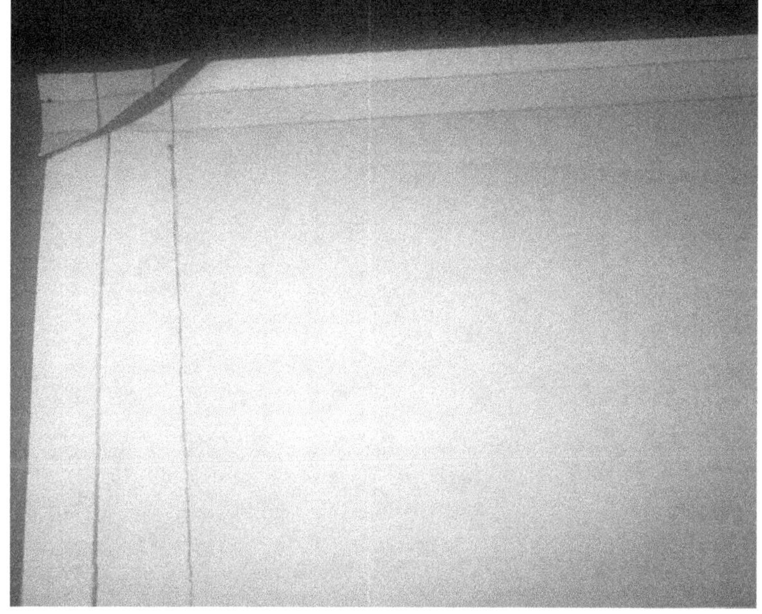

Step 7

Mark another diagonal line on the inner crease fold as shown below.

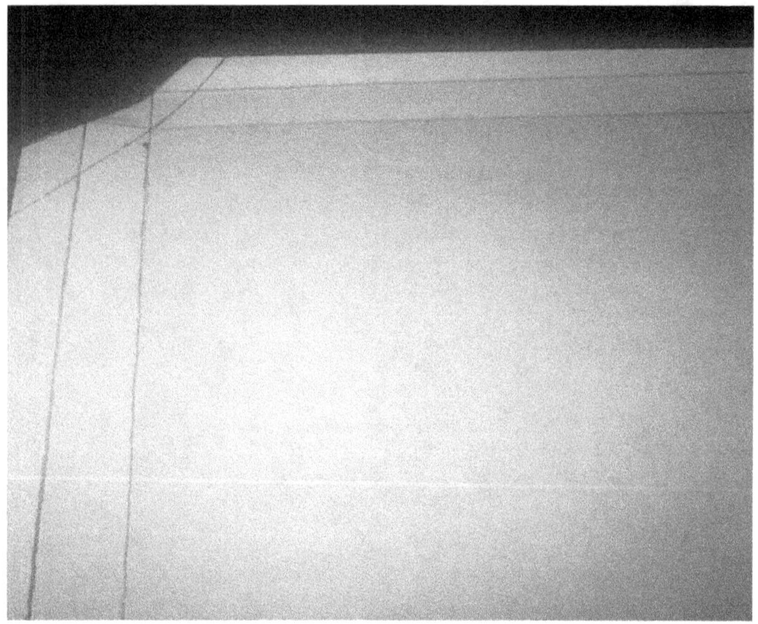

Step 8

Fold along the mark and press it.

Step 9

Now fold again the pressed edge and pin the corner. Repeat the same steps for the remaining corners.

Step 10

Stitch hem edges all around the napkin.

Image source: Maraze/Shutterstock

Now your napkin is ready for use.

Folding a napkin tree

If you already have the napkins, you can go ahead and fold them into a Christmas tree.

Materials required

- Cotton napkin (16 inches * 16 inches)

- Tiny bow

- Pin

Steps to fold the napkins into tiers

Folding the napkins to look like a Christmas tree is a great addition to your table décor this festive season. You can make a good tree napkin using fabric made of 100% natural fibers such as cotton and linen. You can also use fabrics made from a blend of cotton/polyester.

Step 1

Iron the napkin to have a crisper looking tree napkin, although ironing is optional. Place the square napkin on a flat surface. It doesn't matter which side is facing up. If the napkin already has a tag, remove it because you don't want it to show on your final design.

Step 2

Pick your square napkin and fold it in half to form a rectangle shape.

Step 3

Fold it again to get a smaller square. All the corners of the napkin should line up with each other.

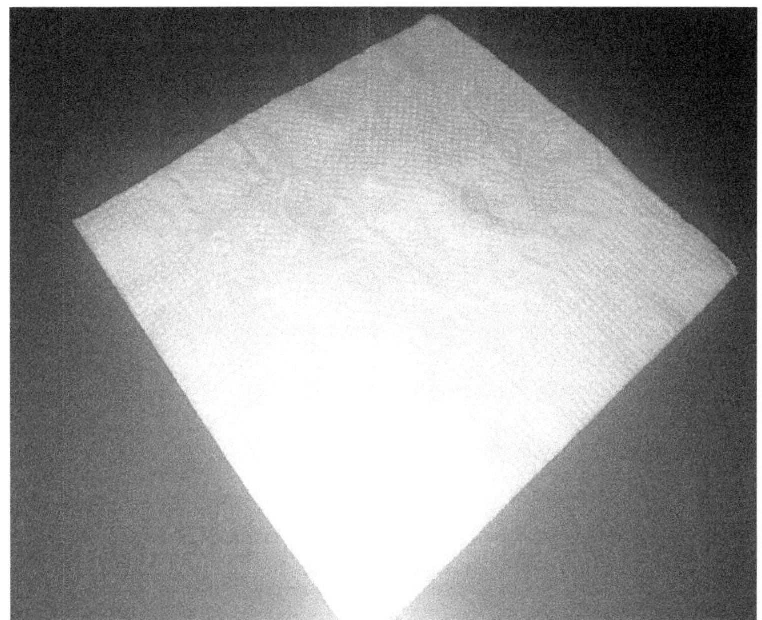

Step 4

Rotate the folded napkin so that it creates a diamond shape. The loose corners should be at the bottom as shown above.

Step 5

Pick the first bottom layer and fold it towards the top point.

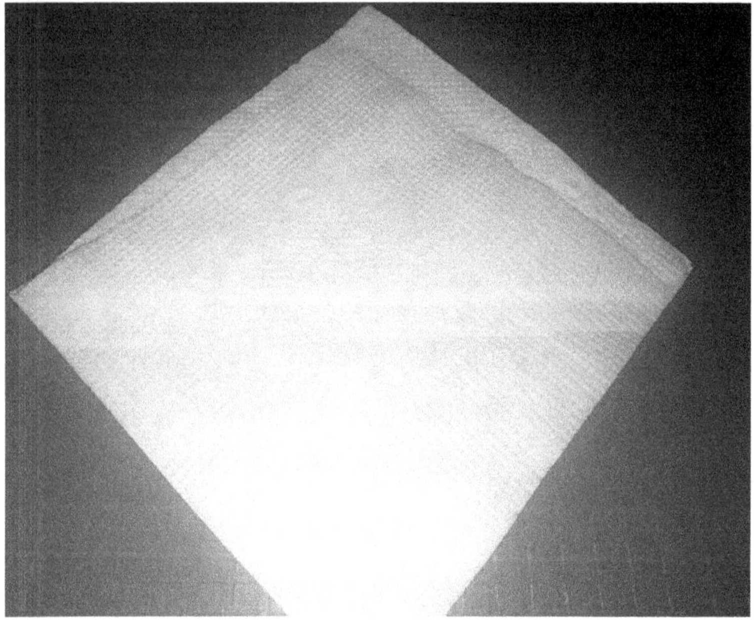

Step 6

Continue to fold the corners up with each corner layer staggering slightly below each other. Fold each layer of the napkin to the top leaving an inch between the folds. Press the folds in place.

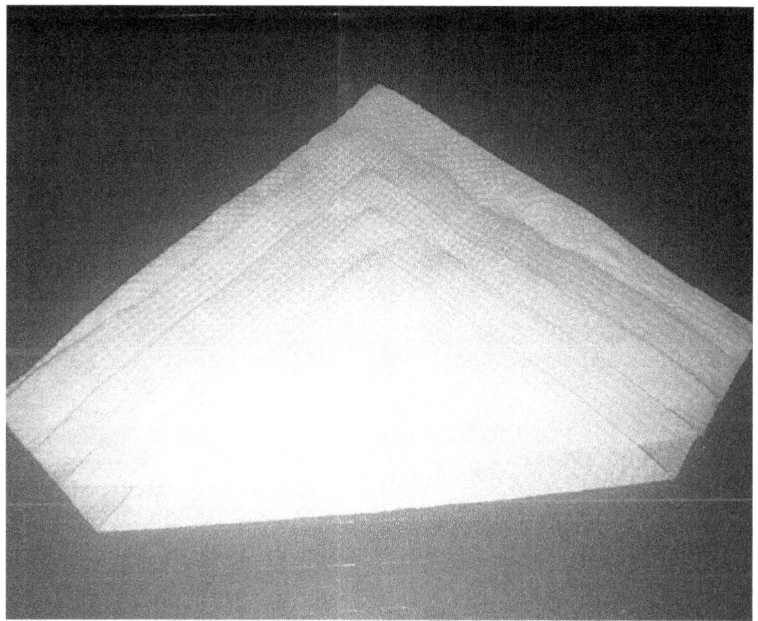

Step 7

Flip the napkin over while holding the folds. You can easily flip the napkin by placing one hand at the bottom while the other is holding the folds at the top then carefully flip the napkin. Press each layer as you fold.

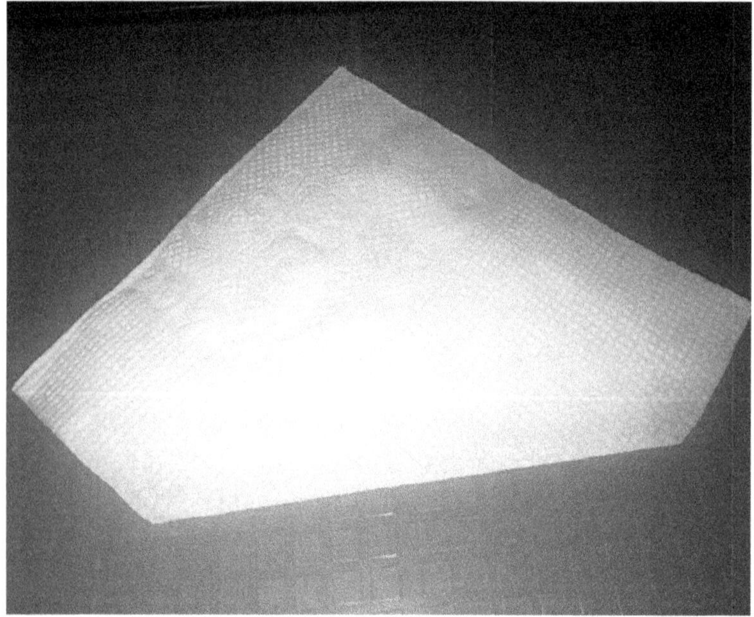

Step 8

Now fold both sides of the napkin together. Fold the lower outside to the opposite side and align each of the panels at the top to form a triangle shape.

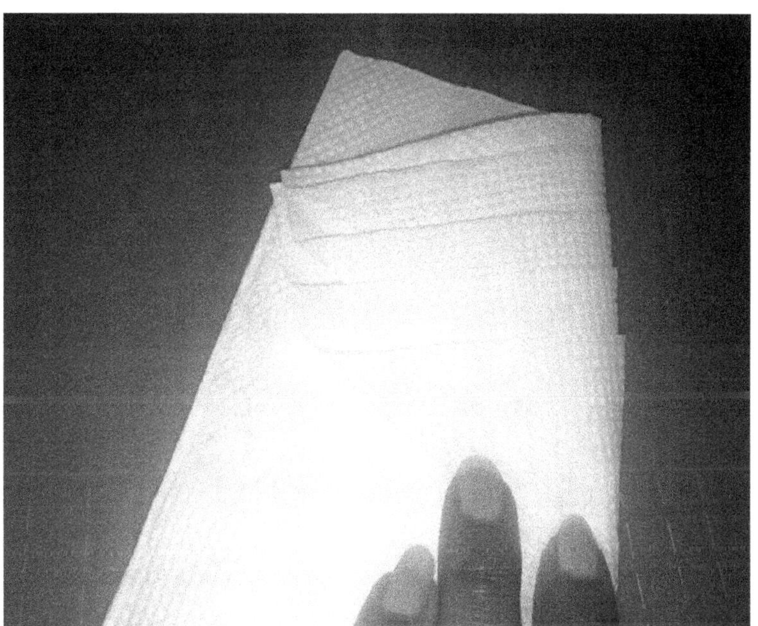

Step 9

Repeat the same process to the other corner. This will create a sharp pointed edge at the bottom of the fabric.

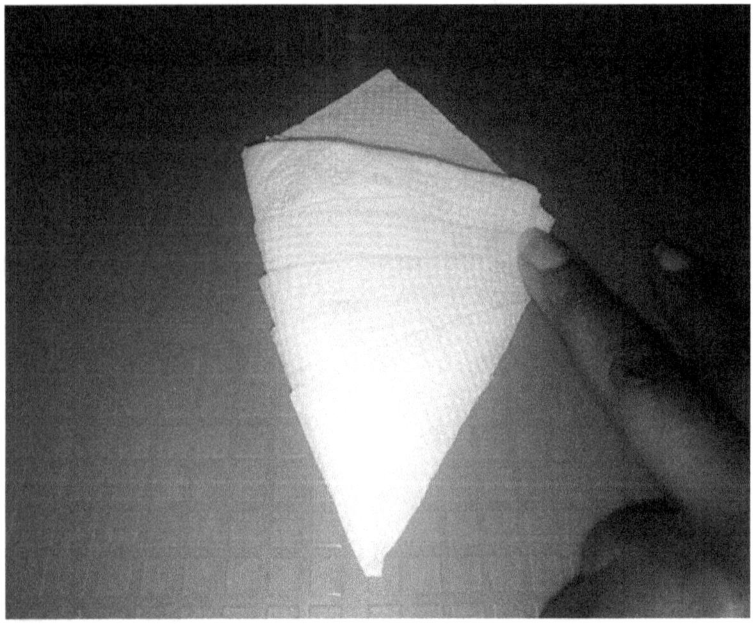

Step 10

Hold the top folded layers so that they don't unfold then flip the napkin over to the front side. Rotate the napkin to have a cute Christmas tree napkin fold. You can stop here or continue adding more decorations to your Christmas tree.

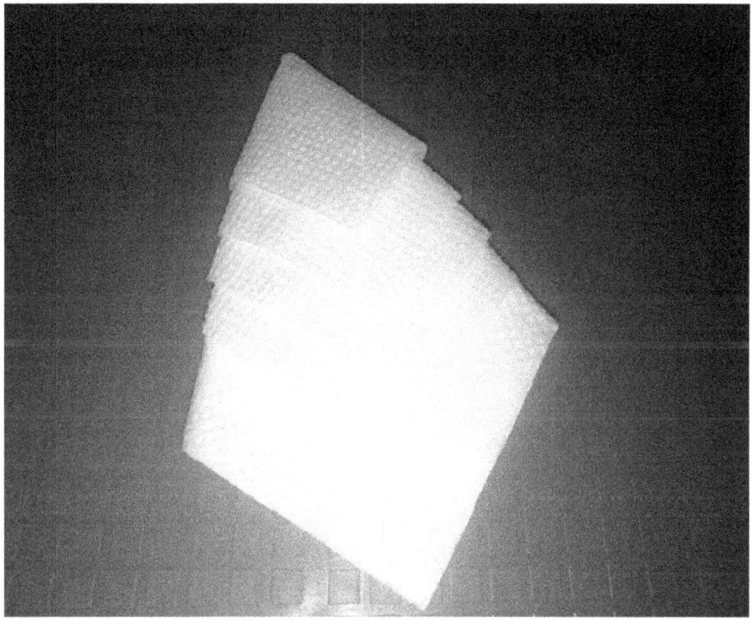

Step 11

Fold the top layer of the napkin to the top to create the peak of your Christmas tree. You can also fold the top layer underneath itself to form a neat triangle shape.

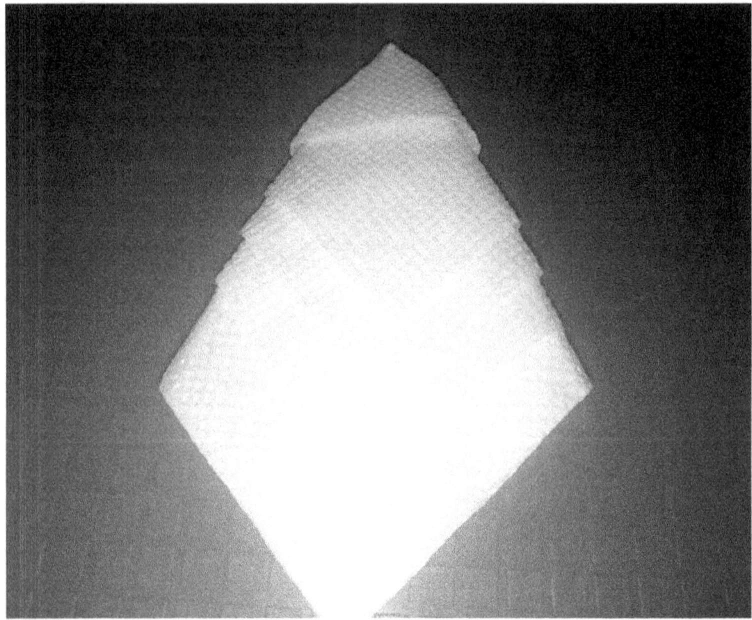

Step 12

Tuck the second layer underneath the upper layer to a triangle-like shape. Press the fold.

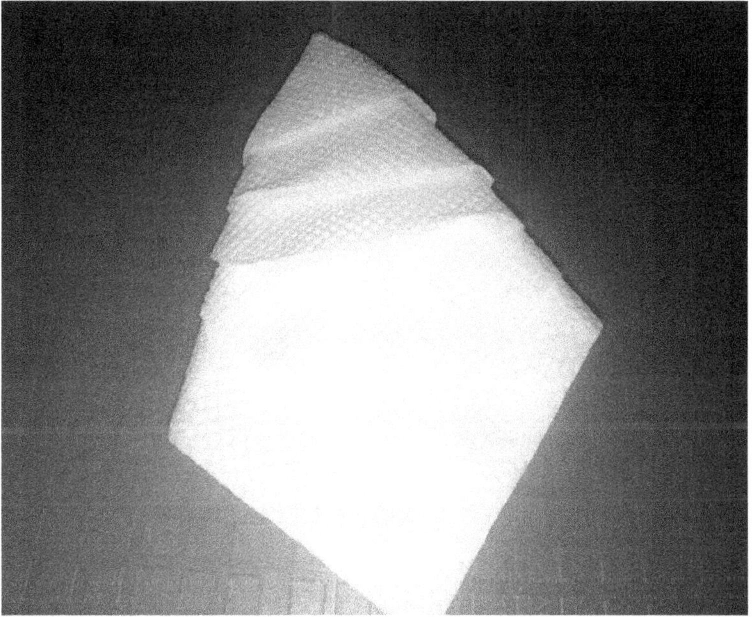

Step 13

Tuck the other layers underneath each of the upper layers and create a beautiful Christmas tree.

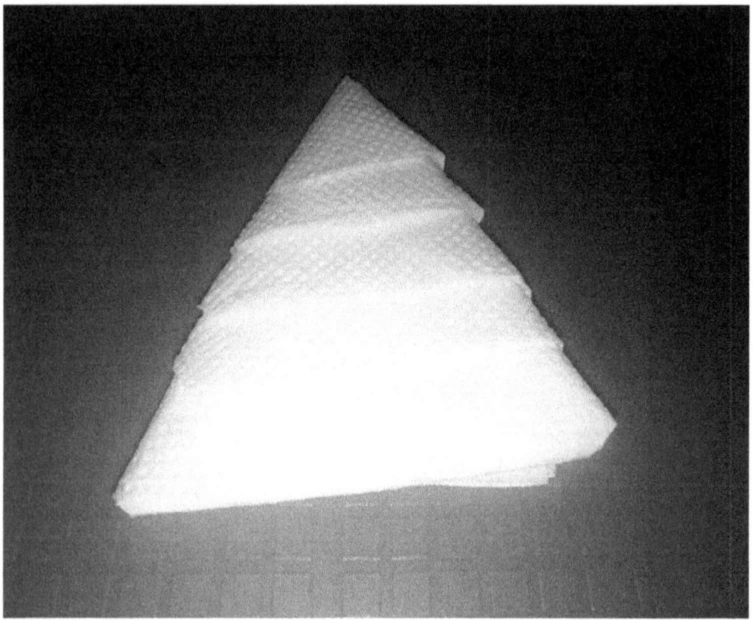

Step 14

You can add a tiny bow at the peak to add more finishing to your Christmas tree. Pin it at the peak.

Step 15

Place the folded napkin on an empty plate and make sure the folds are still in place. Now your Christmas tree folded napkin is ready.

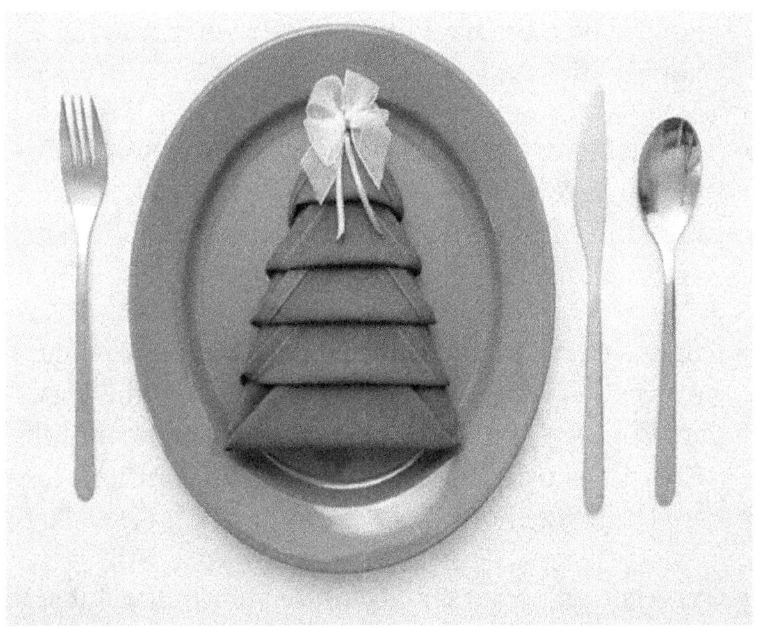

Image source: Alenkadr/Shutterstock

To prevent the folds from coming undone, you can use pins to pin them in place. You can also add some decorations to the folded napkins. For example, you can tie a skinny ribbon to form little bows, use cinnamon sticks at the bottom to make the napkin resemble a real tree, or use paper cut-out stars and other ornaments.

You can also make your folded napkin sit on the plate instead as shown below. All you need is to open the bottom of the napkin.

Chapter Summary

- Creating your own DIY napkin gives you a personalized look at your dining setting. You can use any absorbent fabric like cotton or linen or a blend of the two. The cotton fabric or linen makes it easy to add folds to the napkin especially when making a napkin Christmas tree.

- There are two methods you can use to make your napkins: reversible napkins and mitered corner napkins. Mitered corner napkins using plain material are great for making a Christmas tree.

- Choose a napkin with the color of your choice then proceed to make the napkin tree. Follow the above step by step guide to making a neat and beautiful Christmas tree. You can add some decorations to your tree or just leave it like that and place it on a plate.

- You can go ahead and decorate your dining table with these Christmas tree napkins.

In the next chapter, you will learn how to make your own facemask.

Chapter Eleven:
How To Make Face Mask

In these times when face masks are a necessity, you can easily make one at home using your serger machine.

Since you need a face mask every day when going out, you can make several for your family to protect them. Homemade face masks can add a degree of protection although they may not be as effective as medical-grade masks.

Homemade masks are great for running errands and provides you with a visual cue that you have to maintain social distancing protocols. They also ensure you don't touch your face, nose, and mouth during this COVID 19 pandemic.

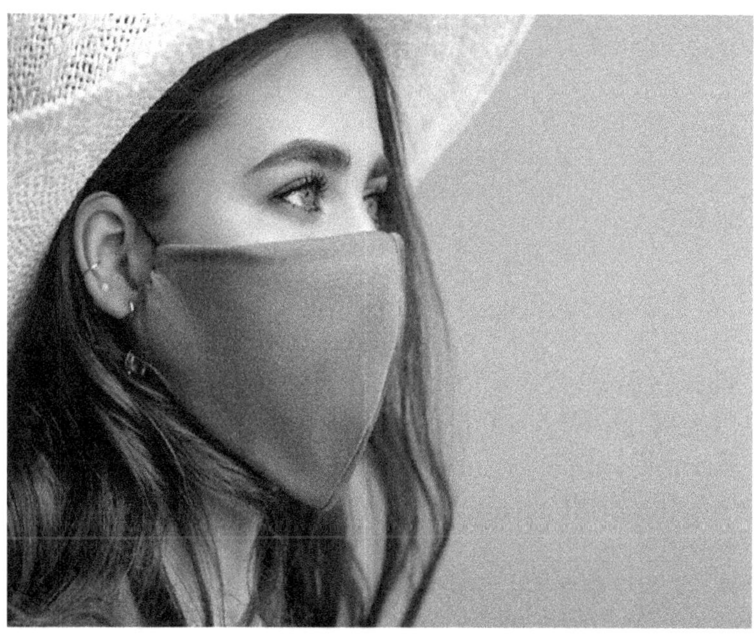

Today, face masks are becoming part of our fashion as a response to providing protection; more reason why you should custom fit them. There are different designs you can use to make your face mask. In this tutorial, I will show you how to make face masks in two ways.

Making an easy design face mask

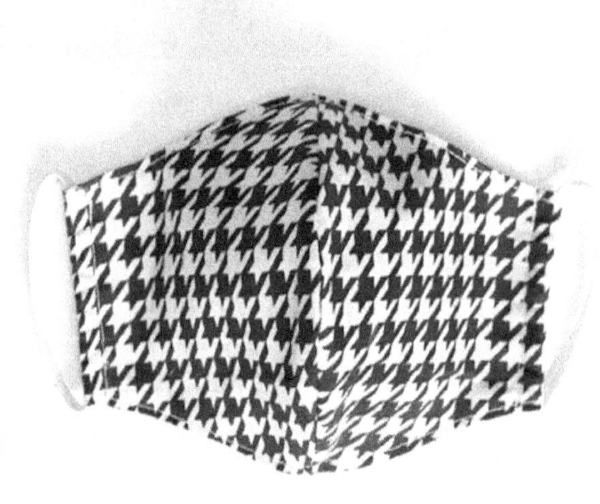

This is one of the most common self-made designs. It is great for those who wear glasses since it has a more comfortable shape. You can easily make this design with your overlock stitch or even the regular sewing machine.

With this design, you can add an additional layer of filter fabric to maximize your protection. Any 4-thread overlock machine can do a marvelous job in sewing this mask. The

MTC (micro thread control) feature in your machine will give you excellent results when sewing the rounded seam.

Material required

- 2 pieces of the outer fabric

- 2 pieces of the middle lining (mouth lining)

- 2 pieces of side-lining (cheeks)

- 4 pieces of cut straps (knit cross-cut)

Machine settings

To start sewing, you have to adjust your tension to default settings or increase the upper looper tension and reduce the lower looper tension. Use a scrap material to test your stitch formation. If your needle thread is loose, then adjust the needle thread tension to default.

Alternatively, you can increase the tension of the left needle thread and reduce tension on the lower looper. If the right needle is loose, you can adjust the tension settings to default. Otherwise, increase the right needle thread tension.

Based on your fabric and thread, you can adjust the stitch length from 0.8 to 4. Adjust your differential feed from 0.7 to 2. If you need flat seams, set your differential feed to be between 1 and 2. To accommodate the fabric stretch, adjust the differential feed to between 0.7-1.

You also need to adjust the seam width based on your needs.

When using the right needle, the stitch formation should be set to a minimum of 3mm seam as shown in the first stitch. The last stitch formation shows a stitch using the left needle with the seam length set to 9mm.

If you have a balanced stitch, you can go ahead and start sewing.

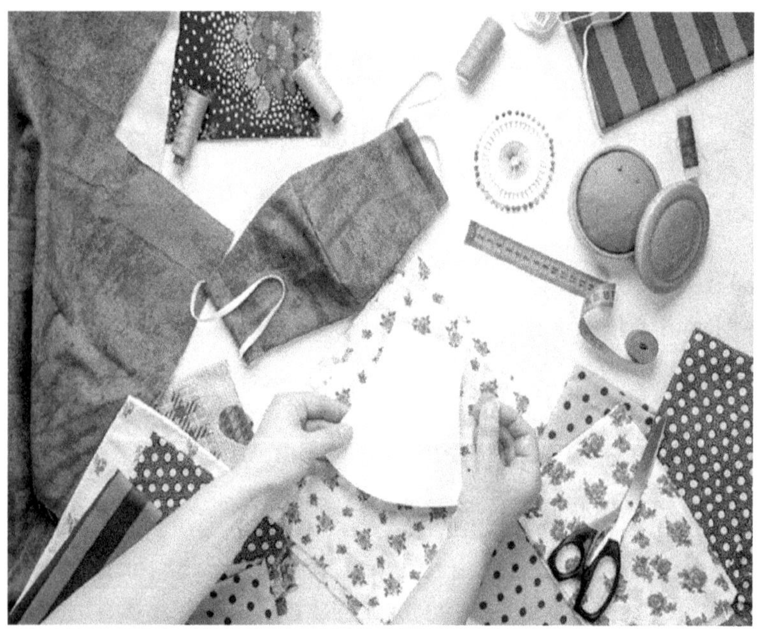

Image source: NatalyaBond/Shutterstock

Step 1

You can use a free downloaded Olson Mask pattern by Clayton Skousen & Rose Hedges to guide you in cutting the pieces of the fabric.

Step 2

Place the rounded outer fabric and the middle lining together with the right side facing each other. Pin them together.

To get better results for the curved seam, pick a scrap fabric, and test the stitch. Set the MTC to +plus because you need loose loops for the curve so that the seam allowance remains flat and no bulkiness on the seam of the curve. You can adjust the MTC while sewing to get the right balance.

Step 3

Once you're satisfied with the results sew the seam on the middle lining and outer fabric curves.

Step 4

Reset the MTC back to the default settings and stitch the next seam.

Step 5

Iron the seam allowance so that it lies flat on one side in the outer fabric and on the other side of the middle lining. This will prevent the formation of thick spots under your chin and on your nose that causes discomfort.

Step 5

Neaten the straight edges of your middle lining and those of the side-lining to securely hold them in place. Neatening stitches prevent fraying of raw edges as well as hold hems securely.

Step 6

Align the top edge of the outer fabric and the middle lining with the right side facing each other. Ensure the curved seam match and the seam allowance face away from each other. Pin the fabrics together.

Align the parts of the side linings and ensure the center lining is overlapping and pin them together.

Step 7

Place the mask sideways with the outer fabric on the outside. Cut the seam allowance of the middle lining to 3mm to prevent it from showing after sewing the mask.

Pin the bottom edge of the mask. Use pins with a clear head so that you can easily remove them as you stitch.

Step 8

Start stitching the mask. Adjust the stitch length to 2 or 2.5 and blade cutting width to be 6mm. Adjust your speed to be slow so that you can get a nice rounded shape. Do not stitch over the pins so you should remove them as you stitch.

To ensure your fabric doesn't slide, you can remove the pin in front of the presser foot.

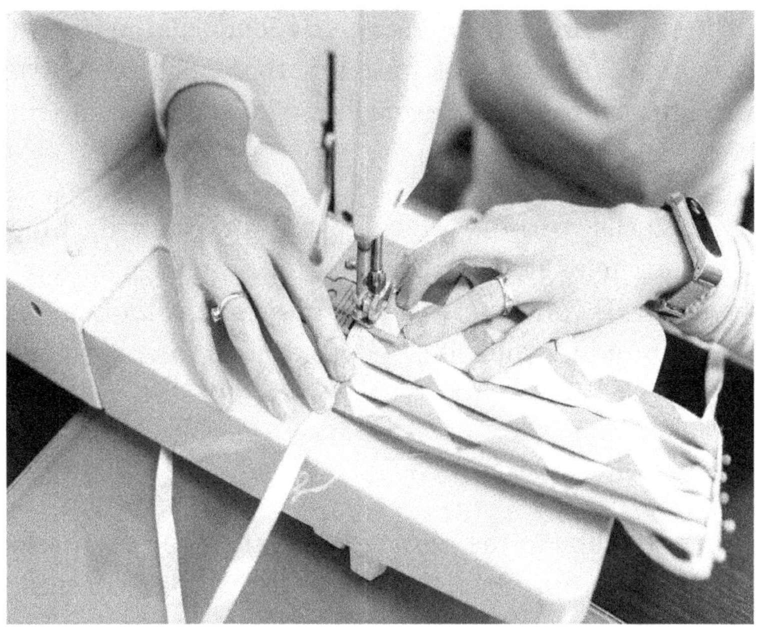

Step 9

When you get to the curved seam, ensure the seam allowance face away from each other to avoid bulkiness. It ensures you don't have unnecessary thick material around your nose or chin.

Step 10

After stitching both sides of the long edges, you can try the mask. If you want your ears to remain free, you can cut off 2cm from the sides of the fabric. You can adjust this after you have tried the mask on your face.

Step 11

Stitch the straps for your mask. You can stitch a tunnel strap using a 2cm seam allowance.

The stretch of your knit straps depends on the type of fabric you use. Always look for fabric that will be comfortable to wear. In this face mask, we will use knit fabric remnants to make the straps.

Sew an easy turning tube with your overlock machine. Set your stitch length to two so that the stitch can stretch to fit the fabric. If you're sewing a highly stretchy knit cross-cut fabric, then reduce the stitch length to 1.5 to increase the elasticity.

Step 12

Turn the tube to the right side out and proceed to insert the straps into your mask. Insert the straps from the middle to the side seams on both the top and bottom edges of the mask and pin the straps. Do the same on the other side of the mask and pin them.

Step 13

Stitch the side seam and remove the pin at the front of the presser foot.

Step 14

Secure the seam at the beginning and at the end by tying a knot on the thread chain and cut the excess chain. You can also use an inserter to insert the thread chain inside the seam.

Iron the seams to get better results and stability. Press seam allowance around the corners such that they are away from each other. You can easily turn the corners by inserting your finger around the corner to form a pyramid and then turn the corners.

The straps can also help in shaping the corners of the mask

Step 15

Now turn the right side out and iron your mask to ensure the seams at the middle lining are flat and all the other seams from the four sides including the middle lining remain hidden.

Step 16

You can also secure the end of the strap by pushing the edges back to the tunnel by 1 cm. you can use any tool that has a rounded tip to insert the edges. Iron the straps.

Step 17

Now your mask is ready for use. The mask has finished edges that make it look more professional.

Face Mask Design 2

If you want to make a more easy face mask, you can follow these few steps to make one for your family and friends.

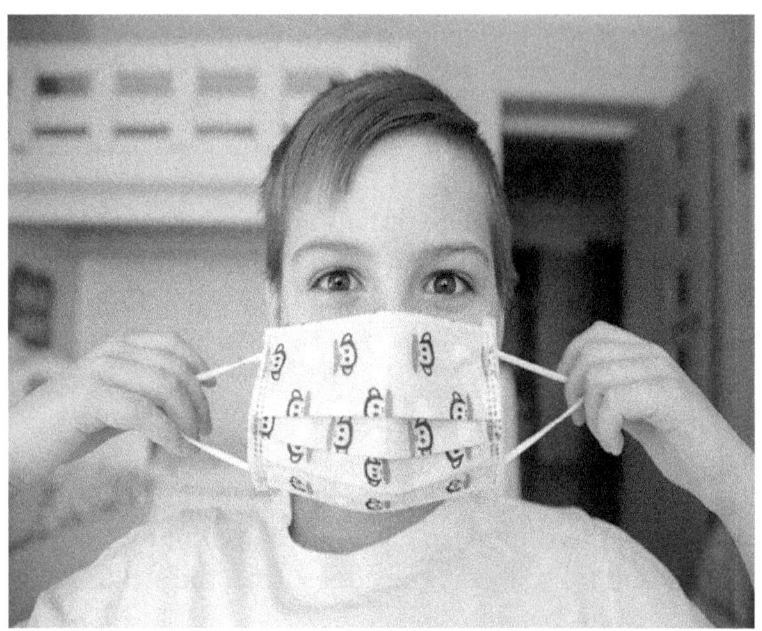

Image source: Tatjana Efimkina/Shutterstock

Required materials

- 100 percent quilting cotton

- Cotton flannel

- Strip ¼ inch wide or Stretchy knit fabric 1 inch

- Twisty tie, pipe cleaner, or ribbon piece (optional)

- Filters (optional)

- Safety pin

- Serger Machine

Step 1

Wash and dry the fabrics. Cut two square pieces of fabric measuring 10.5 inches * 7 inches for adults and 9 inches * 7 inches for kids.

Step 2

Match the two pieces of fabric with the right sides facing each other and ensure the edges are aligned to each other and pin the pieces together.

Step 3

Shape the nose piece by using a twisty tie. You can also use a pipe cleaner or a wired ribbon to shape the nose piece. Place the wire or the twisty pie in the top center of the fabric. You can use either of the sides.

Step 4

Stitch the two pieces together at the top and bottom sides. You can use a cording foot that ensures the wire doesn't get caught up under the needles. If you don't have a cording foot, line up the pipe cleaner such that it runs between the two needles.

Slow down your serging speed as you stitch around the wire. If you don't have a serger machine, you can use a zigzag stitch to sew both the top and bottom edges of the fabric.

Step 5

Turn the fabric to have the right side out and press the seam to have a neat rectangle shape. Use your iron to make the seams sit as flat as possible.

Step 6

Turn your mask so it's upside down with the front fabric facing up. Start forming the pleats of the fabric. The newsprint checked the red & black fabric and the patterned fabric on the ruler mat.

Step 7

Use a light mist on the fabric to make it easy to create crisp pleats as you iron the fabric. Pinch a small piece of fabric on the side edges with your finger to form the first pleat. Make sure the pleat is pointing away from you. When you turn the mask, the outside pleat will face down.

The mask is upside down so add pleats facing away from you starting from the top edge. After forming your first pleat, press it hard and hand folds it on the ruler mat.

Step 8

Do the same process for the remaining pleats. You can form at least 2 more pleats of 3 inches on each side. Form masks on the newsprint fabric on the ruler mat.

Step 9

Press the pleats and use a little steam to help in pressing the pleats. Therefore, it is not necessary to pin the pleats before you can stitch them. Hold the pleats with your hands as you serge along the edges of the mask.

Image source: Texture World/Shutterstock

Do the same procedure to the other short side of the mask

Step 10

Trim off the extra threads from your mask. Make sure you tie a knot at the chain of threads before you cut them to secure the seam. Alternatively, you can use a large needle to tuck the chain of threads into the seam.

Step 11

Create a tunnel to secure the strap into your mask. Turn the sides of the mask to the back by about ½ inch and press. Since it is difficult to thread an elastic or knit strap over the pleated tunnel, the ½ inch space will be of great help.

Press the seam or pin it though the pins are not necessary at this time. It will be much faster to stitch without the pins. All you need is to turn the sides of the mask and hold the seam with your fingers.

Step 12

Stitch a single seam around the serged threads. Serge from the back of the fabric to make it easy to capture the whole length of the mask on the sides.

Step 13

Stitch the strap to the fabric. You can use elastic cording, or knit strapping 1 inch wide. If you don't have an elastic or knit fabric, you can cut 1-inch strips from a t-shirt and use them to make the straps for your mask.

Before you fix the straps, place the mask with the front side up and the top side of the mask up.

Step 14

Use the safety pin to securely fix the strap into the mask. Securely pin the end of the strap with the safety pin then use the safety pin to run the strap through the tunnel on the side of the fabric.

Step 15

Insert the safety pin at the tunnel on the bottom right-hand side of the mask. Wiggle the safety pin inside the tunnel until you can pull it at the top of the tunnel. Don't pull the pin through the tunnel.

Insert the pin from the top left side and continue wiggling until you grab it on the other side. This will leave you with a strap connected across the top of the mask and two loose straps hanging at the bottom side of the mask.

Step 16

Remove the safety pin and your mask is ready for use. Once you wear the mask, you can adjust the straps to comfortably fit you. Tie the bottom straps at the back of your head. If the strap is long, you can cut the excess strap.

Alternatively, you can cut the strap at the top side then tie the top piece with the bottom piece on each side to form straps you can wear around your ears. The choice is yours.

It is very easy to make the mask with your serger machine. You only need to learn the basics and you're good to go.

Tips to speed up face mask sewing

- Start by creating an assembly-line style for your face mask. This involves cutting the fabric into pieces and aligning them so that the pieces can match each other. The assembly line style helps you reduce the number of times you have to stand up from the chair to pick something. If you have several masks to serge, prepare the pieces, and then sew them one after the other. Do not cut the threads until you have sewn all the masks. This saves you a lot of time!

- You can skip pinning the pieces of fabric together. Instead, fold and use steam to press the pieces. The steam holds the shape in place making it easy to stitch the fabric.

- Use your serger machine to form the pleats and create a strap tunnel at the same time. In just a single step you can create pleats and tunnel

- You can serger the top and bottom edges of the mask on the right sides out without using the nose shaper. This eliminates the need for you to turn the mask right side out and press the tube.

- Get the assistance of making the straps from your family members.

Mask evaluation

The World Health Organization recommends the use of different types of masks depending on where you go, who you are, and the amount of cases of the virus circulating in that area.

You can wear a fabric mask when carrying out your daily chores unless you're interacting with a high-risk group, for example, if you find yourself in a crowded area where there is poor ventilation. You should wear a surgical mask if you're taking care of an ill family member, if you have an underlying medical condition, and if you're above 60 years of age.

Depending on any of the conditions, make sure you wear the right type of mask to protect yourself.

According to CDC guidelines, a good face mask should have at least two layers and be easy to wash without any damage. To know whether you have made the right mask for yourself, use a candlelight test.

The efficiency of the mask is determined by the mask's weave. It should have a tight weave to prevent light from showing through. It should also be thick enough such that you can't blow a candle when wearing the mask

Mask maintenance

You should wash the mask regularly. You can wash them with your regular laundry, using regular laundry detergent. Based on the type of fabric used to make the mask, you can use an appropriate warmest water setting. You should also use the highest heating and leave the mask in the drier to completely dry out.

Chapter Summary

- Making your own face mask is a great way to protect yourself and your family. Currently, masks are being used as a comprehensive strategy measure to reduce the transmission of disease and save lives.

- When using a mask, ensure it covers your nose, mouth, and your chin in order to get maximum protection from them.

- Since you're required to wear a mask daily, making your own mask can help cut costs. You can also make fashionable masks that match your daily outfit.

- It is very easy to make your own face mask. In our tutorial, we have discussed two designs you can use to make your own mask. If you have any scrap fabric at home, use it to make custom-made a mask for yourself and your family. You can also make a mask as a gift to your friends. You can make a complete mask within 10 minutes or less based on your design.

Final Words

Serger machines are more preferred than a regular sewing machine because they're much faster. The motor not only runs faster but the machine produces more stitches. Serger machines can create different types of stitches, allowing you to perform several tasks simultaneously.

Apart from creating seams in the fabric, it trims excess fabric and overcast. Due to the various functions, they're preferred for excellent results and ease of use.

When creating stitches, there are different types of stitches you can create with your serger machine. In the above projects, we have used 4-thread stitches on woven and knit fabrics. The 3-thread overlock stitch has been great for creating curved seams and also for the professional finishing of the raw edges of woven fabrics. In most of the projects, we have alternated between the three-thread and four-thread overlock stitch.

For example, our first project was using the blind hem technique to create nearly an invisible seam on the outside of your garment. The stitches are hidden under the folded edges of your fabric.

You can easily join two pieces of raw edges using the blind hemstitch. If you want to attach a pocket to your garment or you simply want to add hemming to your garment, this stitch will give you a neat and clean finish. Blind hem stitches are created using a bling hem foot. Learning how to use this foot will be a great advantage for your serging projects. With the foot, you're able to create super-fast hems that have a professional look.

Another type of stitch you can create for lightweight fabrics is the rolled hemstitch. Serging rolled edges is one of the greatest and fastest hemming techniques you can apply to obtain professional finishings. Rolled hems help you create professional finishing on lightweight and medium weight fabrics. If you're serging a sheer fabric or you want to hem the edges of a scarf or chiffon blouse, then rolled hems will do marvelous work for you.

When using a rolled hem foot, you can use both three-thread stitches. However, some machines will allow you to do rolled hems using a 2-thread overlock stitch although the hem will not be as strong as that done by the 3-thread overlock stitch.

If you're dealing with curved seams like those applied on necklines or armscyes, you can use narrow stitches.

A narrow stitch will result in having a smooth curve since you will have less clipping of the raw edges and notching in order to achieve an efficient turn on your garment.

You're also able to learn how to use the gathering foot to create excellent gathers for your skirts and other garments. This serging tool will make your gathering much easier and you will be able to generate even gathers for your garment. The gathering foot not only helps you to create neat gathers but also helps you to create fabric ruffles.

The gathering foot resembles your regular presser foot but it automatically gathers ruffles as you stitch your fabric, saving you a lot of time and energy. You can use your gathering foot in three ways: to gather ruffle, to shirr your fabric using elastic thread, and to gather ruffle while at the same time you create seams on the non-ruffled fabric. The shirring effect improves the texture of your fabric and makes it look more beautiful.

Depending on the stitch length of your machine, you can create long or small gathers. If the stitch length is short, then you will have small gathers in your garment and vice versa. If you need fuller gathers, you have to set the highest stitch length and increase the differential feed. When adjusting the stitch settings, you can use a piece of scrap fabric to test the stitches. If you have loose threads, adjust them accordingly so that you have a balance of the threads and the stitches. Only when you're satisfied with the stitch setting can you begin your gathering. Otherwise, if you have a gathering fabric at the same time create a seam on non-gathered fabric, you will have a garment with loose stitches that come off when pulled.

Once you have learned how to use your serger machine and serge different types of stitches, you need to learn how to maintain the machine. As we have discussed, you have to clean and oil your machine on a regular basis to boost the life-time of your machine. Proper maintenance ensures your overlock machine remains functional and you don't have any issues with the breaking of needles or threads.

Overlock maintenance involves cleaning, removing lints and pieces of threads, and oiling the movable parts of your serger machine. Not all overlock machines require oiling so you should confirm with your machine manual what type of lubricant or oil to use. Most of the machines come with a soft nylon brush to clean the insides of the machine. You can also use a narrow paint brush to clean around the feed dogs and under the needle plate. Changing needles is also another part of maintaining your machine. You should change them often.

You were also able to learn how to make baby blankets that are more personal between you and your baby. There are different types of materials you can use to make a warm blanket for your baby. Making your own baby blanket gives you the freedom to choose your own design and style. You can also incorporate cartoon themed fabrics to make the blankets.

There are different designs you can choose from and sizes that suit your needs. You can make a blanket with rounded corners or even add embroidery to the top fabric. Always make sure you use the recommended baby clothing fabrics because they're very soft for your baby. You can also make a baby blanket as a gift to your friends.

In Chapter Five, you're able to learn how to make your own pillow covers. Making a pillow cover is effortless and you can personalize them based on your preferences. You don't have to rely on hem tape covers with bulging seams. You can easily make a zippered pillow cover using your machine. Serger machine makes it easy to add zippers so it doesn't have to be scary.

The advantage of making your own pillow covers is that you can select the best fabric that complements your living space. With more practice, you can make pillow covers with different patterns and colors for your living room. Use invisible zippers to make the cover look neat and professional. Home décor fabrics are great for making your pillow covers because of their thicker material that maintains the cover's great shape.

Use a matching thread to stitch the cover and have pillow inserts proportional to the size of your pillow cover so that it can look good on your sofas.

Another DIY sewing project you're able to learn is making a drawstring bag. The drawstring can be great for holding smaller items, using them as a picnic bag, or use the bag to separate different types of clothing when traveling. You can use this bag when going to parties, games, gym or give it as a gift during birthday parties or baby showers.

Making your own drawstring bag is very easy and doesn't need a lot of fabric. You can use scraps of fabric left after making your garment to make the drawstring.

Drawstring bags have wide uses and you can make different sizes that suit different occasions. Different types of fabrics are used to make these types of bags. Make your own stylish designs drawstring bag that you can bring with you at any event. If you're using ribbon pieces as straps to your drawstring bag, then apply fray check at the cut ends of the ribbon to prevent unraveling.

Alternatively, you can make drawstrings with a box bottom. The box bottom makes it easy to place the drawstring on any flat surface. Box bottom requires you to clip part of the fabric to avoid any creases when you stitch the seam around the bottom edges of your drawstring bag. Box bottom drawstring bags look awesome.

We also learned how to make a snack bag that you can bring with you anywhere. If you love going on a picnic, a snack bag will be great for packing different types of snacks. A snack bag can also be referred to as a sandwich bag.

If you pack snacks for your children when going to school then you need one or more snack bags. Making your own snack bag enables you to add a personal touch to them and you will pack fruits and other snacks for your children with a lot of love.

Your children can also choose the design and favorite color for their snack bags. The bags are also eco-friendly and re-usable. You can make different sizes of snack bags to pack different types of snacks.

You can also make snacks using microwave-safe fabrics and that you can dish wash anytime. You can also choose colors that match your outfit.

You have had your serging machine for a while now and having a dust cover will help extend the lifetime of your machine. When you're not using your machine, you should cover it to prevent the accumulation of dust.

Learning to make your own dust cover is very important. Although you can buy a dust cover in the market, you may not get the right size for your machine. Making your own dust cover makes it easy to choose a fabric and color that complements your sewing room. You can make your dust unique and add some pockets that you can store small serger tools or accessories. You also have the freedom to choose the best fabric for your dust cover.

Following the above-discussed steps will help you create your own customized dust cover that suits your serger machine.

In the next chapter, we have talked about how to make a Christmas stocking for your loved ones. Christmas stocking is a large sock crossed with a bag that is used to store gifts from Father Christmas. Children hang Christmas stockings in their room during Christmas Eve because they believe Santa will fill them with gifts if they have behaved well throughout the year.

Instead of buying Christmas stockings for your family, you can make a custom made Christmas stocking. Making the stocking is very easy and cheap and you can make the size as big as you want.

When sewing around the toe curve, cut notch curves so that your stocking looks neat when you turn right side out. You should also avoid clipping the seams around the curve. After making the stocking, you can add a decorative stitch to make the stocking look more attractive. Creating a hanger for your stocking makes it easy to hang it anywhere.

Christmas is here and learning how to make a holiday napkin tree will make your dining table look great. You can create your own modern napkins then transform them into a Christmas tree. If you don't have enough time to make your own napkin, you can use existing napkins and make a Christmas tree with them. These Christmas tree napkins make your dining table look welcoming and your guests will be happy to have them.

When creating your own napkins, you can do it in two ways: creating reversible napkins or creating mitered napkins. Reversible napkins are great for adding color to your dining table and you can use any of the sides while mitered napkins have hemmed edges and are mostly made from linen material.

For you to fold a napkin tree, you need napkins made of natural fibers such as cotton and linen or a blend of cotton and polyester. This will help make it add folds and you don't have to worry about the napkins unfolding themselves when you press them together. The explained steps will guide you in making an excellent Christmas tree napkin. You can also add a bow at the peak and a cinnamon stick at the bottom to make the napkin resemble a real tree. Having several napkins set on your dining table can complement your dining décor.

Lastly, we learned how to create a face mask. Face masks have a variety of uses but currently, we are using face masks to protect ourselves against COVID 19. Since you're required to use masks every day, learning how to make them is very beneficial.

You can make fashionable homemade masks for your family and friends. There are different designs you can use to make the face mask, you can practice several designs and go for the ones you feel comfortable with. Make sure the mask you make has at least two layers for them to give you the protection you deserve. You can also make a face mask with three layers, you only need to make sure the materials used are breathable.

Since most of the face masks sold at the market are for adults, you can make smaller masks for your children. Children below two years are not supposed to wear a face mask.

If you have a scrap fabric at home, use it to make a face mask that matches your outfit. You can make several of them depending on the number of family members. Once you use the mask, you should wash it just like you would wash a regular laundry and dry them.

When cutting the pieces, you can use downloadable online patterns to help you quickly cut the pieces you need for your face masks. There are different patterns you can download, just find the one equivalent to the type and design of mask you want to make and use it to cut the fabric for your new face masks. Sew several of them and donate some to your friends.

With these simple steps, you can create great projects with your server machine. It is also easy and fast compared to a regular sewing machine.

Projects created with a serger machine have a more professional look. Learning the basics of serging will enable you to create more DIY projects. You no longer have to spend money buying various garments. You can create your own customized garments at home.

References

https://blog.bernina.com/en/2020/05/sewing-self-made-face-masks-with-the-overlocker-serger-instruction-for-the-more-elaborate/

https://thegirlinspired.com/fast-and-easy-serger-face-mask/

https://www.thedailysew.com/2016/12/a-very-easy-to-make-drawstring-bag/

https://www.avera.org/app/files/public/76443/Olson-Mask-with-Pattern.pdf

https://weallsew.com/sewing-machine-dust-cover-tutorial/

https://www.closetcorepatterns.com/free-pattern-alert-make-our-serger-sewing-machine-cover/

https://redandhoney.com/diy-reusable-snack-bags/